Enterprise Blockchain Applications and Use Cases

Copyright © 2024 by NOB TREX L.L.C.

All rights reserved. No part of this publication may be reproduced, distributed, or transmitted in any form or by any means, including photocopying, recording, or other electronic or mechanical methods, without the prior written permission of the publisher, except in the case of brief quotations embodied in critical reviews and certain other noncommercial uses permitted by copyright law.

Contents

1 Preface   **9**

2 Introduction to Blockchain for Enterprises   **11**
     2.1 Overview of Blockchain Technology 11
     2.2 Why Blockchain Is Important for Enterprises 13
     2.3 Types of Blockchain: Public, Private, and Consortium . . 15
     2.4 Key Features of Blockchain for Enterprises 17
     2.5 Benefits of Implementing Blockchain in Business Processes 19
     2.6 Challenges and Considerations in Adopting Blockchain . 21
     2.7 Potential Impact of Blockchain Across Various Industries 24
     2.8 Case Studies: Successful Enterprise Blockchain Implementations 26
     2.9 Future Trends and Evolutions in Enterprise Blockchain . 29
     2.10 Summary and Key Takeaways 31

3 Blockchain Technology Fundamentals   **35**
     3.1 What is a Blockchain? 35
     3.2 Characteristics of Blockchain Technology 37
     3.3 How Blockchain Works: Blocks, Transactions, and Chain 39
     3.4 Cryptography in Blockchain: Hashing and Digital Signatures 41

- 3.5 Consensus Mechanisms: Proof of Work, Proof of Stake, and Others 43
- 3.6 The Role of Nodes and Networks in Blockchain 45
- 3.7 Immutable Ledger: Benefits and Limitations 48
- 3.8 Understanding Smart Contracts: Basic Concepts 50
- 3.9 Introduction to Decentralized Applications (DApps) . . . 52
- 3.10 Challenges in Blockchain Development and Maintenance 54
- 3.11 Evaluating the Scalability, Privacy, and Interoperability in Blockchain 56

4 Private vs Public Blockchains for Business — 59
- 4.1 Defining Private and Public Blockchains 59
- 4.2 Core Differences between Private and Public Blockchains 61
- 4.3 Advantages of Private Blockchains for Enterprises 63
- 4.4 Use Cases of Public Blockchains in Business 65
- 4.5 Security Aspects: Comparing Private and Public Options 68
- 4.6 Cost Implications: Setup and Ongoing Maintenance . . . 69
- 4.7 Regulatory Considerations for Private and Public Blockchains 72
- 4.8 Performance and Scalability: Which Suits Business Needs? 73
- 4.9 Choosing Between Private and Public Blockchains for Your Business 75
- 4.10 Hybrid Blockchain Models: Combining the Best of Both Worlds 77
- 4.11 Future Outlook: Trends in Blockchain Adoption for Business 79

5 Blockchain Security and Encryption Techniques — 83
- 5.1 Introduction to Security in Blockchain 83
- 5.2 Fundamentals of Cryptography in Blockchain 85
- 5.3 Hashing Algorithms: Ensuring Data Integrity 88
- 5.4 Digital Signatures for Authentication and Non-Repudiation 90

5.5 Encryption Techniques for Blockchain Data Security . . . 92
 5.6 Smart Contract Security: Best Practices and Common Pitfalls 94
 5.7 Security Challenges in Decentralized Networks 97
 5.8 Quantum Resistance: Future-proofing Blockchain Security 99
 5.9 Security Tools and Protocols for Blockchain Environments 101
 5.10 Implementing Multi-layer Security in Blockchain Systems 104
 5.11 Auditing and Monitoring for Enhanced Blockchain Security 106
 5.12 Conclusion: The Importance of Robust Security in Blockchain Implementations 107

6 Smart Contracts and Their Applications 111
 6.1 Introduction to Smart Contracts 111
 6.2 How Smart Contracts Work: A Technical Overview . . . 113
 6.3 Programming Languages for Smart Contracts 115
 6.4 Benefits of Using Smart Contracts in Business 118
 6.5 Smart Contract Deployment: Steps and Best Practices . . 120
 6.6 Verification and Testing of Smart Contracts 123
 6.7 Common Use Cases for Smart Contracts 125
 6.8 Smart Contracts in Financial Services 127
 6.9 Smart Contracts in Supply Chain Management 129
 6.10 Integrating Smart Contracts with IoT 131
 6.11 Challenges and Limitations of Smart Contracts 134
 6.12 Future Developments in Smart Contracts Technology . . 136

7 Blockchain in Supply Chain Management 139
 7.1 Overview of Supply Chain Management 139
 7.2 The Role of Blockchain in Enhancing Supply Chain Transparency 141
 7.3 Blockchain for Traceability in Supply Chains 143

7.4 Improving Efficiency in Supply Chains through Blockchain 145
  7.5 Reducing Costs with Blockchain in Supply Chain Management 147
  7.6 Ensuring Product Authenticity and Compliance 149
  7.7 Integration Challenges: Blockchain and Existing SCM Systems 151
  7.8 Blockchain-Powered Smart Contracts in Supply Chains . 153
  7.9 Case Studies: Blockchain Implementations in Supply Chain 155
  7.10 Future Trends: Blockchain Technology in Supply Chain Management 157
  7.11 Conclusion: The Impact of Blockchain on Supply Chain Operations 159

8 Blockchain for Finance and Banking   163
  8.1 Introduction to Blockchain in Finance and Banking . . . 163
  8.2 Benefits of Blockchain in Financial Services 165
  8.3 Blockchain for Payment Systems and Money Transfers . 167
  8.4 Enhancing Loan and Credit Processing through Blockchain 169
  8.5 Blockchain Solutions for Securities Settlements 171
  8.6 Use of Smart Contracts in Financial Products 173
  8.7 Regulatory Compliance and Reporting with Blockchain . 175
  8.8 Security and Fraud Prevention in Banking using Blockchain 177
  8.9 Challenges of Implementing Blockchain in Financial Institutions 179
  8.10 Case Studies: Successful Blockchain Adoption in Finance 182
  8.11 The Future of Blockchain in the Financial Industry 184

9 Blockchain in Healthcare   187
  9.1 Overview of Blockchain Application in Healthcare 187
  9.2 Challenges in Healthcare Data Management 189

- 9.3 Blockchain for Medical Records and Patient Data Security 191
- 9.4 Ensuring Data Interoperability with Blockchain 193
- 9.5 Blockchain for Drug Traceability in the Pharmaceutical Industry 195
- 9.6 Use of Smart Contracts in Healthcare Services 197
- 9.7 Blockchain for Clinical Trials and Research Data 200
- 9.8 Improving Health Insurance Claims Processing through Blockchain 202
- 9.9 Regulatory and Compliance Concerns in Healthcare Blockchain 204
- 9.10 Case Studies: Blockchain Impact on Healthcare Organizations 206
- 9.11 Future Directions for Blockchain in the Healthcare Industry 208

10 Integrating Blockchain with Existing IT Infrastructure 211

- 10.1 Assessing Current IT Infrastructure for Blockchain Integration 211
- 10.2 Key Considerations Before Integrating Blockchain 214
- 10.3 Blockchain Integration Strategies 216
- 10.4 Technical Requirements for Blockchain Deployment . . . 218
- 10.5 Handling Data Migration and Interoperability Issues . . 221
- 10.6 Modifying Existing Applications to Work with Blockchain 223
- 10.7 Securing the Blockchain within Existing IT Ecosystems . 225
- 10.8 Monitoring and Managing Blockchain Operations 228
- 10.9 Training and Support for Blockchain Integration 230
- 10.10 Evaluating the Impact of Blockchain on IT Operations . . 232
- 10.11 Case Studies: Successful Integrations of Blockchain in Existing IT Infrastructures 234

11 Legal and Regulatory Considerations of Blockchain 237

- 11.1 Understanding the Legal Framework Surrounding Blockchain 237

11.2 Global Regulatory Landscape for Blockchain Technology 239
11.3 Contract Law and Smart Contracts: Legal Recognition . . 241
11.4 Privacy Laws and Data Protection in Blockchain Systems 243
11.5 Regulatory Compliance in Financial Blockchain Applications 245
11.6 Intellectual Property Issues in Blockchain Development . 246
11.7 Cross-border Transactions and Jurisdictional Challenges 249
11.8 Legal Concerns with Decentralization and Anonymity . 251
11.9 Blockchain and Anti-Money Laundering (AML) Regulations 253
11.10 Consumer Protection and Dispute Resolution Mechanisms 255
11.11 Future Legal Trends and Potential Regulations for Blockchain 257

Chapter 1

Preface

Blockchain technology, since its inception, has grown beyond its initial application as the backbone of cryptocurrency, evolving into a revolutionary solution for various industries, especially within the enterprise sector. This book, "Enterprise Blockchain: Applications and Use Cases," aims to elucidate the multifaceted concepts of blockchain technology, discuss its practical implementations, and provide a thorough investigation of its use across multiple business domains. The target readership includes business leaders, IT professionals, and those aiming to understand the implications, benefits, and challenges of blockchain technology in the enterprise environment.

The content of this book is structured to provide a clear exposition of blockchain fundamentals followed by discussions on privacy, the differences between public and private blockchains, security enhancements, and the integration of blockchain into existing IT infrastructure within a business context. Dedicated chapters explore significant applications in fields such as finance, healthcare, and supply chain management, detailing how blockchain can improve transparency, efficiency, and security. The discussions extend to legal and regulatory considerations, ensuring that readers are aware of the compliance and legal frameworks affecting blockchain implementation in businesses.

Our aim with this publication is to deliver high-caliber, actionable knowledge that empowers decision-makers to make informed choices regarding blockchain technology adoption and integration. We focus on delivering content devoid of undue complexity or technical jargon; instead, we explore real-world applications and case studies to demonstrate the tangible benefits and potential limitations of blockchain in a professional setting.

"Enterprise Blockchain: Applications and Use Cases" is more than just a guide; it is a comprehensive resource designed to enable a deep understanding of blockchain technology from a corporate perspective, helping professionals harness this potential in their strategic operation frameworks. This book stands as an essential read for anyone poised to lead their organization through the evolving landscape of digital transformation influenced by blockchain technology.

Chapter 2

Introduction to Blockchain for Enterprises

Blockchain technology offers transformative potential for enterprises looking to enhance security, efficiency, and transparency in their operations. This chapter introduces the fundamentals of blockchain, explores its key features, and discusses its various applications within the business sector. It further examines the advantages and challenges associated with implementing blockchain in an enterprise setting, providing insights into how industries are leveraging this technology to innovate and gain competitive advantages.

2.1 Overview of Blockchain Technology

Blockchain technology, fundamentally a distributed database, presents an innovative leap in the way data is stored and managed. Instead of relying on a central authority or repository, blockchain decentralizes the data storage, making it essentially managed by all participants in the network. This decentralization is critical in enhancing the security and integrity of data, as it removes a single point of failure and distributes the data across multiple nodes in the network. Each participant (or node) holds a copy of the entire ledger, and any amendments to the ledger must be validated by consensus among these nodes.

Blockchain operates on the principle of forming blocks of data, which are then linked together in a chain using sophisticated cryptographic methods. Specifically, each block contains a cryptographic hash of the previous block, a timestamp, and transaction data, represented typically as a Merkle tree. The cryptographic hash function—an algorithm that takes an input (or 'message') and returns a fixed-size string of bytes, typically a hash value that is unique to each specific input—is crucial here because any slight change in input data will generate a completely different hash output. This property is called hash sensitivity and it is fundamental for the integrity and security of blockchain technology.

Moreover, blockchain employs consensus algorithms to ensure the agreement on a single data value among distributed processes or systems. Examples of such algorithms include Proof of Work (PoW), Proof of Stake (PoS), and Delegated Proof of Stake (DPoS), among others. These protocols help prevent fraudulent activities and ensure the authenticity of the data recorded on the blockchain.

- PoW involves solving complex mathematical puzzles, which requires computational power. The first node to solve the puzzle gets the right to add a new block to the blockchain. This mechanism provides security but can be energy intensive.

- PoS selects validators in proportion to their holdings of the blockchain's base cryptocurrency. This method is less resource-intensive compared to PoW.

- DPoS enhances the basic PoS mechanics by introducing a voting and delegation mechanism where stakeholders elect delegates to validate and add blocks to the blockchain.

Smart contracts are another innovation within blockchain technology. These are self-executing contracts with the terms of the agreement between buyer and seller being directly written into lines of code. The code and the agreements contained therein exist across a distributed, decentralized blockchain network. This automation increases transaction speed and reduces or eliminates the need for intermediaries, thereby reducing costs.

```
1  contract SimpleStorage {
2      uint storageData;
3      function set(uint x) public {
4          storageData = x;
5      }
6      function get() public view returns (uint) {
7          return storageData;
```

```
8     }
9 }
```

In the above example, a simple smart contract in Solidity (a programming language used for Ethereum smart contracts) is illustrated. It allows for storing and retrieving a number ('uint') on the blockchain. The 'set' function is used to input a value, and the 'get' function retrieves the value.

```
Output:
Value of storageData returned by the get() function
```

As enterprises adopt blockchain technology, they must carefully consider the implications for their specific operational environments. The immutability and transparency offered by blockchain can significantly enhance trust and security in enterprise applications. Furthermore, the blend of cryptographic security with decentralized consensus protocols not only mitigates traditional cyber threats but also introduces new efficiencies in how transactions are processed and verified.

The inherent complexities of blockchain, particularly those associated with the integration and operation of such transformative technology within existing IT infrastructures, necessitate a thorough understanding and strategic plan for implementation. However, with careful design and deployment, blockchain stands to offer significant value in terms of operational efficiency, security, and transparency. As this technology evolves, it will continue to expand its influence and potential applications in enterprise settings, making it an indispensable component of modern IT strategies.

2.2 Why Blockchain Is Important for Enterprises

Blockchain technology's underpinning design delivers several crucial benefits critically important for enterprise applications, notably in its ability to ensure data integrity, transparency, and security simultaneously. As businesses increasingly operate in digitally interconnected environments with significant data exchanges, these attributes become paramount.

The primary importance of blockchain for enterprises revolves around its inherent system architecture. At its core, blockchain is a distributed ledger technology where each transaction on the network is recorded in a block linked to a preceding block, forming a chronological chain. This structure is fortified by cryptographic hashes, ensuring that once a transaction is added to the blockchain, it cannot be altered retroactively without detection.

- **Enhanced Security**: Each transaction on a blockchain is secured through a consensus mechanism before it is recorded. This, coupled with the cryptographic linkage between blocks, makes the system highly resistant to unauthorized changes and fraudulent activities. Unlike traditional databases where security might rely on one or a few servers, the decentralized nature of blockchain spreads the risk across numerous nodes in the network, reducing potential single points of failure.

- **Increased Transparency**: Due to the decentralized and immutable ledger that blockchain provides, all transactions are transparent and verifiable by all parties with the necessary permissions. This transparency is critical for enterprises needing a verifiable audit trail of asset provenance, transaction history, and data integrity without relying on a trusted third party.

- **Reduced Costs and Efficiencies**: Blockchain technology can streamline internal processes by removing intermediaries or administrative overheads involved in cross-verification and validation of transactions. This trimming of unnecessary intermediaries translates directly into cost savings and speedier transactions. Additionally, the automation potential through smart contracts — self-executable contracts with the terms directly written into code — can further enhance operational efficiencies.

Moving from generalized advantages to specific industry applications, blockchain technology significantly influences areas such as supply chain management, financial services, healthcare, and more. For instance, in supply chain management, blockchain enables enterprises to track product movement transparently and in real-time from production to delivery, ensuring authenticity and compliance. This traceability is not only crucial for quality assurance but also essential in combatting issues like counterfeiting and ensuring regulatory compliance.

In financial services, blockchain introduces improvements in transactions processing times, settlements, and even cross-border payments. By directly connecting parties involved in a transaction without the need for intermediary financial institutions, enterprises benefit from quicker settlements and reduced transactional costs. Moreover, blockchains can enhance the security and efficiency of transactions by reducing or eliminating the scope for human error and the need for prolonged validations typically required by conventional banking systems.

Similarly, in the healthcare sector, blockchain can secure and streamline the exchange of sensitive medical records, ensure compliance with privacy regulations, and improve the traceability of pharmaceuticals to fight counterfeit drugs. Each stakeholder in the healthcare value chain, from providers to patients to regulatory bodies, stands to gain from the increased data integrity and accessibility that blockchain offers.

These specific cases underscore the multidimensional importance of blockchain across various enterprise domains, highlighting not only its role in enhancing operations but also its potential to drive fundamental industry transformations. This aligns with the broader enterprise objectives of improved security, reduced operational costs, and enhanced transparency.

While the implementation of blockchain comes with its complexities, the long-term benefits derived from its strategic application in business processes are compelling. Businesses that understand and leverage the strengths of blockchain technology can expect not only to optimize their operations but also to position themselves competitively in an increasingly digital and data-driven market landscape.

2.3 Types of Blockchain: Public, Private, and Consortium

Blockchain technology is typically segmented into three distinct types: public, private, and consortium blockchains. Each type serves unique purposes and is suited to specific business needs and operational frameworks. This section delves into the defining characteristics, use cases, advantages, and limitations of each type.

Public Blockchain Public blockchains are characterized by their entirely open and decentralized nature. These blockchains allow anyone to join and participate in the core activities of the network, such as validating transactions, without any restrictions. Bitcoin and Ethereum are prominent examples of public blockchains.

- **Decentralization:** No single entity has control over the entire blockchain, making it resistant to censorship and centralized points of failure.
- **Transparency:** All transactions are visible to everyone on the network, ensuring full transparency in the system.
- **Security:** Utilizing consensus algorithms like Proof of Work (PoW) or Proof of Stake (PoS), public blockchains are secured by a large network of participants.

However, this openness comes with the cost of scalability and speed. Public blockchains often experience slower transaction times and higher transaction costs compared to their private counterparts because each transaction must be verified by a multitude of participants across the globe.

Private Blockchain Unlike public blockchains, private blockchains are permissioned systems where access is restricted to a specific group of users. Organizations often deploy private blockchains when they need to control accessibility, maintain privacy, yet want to leverage blockchain's benefits within the organization or a closed community.

- **Efficiency:** With fewer nodes to validate transactions, private blockchains can process transactions faster than public blockchains.
- **Privacy:** Transactions are only visible to authorized participants, enhancing privacy.
- **Control:** Governance is streamlined, and rules can be altered as per the network admin's requirements.

Despite providing greater control and efficiency, private blockchains sacrifice a degree of security and decentralization since the limited number of participants increases the risk of collusion and central control.

Consortium Blockchain Consortium blockchains represent a middle ground between the public and private varieties. A consortium blockchain is typically governed by a group of organizations, rather than a single entity, which participate collaboratively. This type of governance offers a higher level of security than private blockchains but more control over the network compared to public blockchains.

- **Governance:** Controlled by a consortium of firms, enabling balanced decision-making.
- **Scalability:** Better transaction speed and handling capacity as compared to public blockchains due to less crowded network.
- **Security:** More secure than private blockchains as multiple unrelated parties validate transactions.

Consortium blockchains are particularly suited for business scenarios where multiple entities need to engage in secure, controlled data exchange while maintaining trust among each other, such as in banking, supply chain management, or health care sectors.

Each type of blockchain offers distinct advantages and faces particular challenges. Deciding which blockchain to implement should be guided by the specific requirements, goals, and context of usage within an enterprise. While public blockchains offer transparency and are tamper-evident, they lack in speed and cost-effectiveness. Private blockchains, offering efficiency and privacy, give up the robustness associated with decentralization. Consortium blockchains, meanwhile, provide a balanced approach with shared control, but require collaboration and consensus from all participating parties, which can complicate governance and operation. Enterprises must weigh these aspects carefully to choose the optimal blockchain approach that aligns with their strategic objectives and operational frameworks.

2.4 Key Features of Blockchain for Enterprises

Blockchain technology is distinguished by several pivotal features that render it highly suitable for use in enterprise applications. These features include decentralization, immutability, enhanced security, transparency, and tokenization. Each of these characteristics plays a crucial role in enhancing the efficiency and security of business operations.

Decentralization Blockchain operates on a decentralized network that distributes data across multiple nodes, which are essentially computers or servers participating in the blockchain network. This means that no single entity has control over the entire blockchain, leading to a significant reduction in risks associated with centralized data management systems, including single points of failure and central points of attack.

A typical scenario illustrating decentralization is when a blockchain is used for supply chain management. Here, information such as product origin, batch numbers, and shipping details are recorded on a blockchain. Each participant in the supply chain, from producers to distributors, operates a node, thus facilitating a transparent and verifiable record without relying on a central authority.

```
1  // Example of setting up a decentralized blockchain node
2  BlockchainNode node = new BlockchainNode();
3  node.connectToNetwork("supplyChainNetwork");
4  node.addRecord("productID123", "Origin: Farm A, Batch No: 009, Shipped: 01-03-2023"
       );
```

Immutability Once data is entered into the blockchain, it cannot be altered or deleted. This immutability is ensured through cryptographic hash functions. Each block contains a unique hash, along with the hash of the previous block, creating a chain link that secures all information.

For instance, in financial transactions, once a transaction detail is recorded on a blockchain, it cannot be changed, thereby preventing fraud and ensuring the integrity of the financial records.

```
Transaction Record:
Hash: 000a113f...9c5
Previous Hash: 000cf44f...6b2
Details: Transfer $5000 from Account A to Account B
TimeStamp: 01-04-2023 12:00 UTC
```

Enhanced Security Blockchain employs advanced cryptographic techniques to ensure that the information is secure. Public-private key pairs are used to create a secure and verifiable identity for each participant. Only the holder of the private key can authorize transactions, which safeguards against unauthorized access and cyber threats.

```
1  // Example of generating a cryptographic key pair
2  KeyPairGenerator keyGen = KeyPairGenerator.getInstance("RSA");
3  keyGen.initialize(2048);
4  KeyPair pair = keyGen.generateKeyPair();
5
6  PublicKey pubKey = pair.getPublic();
7  PrivateKey privKey = pair.getPrivate();
```

Transparency Each transaction on the blockchain is visible to all participants and can be audited in real-time. This transparency helps in building trust among stakeholders by ensuring that all actions are traceable and visible.

- All transactions are logged and time-stamped,
- Transactions are visible to all network participants,
- Real-time auditing is possible.

Tokenization Tokenization refers to the conversion of assets into digital tokens on the blockchain, representing ownership or rights over assets. This can significantly streamline the process of asset trading and management, enhancing liquidity and reducing the time and cost associated with traditional asset transfer methods.

```
// Example of asset tokenization
Blockchain blockchain = new Blockchain();
Asset asset = new Asset("Real Estate", "Commercial Property, 123 Main St");
Token token = blockchain.tokenizeAsset(asset, 1000000); // Create 1 million tokens

System.out.println("Asset tokenized into " + token.getTotalUnits() + " units.");
```

The synergy of these features — decentralization, immutability, enhanced security, transparency, and tokenization — provides a robust framework for enterprises seeking to enhance their operations through technology. These functionalities of blockchain foster a new paradigm of efficiency and trust in business processes, as it caters to the diverse needs and challenges faced by today's enterprises. These attributes not only promote accountability but also facilitate a higher degree of automation and innovations in business models.

2.5 Benefits of Implementing Blockchain in Business Processes

The integration of blockchain technology into business processes offers manifold advantages that can significantly enhance operational efficiency, security, and transparency. This section delves into these benefits, highlighting how blockchain's inherent characteristics align with the needs of modern enterprises.

1. Enhanced Security: Blockchain's cryptographic foundation is pivotal for enhancing the security aspect of business processes. Each block within the blockchain is linked to its previous one via a cryptographic hash, a mechanism that ensures data integrity and prevents unauthorized alterations. For example, suppose a malicious actor attempts to alter information in a transaction.

```
1  data = "original_transaction_data"
2  hash = encrypt(data) // Assuming a simple hash function for explanation
3
4  // Now the malicious actor attempts to alter the data
5  malicious_data = "altered_transaction_data"
6  malicious_hash = encrypt(malicious_data)
7
8  // Verification process in blockchain
9  verify_transaction(original_hash, malicious_hash)
```

The blockchain will detect any discrepancy in the hash values during its validation process, thereby averting potential frauds.

2. **Decentralization:** By enabling a distributed ledger system, blockchain eliminates the need for a central authority, thus reducing bottlenecks and risks associated with a single point of failure. This decentralization not only contributes to reducing administrative costs but also expedites transactions, as the consensus can be achieved directly between the involved parties. Thus, blockchain fosters a more autonomous and efficient operational flow.

3. **Increased Transparency:** With blockchain, every transaction is logged in a tamper-evident ledger and is accessible to all participants (or nodes) in the network, enhancing the transparency of transactions. This visibility is particularly beneficial in sectors where stakeholders need to verify the authenticity of products or the integrity of data without depending on third-party verification. Here, the blockchain serves as a single source of truth.

4. **Traceability:** In supply chain management, blockchain provides exceptional traceability of goods and assets. As items are traded through various hands, each transaction is recorded on the blockchain, creating an immutable history of product movement. This capability not only helps in verifying the authenticity of products but also enhances the accountability in supply chains.

```
1  transaction_block = {
2    'previous_hash': '123456',
3    'transaction_details': 'Product shipped from A to B',
4    'timestamp': '2023-09-21T12:00:00'
5  }
6  append_to_ledger(transaction_block)
```

5. **Improved Efficiency:** By automating complex processes through smart contracts, blockchain can execute agreements automatically when predefined conditions are met. Smart contracts eliminate the need for intermediaries, thereby reducing delays, costs, and human errors associated with manual processes.

```
Contract executed successfully:
Transaction ID: 987654321
Timestamp: 2023-09-21T12:05:00
Participants: Party A, Party B
Status: Completed
```

6. Reduced Costs: By streamlining processes and removing intermediaries, blockchain substantially lowers various operational costs, such as those associated with audits, compliance, and transaction processing. Automation via smart contracts further reduces the expenses related to manual oversight and error resolution, making business transactions more cost-effective.

- Reduced reliance on paper-heavy processes
- Lower transaction fees due to elimination of middlemen
- Decreased costs related to fraud prevention and data breaches

Enterprise adoption of blockchain technology not only aligns with present-day demands for more robust, transparent, and efficient systems but also positions businesses strategically for the challenges and opportunities of the digital age. The foregoing benefits highlight the potential transformative impact of blockchain across various business functions, demonstrating its capacity to not only solve traditional problems but also unlock new value streams in an increasingly interconnected business environment.

2.6 Challenges and Considerations in Adopting Blockchain

Adopting blockchain technology in enterprise settings involves a variety of challenges and considerations that must be thoroughly analyzed and addressed to ensure successful implementation. These challenges can be technical, organizational, and regulatory in nature.

Technical Challenges:

- **Scalability:** Blockchain technology, particularly public blockchains, suffers from limited transaction throughput. For example, Bitcoin can handle about 7 transactions per second, and Ethereum around 15, which is significantly lower compared to traditional payment networks like Visa, which can process over 24,000 transactions per second. Enterprises must consider blockchain platforms that offer improved scalability to meet their operational demands.

```
// Example of a blockchain scalability solution
class Blockchain {
    constructor() {
        this.chain = [];
        this.pendingTransactions = [];
        this.addBlock(new Block(1, "01/01/2020", "Genesis block"));
    }

    addBlock(block) {
        this.chain.push(block);
    }
};
```

- **Interoperability:** Different blockchain systems often operate in isolation. This lack of interoperability can limit the ability of enterprises to transfer data or assets across various blockchain networks, essential for applications that span diverse industries or geographies. Solutions such as blockchain bridges and protocols that facilitate interoperability must be employed.

```
Interoperable Transfer Output:
Cross-chain asset transfer successful.
```

- **Energy Consumption:** The proof-of-work mechanism used by some blockchains, such as Bitcoin, requires substantial computational power, leading to high energy consumption. Enterprises need to consider the environmental impact and potential PR fallout from the use of such energy-intensive technologies.

Organizational Challenges:

- **Cultural Resistance:** Implementing blockchain requires a culture shift within an organization. The decentralized nature of blockchain is often at odds with existing centralized operational models, and resistance can arise from stakeholders who are accustomed to traditional systems.

- **Understanding and Expertise:** There exists a significant gap in blockchain expertise that can hinder its adoption. Enterprises must invest in training and hiring qualified personnel or seek external expertise to navigate the complex aspects of blockchain technology.

```
// Training module outline for blockchain education
```

2.6. CHALLENGES AND CONSIDERATIONS IN ADOPTING BLOCKCHAIN

```
2   class BlockchainTraining {
3       constructor(participants) {
4           this.participants = participants;
5       }
6
7       startModule(module) {
8           console.log(`Starting ${module} module...`);
9       }
10  };
```

- **Cost Implications:** Initial setup costs for blockchain technology can be substantial. Beyond implementation, ongoing maintenance and updates require additional financial outlays. Decision-makers must perform cost-benefit analyses to ensure that the investment in blockchain technology aligns with long-term strategic goals.

Regulatory Challenges:

- **Unclear Regulation:** The legal and regulatory framework governing the use of blockchain technology is still in its nascent stages in many territories. This uncertainty can pose risks to businesses, including compliance issues and potential legal challenges.

- **Data Privacy:** Blockchains immutable nature means once data is added, it cannot be altered or deleted. This characteristic raises significant data privacy concerns, particularly with laws like the General Data Protection Regulation (GDPR) in Europe, which includes the right to erasure or "right to be forgotten."

```
Legal Compliance Report:
- GDPR Compliance: Non-Compliant
- Recommended Actions: Implement data masking before inserting personal
  data into the blockchain.
```

Successfully navigating these challenges requires a clear understanding and a strategic approach tailored to each organization's specific circumstances. Through the careful consideration of these factors, enterprises can leverage blockchain technology effectively and responsibly, enhancing their operations while paving the way for innovation and transformation in their industry sectors.

2.7 Potential Impact of Blockchain Across Various Industries

The potential impact of blockchain technology across various industries can be substantial as it provides solutions that enhance transparency, security, and efficiency. Each industry has its unique requirements and challenges, and the adaptiveness of blockchain offers tailor-made solutions that can profoundly alter their traditional processes.

Finance and Banking

The finance and banking industry stands to benefit immensely from blockchain technology. The inherent features of blockchain such as decentralization, immutability, and transparency can address core needs in this sector.

- Reduction in Fraud: Blockchain's immutability helps in significantly reducing fraud related to financial transactions and operations.
- Streamlining of Processes: The technology can automate and streamline back-office operations through smart contracts, reducing costs and human errors.
- Enhanced Security: Enhanced security measures are inherent due to the cryptographic nature of blockchain.

Finance organizations can employ blockchain to reform how they handle payments, optimizing not only local but also international transactions. An example of this is the use of blockchain for cross-border payments which facilitates quicker and less expensive transactions as opposed to traditional systems.

Supply Chain Management

In supply chain management, blockchain can provide transparent and immutable record-keeping, making it easier to track the origin, quality, and delivery of goods and materials. Here are some specific potential impacts:

- Provenance Tracking: Enterprises can trace the product journey from manufacture to end-sale, ensuring authenticity and compliance.

- Reduction in Counterfeits: Enhanced traceability helps in reducing the chances of counterfeit goods entering the market.

- Improved Efficiency: Real-time tracking and automated smart contracts can significantly speed up administrative processes and reduce disputes.

Walmart, for example, uses a blockchain system to trace the origin of food products, enhancing safety standards and response speed to food safety incidents.

Healthcare

Blockchain technology in healthcare promises to solve issues related to data security, accessibility, and integrity. The impacts include:

- Secure Patient Data: Blockchain can secure patient records, ensuring they are immutable and accessible only by authorized entities.

- Enhanced Data Sharing: With patient consent, blockchain facilitates a more efficient data sharing between practitioners, improving diagnostic and treatment accuracy.

- Drug Traceability: It can help in tracking drug supply chains, ensuring the drugs remain safe and unaltered throughout their journey from manufacturer to consumer.

Implementations like these can revolutionize how sensitive and critical data is handled within the healthcare industry, potentially reducing fraud and errors significantly.

Real Estate

Blockchain introduces a level of record-keeping and transaction efficiency previously unseen in the real estate market. Key benefits would include:

- Transparent Transactions: Blockchain can store property records, making them easily accessible and reducing the likelihood of transaction disputes.

- Reduced Costs: By eliminating middlemen and reducing the need for paper-based processes, both time and money can be saved.

- Smart Contracts: These can automate various aspects of real estate transactions, including payments and compliance checks.

Education and Credentialing

Education systems can use blockchain to issue and verify academic credentials, reducing fraud and making the process more efficient:

- Secure Credential Storage: Academic and professional certificates can be securely stored on a blockchain, making forgery extremely difficult.

- Simplified Verification Process: Employers and institutions can verify credentials without needing to contact each issuing institution.

The implementation of blockchain in these sectors demonstrates its potential to drive significant changes in the traditional processes. The technology not only addresses inherent shortcomings such as inefficiencies, susceptibility to fraud, and lack of transparency but also introduces operational improvements such as cost reduction, speed, and user empowerment. Through continuous advancements and integration, blockchain stands poised to significantly reshape the way industries operate, hinting at an evolutionary leap in enterprise operation.

2.8 Case Studies: Successful Enterprise Blockchain Implementations

Supply Chain Optimization at Maersk

One significant application of blockchain technology in enterprises is demonstrated by Maersk, the world's largest shipping company. They

2.8. CASE STUDIES: SUCCESSFUL ENTERPRISE BLOCKCHAIN IMPLEMENTATIONS

collaborated with IBM to develop 'TradeLens', a blockchain-based supply chain solution. TradeLens facilitates the secure and transparent sharing of information among various stakeholders in the shipping and logistics ecosystem.

- Efficiency: By digitizing the supply chain process, TradeLens has significantly reduced the processing time of shipping documents and transactions.

- Visibility: Each stakeholder in the supply chain, from the port operators to customs authorities, can track the cargo in real-time, enhancing the overall visibility and predictability of logistic operations.

- Security: The blockchain's inherent characteristics ensure that records on TradeLens are immutable and tamper-evident, increasing security across the supply chain.

The implementation has reported a 40% reduction in the cost of shipping documentation processing and has improved overall transit times through quicker documentation turnover.

```
1  BlockchainAPI.connect("TradeLens")
2  BlockchainAPI.query("shipment", "status", shipment_id="#1234")
```

```
Output:
{
  "shipment_id": "#1234",
  "status": "In transit",
  "current_location": "Port of Singapore",
  "estimated_arrival": "2021-12-23",
  "security_checks": "Passed"
}
```

Financial Transactions in HSBC

HSBC, one of the leading financial organizations worldwide, has harnessed blockchain technology to rationalize its financial transaction processes. The primary focus has been on foreign exchange transactions, which benefit immensely from blockchain through increased speed and reduced costs.

Blockchain implementation in HSBC has resulted in:

- Reduced latency: Transactions that typically took days are now completed in seconds.

- **Lower costs:** Decreased dependency on intermediaries translates into lower transaction costs.

- **Enhanced security:** Encrypted transactions and immutable record-keeping enhance the security of sensitive financial data.

A significant achievement was the execution of the first scalable multi-nodal live transaction on R3's Corda platform, demonstrating feasibility across international boundaries.

```
1  CordaAPI.initiateTransaction("FX", sourceCurrency="USD", targetCurrency="EUR",
       amount=10000)
```

```
Transaction status: Success
Transaction ID: FX293842034
Effected Date: 2021-10-05
```

Retail Loyalty Programs at Walmart

Walmart has developed a blockchain for managing its retail loyalty programs, allowing for greater customer engagement and operational efficiency. The system is designed to cater to a large customer base with the ability to handle millions of transactions securely and transparently.

- **Customer Satisfaction:** Enhanced transparency and real-time updates increase customer trust and satisfaction.

- **Operational Efficiency:** Streamlined operations through automated transactions and reduced manual intervention.

- **Fraud Reduction:** Immutable record-keeping on spending and reward points accrual reduces the potential for fraud.

The deployment of this blockchain-based loyalty program has seen a 30% increase in customer participation year-over-year, indicating a profound affect in customer loyalty strategies.

```
1  LoyaltyBlockchain.recordTransaction(customer_id="C123", transaction_type="purchase"
       , amount_spent=300)
```

```
Loyalty Points Update:
Customer ID: C123
Points Earned: 30
Total Points: 150
```

The deployment of blockchain in these varied enterprise applications showcases not only the versatility of the technology but also underscores its potential to revolutionize traditional business operations and systems across industries. The case studies reflect tangible benefits in operational efficiencies, cost reductions, and enhanced security protocols, prompting other enterprises to explore the blockchain landscape for further innovation and competitive advantage.

2.9 Future Trends and Evolutions in Enterprise Blockchain

As enterprise blockchain matures, several key trends and evolutions are shaping its trajectory. These include the increasing integration of artificial intelligence (AI), the growing importance of interoperability and standardization efforts, a shift towards sustainability, expansion of blockchain consortia, and upcoming regulatory frameworks.

Integration with Artificial Intelligence

The convergence of blockchain technology and AI is poised to significantly deepen the capabilities of enterprise applications. Blockchain can secure, and hence, enhance the reliability of AI-generated data, facilitating more trusted machine learning models. Concurrently, AI can manage complex algorithms that pinpoint inefficiencies or automate decision-making processes on the blockchain.

For instance, consider a blockchain that tracks the supply chain for a multinational manufacturing business:

```
contract AIEnhancedSupplyChain {
    // Data structure to store shipment details
    struct Shipment {
        string id;
        address sender;
        uint timestamp;
        string status;
    }

    mapping(string => Shipment) public shipments;

    // Function to update shipment status
    function updateShipment(string memory id, string memory status) public {
        shipments[id].status = status;
        shipments[id].timestamp = block.timestamp;
    }
}
```

This example illustrates how a smart contract might interact with an AI system that predicts shipment statuses based on historical data and external factors like weather conditions.

Interoperability and Standardization

Interoperability between different blockchain platforms and the standardization of protocols are critical areas of focus. Enterprises are increasingly demanding solutions that can seamlessly interact with other blockchains and with existing traditional systems. Efforts such as the InterWork Alliance (IWA) aim to establish a standardized framework for building distributed applications across various platforms.

- Development of universal communication protocols to facilitate blockchain interactions.
- Creation of standardized APIs for easier implementation of blockchain solutions.
- Adoption of common frameworks for smart contracts that ensure security and compliance across platforms.

Sustainability Initiatives

Blockchain's environmental impact, particularly for consensus mechanisms like Proof of Work (PoW), has been a significant concern. The trend towards more sustainable and energy-efficient alternatives like Proof of Stake (PoS) is becoming prevalent among enterprise-oriented blockchains. For example, a shift from traditional PoW to a PoS approach can significantly reduce the energy consumption as demonstrated below:

```
Energy Consumption:
- PoW: ~45 kWh per transaction
- PoS: ~5 kWh per transaction
```

This reduction facilitates a more sustainable blockchain ecosystem while still maintaining security and decentralization.

Expansion of Blockchain Consortia

Blockchain consortia, which are collaborative groups where businesses unite to exploit blockchain's benefits, are expanding. These consortia help standardize and democratize the technology usage, leading to faster adoption and creation of industry-specific solutions.

Projects initiated by consortia allow multiple stakeholders to test and improve blockchain systems collaboratively, effectively reducing costs and enhancing reliability due to shared expertise and resources.

Regulatory Frameworks

With blockchain technology entering mainstream business applications, regulatory frameworks are imminent. Legislation and policies concerning digital assets, smart contracts, and personal data security are actively being discussed and developed. Compliance with these regulations will be essential for businesses implementing blockchain solutions, affecting how they design and execute their blockchain strategies.

Initiatives such as the development of the "Digital Commodity Exchange Act" in the United States showcase steps toward more structured regulatory environments. Enterprises must stay informed and adaptable to integrate these norms effectively.

As these trends advance, enterprises should anticipate not only vast improvements in blockchain functionality and efficiency but also enhanced capability for innovation. By staying ahead of these developments, businesses can strategically position themselves to leverage blockchain technologies most effectively, responding dynamically to new opportunities that these technologies may unveil.

2.10 Summary and Key Takeaways

Throughout this chapter, we have delineated the foundational concepts underpinning blockchain technology and underscored its paramount significance in the enterprise domain. A comprehensive exposition has been provided on the various types of blockchains—public, private, and consortium—and their distinctive characteristics and suitability for different business applications. By examining these types, enterprises can make informed decisions about which blockchain configuration best aligns with their strategic goals.

The key features of blockchain, such as decentralization, immutability, and transparency, have been discussed. These features contribute vitally to enhancing the security and efficiency of enterprise operations. Decentralization eliminates the dependency on a central authority, immutability ensures that data cannot be altered retrospectively, and transparency aids in trust-building among stakeholders. These attributes collectively fortify the integrity and reliability of the data shared across a blockchain network.

The benefits of implementing blockchain in business processes are multifold. Notably, it simplifies transactions, enhances traceability, reduces costs associated with middlemen, and improves data management practices. Despite these advantages, the adoption of blockchain also presents challenges, including scalability issues, the requirement for significant initial investment, and the need for regulatory compliance. The operational impact of these challenges must be carefully evaluated when devising an implementation strategy.

Furthermore, we have illustrated the potential impact of blockchain across various industries such as finance, supply chain management, healthcare, and more. Each of these sectors can leverage blockchain to address specific challenges, such as enhancing supply chain transparency, securing medical records, or simplifying financial transactions. The distinctive needs and compliance requirements of each industry dictate the particular adaptations and innovations necessary for successful blockchain integration.

The real-world applications and benefits of blockchain have been substantiated through multiple case studies. These studies not only underscore the practicality of blockchain but also highlight the innovative approaches organizations are taking to integrate blockchain into traditional business models. By learning from these success stories, other enterprises can envision potential blockchain applications within their own operational contexts.

Looking ahead, the future trends in blockchain technology suggest a continuous evolution in how enterprises will use this technology. Increased adoption of blockchain is anticipated, driven by further advancements that enhance scalability, interoperability, and usability. As the technology matures, more tailored solutions are expected to emerge that address the specific needs of different industries and sectors.

Each business must weigh the potential benefits against the challenges to determine the viability of blockchain technology within their specific context. The key to successful implementation lies in thoroughly understanding the technology's capabilities and limitations, leveraging strategic thinking to align it with business objectives, and maintain-

2.10. SUMMARY AND KEY TAKEAWAYS

ing flexibility to adapt to technological advancements. As enterprises continue to navigate their digital transformation journeys, blockchain stands out as a pivotal technology that can provide substantial value through enhanced transparency, security, and efficiency in business operations.

Chapter 3

Blockchain Technology Fundamentals

This chapter delves into the core components of blockchain technology, elucidating the underlying principles that govern its operation. It addresses the structure of blocks, the process of transactions, and the mechanics of chaining methods in blockchain architecture. Essential concepts such as cryptography, consensus mechanisms, and blockchain types are explained to lay a foundation of understanding, crucial for both newcomers and those looking to deepen their knowledge of how blockchains function and ensure data integrity and security.

3.1 What is a Blockchain?

A blockchain is a distributed digital ledger comprised of a series of records, referred to as blocks, which are interconnected in a chronological order to form a continuous line, metaphorically termed a chain. Each block in the blockchain contains a compact and unchangeable data record of transactions or digital events, which have been agreed upon by consensus of a network of participants. The data recorded on a blockchain is inherently resistant to modification, which is a foundational attribute that drives the trust and security perceptions of this technology.

Each block typically contains a timestamp, transaction data, and a cryptographic hash of the preceding block. This design inherently makes a blockchain secure by design and exemplifies a distributed computing system with high Byzantine fault tolerance. The decentralization aspect is critical—it implies that no single entity owns or controls the entire network, enhancing the immutable nature of the blockchain records.

- Transactions are digitally signed using public-key cryptography to ensure their authenticity and to prevent fraud. This method ensures that only the owner of a digital asset can initiate and authenticate transactions, safeguarding against unauthorized access or alterations.

- Block creation is performed by network participants known as miners in public blockchains who expend computational power to solve complex cryptographic puzzles—a process known as mining.

- New blocks are added to the end of the blockchain and must be confirmed by other nodes through a consensus mechanism before they are recorded on the ledger. This process ensures that each participant in the network agrees with the current state of the ledger and the validity of all transactions hence promoting transparency and trust.

Once data has been written to a blockchain no single participant can alter it without simultaneously altering subsequent blocks, which requires the consensus of the majority of the network. This feature not only makes the data secure and trustworthy but also creates a historically transparent, traceable, and unalterable record of all transactions.

In view of operational mechanics, the blockchain utilizes cryptographic operations to safeguard data integrity and confidentiality. The blockchain protocol employs hash functions; specifically, the SHA-256 hashing algorithm, which transforms an input of arbitrary size into a fixed-size string of bytes, typically a hash code of 256 bits. For instance, when a new block is generated, the transactions are taken as an input, and a hash code of these transactions is included in the new block along with the hash of the previous block. This chaining of hashes serves as the pivotal security feature of the blockchain.

```
1  Example of a SHA-256 function generating a hash:
2
```

```
3   Input: "Sample transaction data"
4   Output: SHA-256("Sample transaction data") = "3
        a7bd3e2360b2a54d3db36ead25f45fc5d5282b369a084307ab5c715d38b4943"
```

Expected console output for the hash:
3a7bd3e2360b2a54d3db36ead25f45fc5d5282b369a084307ab5c715d38b4943

Thus, a blockchain serves multiple roles: it acts as a technology framework, an architectural pattern, and as a decentralized data verification mechanism. This multi-faceted nature is what enables blockchains to be applied across varied sectors not limited to finance, health care, logistics, and even governmental systems where transparency, security, and data integrity are paramount.

By enabling decentralized and transparent transaction verification, while also maintaining data immutability and consistency, blockchains challenge traditional business models and invite innovative approaches to how systems and processes are designed and handled across various industries.

3.2 Characteristics of Blockchain Technology

Blockchain technology is distinguished by several pivotal characteristics that enable its application across various industries and domains. These characteristics are primarily responsible for the technology's robust security features, transparency, and decentralization. This section will explore these defining attributes, namely: decentralization, transparency, immutability, and security.

Decentralization

The traditional model of managing transactions or data typically involves a central authority or server that stores and processes information. Blockchain technology, however, operates on a decentralized network architecture. In blockchain, data is distributed across a network of computers, often referred to as nodes, and each participant on the network possesses an entire copy of the transaction ledger. This means that no single entity has control over the entire network, which can prevent any single point of failure and manipulation.

In a blockchain, when a transaction is conducted, it is broadcast to the network and validated by multiple nodes. This process not only helps in maintaining the integrity and transparency of the data but also ensures that the system remains operational even if parts of the network fail.

Transparency

One of the significant attributes of blockchain technology is its transparency. Changes to public blockchains are publicly viewable by all parties creating transparency, and all transactions are immutable, meaning they cannot be altered or deleted. This level of transparency helps users to track and verify transactions effortlessly and securely.

Moreover, blockchain technology provides mechanisms for enhanced transparency through the use of consensus protocols which are rules and arrangements that decide on the validity of contributions made by various participants. This ensures that each participant can audit the transactions independently without having to trust a central authority.

Immutability

Immutability in the context of blockchain refers to the capability of the blockchain ledger to remain unaltered and indelible. Once a transaction has been added to the blockchain, it is extremely difficult to change. To ensure immutability, blockchain utilizes cryptographic hash functions, which are designed to provide a secure and one-way linkage between sequential blocks in the chain.

Every block contains its own hash and the hash of the previous block. If an attacker attempts to alter any transaction, the hash of the altered block will change as well and disrupt the blockchain's continuity. Such changes would be immediately noticed by other nodes in the network, who will reject the tampered data, preserving the ledger's historical accuracy.

Security

Security in blockchain is enforced through various cryptographic techniques, including the use of digital signatures and hash functions. Each transaction on a blockchain is signed digitally, using the private key of the sender. This signature ensures that the transaction remains linked to the sender and cannot be repudiated or altered by anyone else.

The security of a blockchain is also fortified by the proof of work (PoW) consensus mechanism, which involves solving a complex mathematical problem that requires significant computational resources. The difficulty of these problems ensures that tampering with the blockchain is economically unfeasible for an attacker.

Through the unique integration of these characteristics, blockchain technology offers a revolutionary approach to storing and managing data across various spheres of activities, ranging from financial transactions to administrative operations in public sectors. This paradigm shift not only challenges traditional architectures but also opens up a spectrum of possibilities for enhanced system integrity and transparency.

3.3 How Blockchain Works: Blocks, Transactions, and Chain

Understanding the construction of blocks, the nature of transactions, and the chaining process is fundamental to grasping how blockchains function. Each component is essential and interlinked, providing security and integrity throughout the blockchain.

Blocks are the fundamental units of a blockchain. Each block contains a list of transactions that have been bundled together and confirmed by the network during a particular time period. The composition of a block can typically be divided into a block header and a block body. The header includes the following elements:

- `Previous_Block_Hash`: A cryptographic hash of the previous block's header, linking the blocks securely and ensuring integrity from any alteration of the past block.

- `Timestamp`: The time when the block was created.

- `Nonce`: A variable that is used during the mining process to find a hash that satisfies certain conditions defined by the consensus protocol, such as Proof of Work.

- `Merkle_Root`: A hash of all the transactions in the block, providing a concise and secure way to verify transaction integrity.

The block body primarily lists all transactions that have been validated and agreed upon by network nodes.

Transactions are the second core component of blockchain. A transaction, in essence, is a transfer of value between two parties on the blockchain network. It is comprised of the following elements:

- `Input`: The source of funds, generally referred to as references to previous transaction outputs.

- `Output`: Details of the transaction recipients and the amount of cryptocurrency each is to receive.

- `Digital_Signature`: A cryptographic signature created by the sender's private key. This signature is used to verify the transaction's integrity and the sender's authority by other parties.

When a transaction is initiated, it is broadcasted to a network of nodes. Here, the transaction undergoes a series of verifications, which include the verification of the digital signature and the confirmation that the sender has sufficient balance to complete the transaction. Upon successful verification, the transaction is considered valid and is circulated to the pending transaction pool where it awaits inclusion in a block.

Chaining of blocks happens through the `Previous_Block_Hash` within a block's header pointing to the hash of its previous block. This chaining ensures that any alteration of transaction data in a previously confirmed block would necessitate recalculating all subsequent blocks' hashes, which is computationally impractical. This mechanism fundamentally secures the blockchain against tampering and revision, ensuring immutability and continuity of the ledger.

Here is a simplified pseudocode to illustrate the creation of a block and its addition to the blockchain:

Algorithm 1: Creating and Adding a Block
Data: transactionsToInclude, previousHash
Result: newBlock
1 **begin**
2   sortedTransactions ← sortTransactionsByCriteria(transactionsToInclude)
3   merkleRoot ← calculateMerkleRoot(sortedTransactions)
4   timestamp ← getCurrentTimestamp()
5   nonce ← findNonceForNewBlock()
6   newBlock ← createBlock(previousHash, merkleRoot, timestamp, nonce, sortedTransactions)
7   addBlockToChain(newBlock)
8   **return** *newBlock*

This process, combined with robust consensus mechanisms and distributed agreement, is why blockchain technology is renowned for its enhanced security and trustworthiness. The interdependencies of blocks, transactions, and the chaining mechanism require that each component operate flawlessly within its scope to maintain the operational and security standards that underpin blockchain technology.

3.4 Cryptography in Blockchain: Hashing and Digital Signatures

Cryptography provides the backbone of security within blockchain technology. This section delves deeply into two fundamental cryptographic components: hashing and digital signatures, exploring their roles and mechanisms in ensuring the integrity and authenticity of blockchain transactions.

Hashing is a cryptographic technique that transforms an input of arbitrary size into a fixed-size string of bytes, typically a digest that appears random. Each hash is unique; even a minor change in the input results in a completely different output. This attribute is crucial for blockchain operations, where every block contains a cryptographic hash of the prior block, thus securing the chain's continuity and immutability.

The hash function used in the majority of blockchain applications is SHA-256, part of the Secure Hash Algorithm 2 family, designed by the United States National Security Agency. Below is an example of applying a SHA-256 hash to a string "Blockchain".

```
1  import hashlib
2
3  # Example string
4  input_string = "Blockchain"
5  # Using hashlib to apply sha256
6  output_hash = hashlib.sha256(input_string.encode()).hexdigest()
7
8  print(output_hash)
```

The output would adjust accordingly if the string changes:

4a44dc15364204a80fe80e903396e72af18daf48a683cd4a8d1a3d6904caf0c9

This irreversible and unique nature of hashing makes it infeasible to derive the original input from its hash, hence providing security for the data stored within each block against tampering.

On the other hand, digital signatures are utilized to verify the authenticity and integrity of a message or a document. A digital signature assures that a document or a message was sent by the claimed sender and has not been altered in transit. Blockchain employs public key cryptography to create and verify digital signatures. Each user or node in the blockchain network holds a pair of keys: a private key and a public key. The private key is used to generate the signature and is kept secure, while the public key is distributed and available openly on the blockchain to all participants for signature verification.

Here is how a digital signature is generated and verified within a blockchain network:

1. A user signs a transaction or a document using their private key. 2. The signature and the corresponding public key are broadcast along with the transaction. 3. Other network participants use the public key to validate the signature.

Generating a digital signature in a simulated environment could be illustrated with the following Python example, using the ECDSA (Elliptic Curve Digital Signature Algorithm) method for signing:

```
1   from ecdsa import SigningKey, SECP256k1
2
3   # Generate private key
4   private_key = SigningKey.generate(curve=SECP256k1)
5   # Generate public key
6   public_key = private_key.get_verifying_key()
7
8   # Message to sign
9   message = b'Blockchain transaction'
10  # Sign the message
11  signature = private_key.sign(message)
12
```

```
13  print(signature.hex())
```

To verify this signature, one would perform the following steps:

```
1  from ecdsa import VerifyingKey
2
3  # Verification of the signature
4  is_verified = VerifyingKey.from_string(public_key.to_string(), curve=SECP256k1).
       verify(signature, message)
5  print(is_verified)
```

True

The cryptographic mechanisms of hashing and digital signatures together enhance the security framework of blockchain by protecting the data integrity and confirming the authenticity of transactions. Each block linked in the blockchain is verified through these cryptographic proofs, ensuring that any alteration of data is computationally infeasible. This irrevocability and trustworthiness are what empower blockchain applications in various sectors, from finance to healthcare, and beyond. Thus, effective understanding and application of these cryptographic principles are essential for developers and stakeholders in the blockchain ecosystem.

3.5 Consensus Mechanisms: Proof of Work, Proof of Stake, and Others

Consensus mechanisms are fundamental to the functioning of blockchain technology, as they ensure unanimity in the network despite the absence of a central authority. This section explores three primary consensus mechanisms: Proof of Work (PoW), Proof of Stake (PoS), and others that are less common but equally significant for certain applications.

Proof of Work (PoW) is the original consensus mechanism used in blockchain technology, prominently featured in Bitcoin. PoW requires network participants, referred to as miners, to solve complex mathematical problems to validate transactions and create new blocks. The process demands considerable computational power. When a miner successfully solves the problem, they broadcast the solution to other nodes in the network for verification. The general sequence of actions in a typical PoW cycle can be described as follows:

Algorithm 2: Proof of Work Algorithm

Data: List of pending transactions
Result: New block added to the blockchain

1. initialization;
2. **while** *no valid nonce found* **do**
3.   select transactions from mempool;
4.   create block header with previous block's hash and nonce;
5.   calculate hash of current block header;
6.   **if** *hash meets difficulty criteria* **then**
7.   broadcast block to network;
8.   exit;
9.   increment nonce;

The primary advantage of PoW is its security feature; altering any aspect of the blockchain would require re-mining all subsequent blocks. However, the significant energy consumption and slower transaction processing rates pose substantial drawbacks.

Proof of Stake (PoS) was developed as an alternative to PoW to address these limitations. In PoS, the creation of new blocks is determined by one's stake in the network (e.g., the number of cryptocurrency units held), rather than computational power. Validators are selected to create a new block based on various factors including random selection and wealth or age (i.e., the stake). A typical PoS algorithm involves the following steps:

Algorithm 3: Proof of Stake Algorithm

Data: List of validating nodes, their stakes
Result: New block added to the blockchain

1. initialization;
2. **while** *no new block created* **do**
3.   select validator based on stake and randomization;
4.   validator creates block with pending transactions;
5.   block is broadcast to network for validation;
6.   **if** *block is validated* **then**
7.   append block to blockchain;
8.   exit;

PoS does not require the extensive computational resources that PoW does, significantly reducing the power consumption and allowing for faster processing of transactions. The risk of centralization, though, might be greater if the formation of blocks is dominated by nodes with larger stakes.

Other Consensus Mechanisms: Beyond PoW and PoS, several other mechanisms provide unique advantages tailored to specific situations. These include Proof of Authority (PoA), which vests the power to create new blocks in nodes that are deemed trustworthy by the network; and Proof of Space (PoSpace), which involves using disk space as the resource cost for mining, instead of CPU/GPU power.

Proof of Authority (PoA):

- Used primarily in private networks.
- Validators are pre-approved and trusted identities.
- Faster and more energy-efficient than PoW.

Proof of Space (PoSpace):

- Participants prove that they allocate a certain amount of disk space for storage purposes.
- Reduces energy consumption when compared to PoW.

Each of these mechanisms aims to ensure digital agreement and integrity across the distributed blockchain network.

This comprehensive examination of various consensus mechanisms elucidates their pivotal role in maintaining the decentralized ethos of blockchain technology while highlighting the trade-offs that come with each model.

3.6 The Role of Nodes and Networks in Blockchain

A blockchain network consists of multiple components, of which nodes are the fundamental elements. Nodes are individual computers connected to the blockchain network that perform a variety of roles, from maintaining the blockchain to executing the protocols that powers its functionality. This section discusses the critical roles of these nodes, their types, and the structure of blockchain networks in detail.

Nodes in a blockchain assume a pivotal role by ensuring the integrity, transparency, and availability of data. They are responsible for verifying, storing, and relaying valid transactions to other nodes. When a new transaction is initiated, it is broadcast to the network. Nodes then gather these transactions from the mempool, verify their legitimacy according to the predefined rules, and pass them on to other nodes.

- Full nodes store a complete copy of the blockchain ledger and participate in the transaction verification process. They serve as the bulwark of blockchain's decentralization and security, facilitating consensus by validating the blocks and states of the blockchain.

- Light nodes, in contrast, do not store the entire blockchain but rather depend on full nodes for information. They offer the advantage of requiring significantly less storage and resources, thus being suitable for devices like mobile phones and small-scale IoT devices.

- Mining or Validator nodes actively contribute to consensus mechanisms such as Proof of Work (PoW) or Proof of Stake (PoS). These nodes often require considerable computational power, especially in PoW blockchain systems where complex cryptographic problems must be solved to add a new block to the chain.

The interconnectivity within a blockchain is established through a peer-to-peer (P2P) network structure. This architecture enhances robustness and scalability, as the network does not rely on a central server but rather on direct node-to-node communications. Each node in the network operates both as a client and a server, which promotes data redundancy and fault tolerance.

```
Connection established: Node A (Full Node) <-> Node B (Mining Node)
Data exchanged: Transaction data, Block information, and Consensus communications
Network topology: Dynamic and decentralised
```

Nodes communicate by propagating transactions and blocks, synchronized across the network, thus ensuring all nodes have uniform and up-to-date information about the state of the ledger. This distribution mechanism makes blockchain networks inherently resistant to certain types of attacks, such as single point of failure disruptions or data manipulation.

In blockchain networks, scalability and performance issues are pivotal considerations. The network's capacity to handle a high number of

3.6. THE ROLE OF NODES AND NETWORKS IN BLOCKCHAIN

transactions depends on multiple factors, including network latency, the block size, and the consensus protocol in place. For instance, scalability in Bitcoin's network is impacted by its block size limit and the PoW mechanism, which leads to limitations in the throughput of transactions.

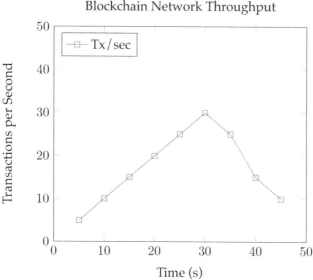

Network modifications and enhancements, like the implementation of second-layer solutions (e.g., Lightning Network for Bitcoin), and adjusting block size or inter-block times are among the adaptive strategies employed to address these challenges while retaining security and decentralization.

Blockchain's resilience is derived significantly from the distributed nature of its network, with nodes playing a critical role in the maintenance, operation, and security of the blockchain. Each node contributes to a larger ecosystem that is greater than the sum of its parts, ensuring continuous operation and integrity of the system against adversarial threats. The continuous evolution of node capabilities and network structures aims to address emerging challenges and needs, showcasing the dynamic adaptability of blockchain technology.

3.7 Immutable Ledger: Benefits and Limitations

An immutable ledger, a core component of blockchain technology, is characterized by its ability to maintain a permanent and unalterable record of all transactions. This immutable property stems largely from the cryptographic linkage between consecutive blocks and the decentralized consensus mechanism employed by nodes within the blockchain network.

Benefits of an Immutable Ledger

The principal advantages of maintaining an immutable ledger are manifold and significantly contribute to the robustness and security that are synonymous with blockchain technology.

- **Data Integrity:** Once a transaction has been recorded on a blockchain, altering this information becomes computationally impractical. This is due to each block containing a unique hash of its contents and the hash of the preceding block, creating a secure link between them. This linkage ensures any attempt to alter the data in a previously confirmed block would necessitate recalculating every subsequent block's hash, a task that requires enormous computational resources.

- **Transparency and Trust:** With every transaction recorded verifiably and indelibly, blockchain technology fosters a transparent operational environment. This transparency, in turn, builds trust among users, as records are easily verifiable and accessible by all parties in the network without the need for intermediaries.

- **Auditability:** The permanent nature of the blockchain ledger makes it simple for auditors to trace and verify transactions. This feature is particularly crucial in financial sectors and other industries where maintaining an accurate and detailed transaction history is necessary for compliance and auditing purposes.

- **Reduction in Fraud:** The integrity of transactions assuaged by the immutability of the blockchain significantly reduces the potential for fraud. This is especially pertinent in scenarios involving contractual agreements and where transaction records are prone to manipulation.

Limitations of an Immutable Ledger

Despite its strengths, the immutable ledger of blockchain also introduces certain limitations and challenges that need meticulous consideration.

- **Storage Constraints:** As every transaction is permanently recorded, the size of the blockchain inevitably grows over time, leading to increased demands on storage capacity. This can become a significant issue, particularly for nodes that are required to maintain a complete copy of the blockchain ledger.

- **Scalability Issues:** The time taken to reach a consensus on each transaction and the subsequent recording process limits the throughput of a blockchain. Therefore, high-volume environments might encounter scalability issues, as the growing number of transactions can lead to increased transaction validation times and higher costs.

- **Data Correction and Removal Difficulty:** The immutable nature of the ledger makes it challenging to correct erroneous entries. Regulations such as the General Data Protection Regulation (GDPR) in the European Union stipulate the right to erasure, which could come into conflict with blockchain data immutability.

- **Energy Consumption:** The consensus mechanisms, such as Proof of Work used by some blockchains, require significant computational power, leading to substantial energy consumption. This environmental impact is a growing concern and the subject of criticism from various sectors.

These key aspects highlight the dual nature of an immutable ledger—its capability to ensure data security and trust, juxtaposed with the operational and ethical challenges it may pose. For successful implementation and operation, stakeholders must carefully weigh the benefits against the potential drawbacks. This balance is crucial for the eternal evolution and adoption of blockchain within enterprise frameworks, ensuring that the technology aligns with both organizational objectives and regulatory frameworks.

3.8 Understanding Smart Contracts: Basic Concepts

Smart contracts represent a pivotal innovation in blockchain technology, offering a robust and transparent way to execute and automate agreements without the need for intermediaries. A smart contract is a self-executing contract with the terms of the agreement directly written into lines of code. The code and the agreements contained therein exist across a distributed, decentralized blockchain network. The code controls the execution, and transactions are trackable and irreversible.

The concept of smart contracts was proposed by Nick Szabo in 1994, long before Bitcoin was conceptualized. Szabo is a legal scholar and cryptographer known for his research in digital contracts and digital currency. The idea was to implement a digital transaction protocol that executes terms of a contract automatically, without requiring external enforcement.

Structure of Smart Contracts: Smart contracts function by following simple "if/when...then..." statements that are written into code on a blockchain. A network of computers executes the actions when predetermined conditions have been met and verified. These actions could include registering a vehicle, issuing a ticket, sending notifications, or releasing funds to appropriate parties.

The key components involved in the creation and operation of smart contracts are:

- **Contract State:** Stored in the blockchain, it represents any variable, such as balance, status, or owner.

- **Functions:** Functions are implemented to modify the state. For example, a function could change the owner of a contract or update the balance.

- **Input Data:** Input data is external information necessary for the contract's functions to execute.

Deployment and Invocation: Deployment of a smart contract in the blockchain is a transaction itself. Once deployed, the contract resides at a specific address on the blockchain. Users or other contracts can invoke the deployed contract by sending transactions to its address, executing its associated functions based on the provided input data.

3.8. UNDERSTANDING SMART CONTRACTS: BASIC CONCEPTS

Here is how a basic smart contract in Solidity, a contract-oriented programming language for writing smart contracts on various blockchain platforms, might look:

```solidity
pragma solidity ^0.5.0;

contract SimpleStorage {
    uint storedData; // State variable

    function set(uint x) public {
        storedData = x;
    }

    function get() public view returns (uint) {
        return storedData;
    }
}
```

In the example above, 'SimpleStorage' is a smart contract with one state variable storedData and two functions. The set function allows the user to update storedData, and the get function reads and returns the value of storedData.

Security Considerations: Since smart contracts automatically execute transactions based on the underlying code, they must be designed with utmost security in mind. Poorly written smart contracts can lead to attacks and significant losses. Common vulnerabilities include reentrancy attacks, issues with random number generation, integer overflow, and underflow. Due to this, many platforms offer standardized templates and testing frameworks to build secure smart contracts.

Advantages Over Traditional Contracts: Smart contracts automate enforcement, management, and execution of agreements, offering several advantages over traditional contracts:

- **Speed and Efficiency:** Automated processes reduce the time needed to complete contractual agreements and eliminate human errors in paperwork.

- **Trust and Security:** Cryptographic encryption ensures secure transaction of data, reducing the chance of manipulation or fraud.

- **Cost Reduction:** With smart contracts, costs associated with intermediaries, including legal advisors, brokers, and banks, are significantly lowered or eliminated.

In practice, the potential applications of smart contracts extend beyond simple transfer of assets: they can enable complex interactions in systems of IoT (Internet of Things), supply chain management, financial services, real estate, and beyond. As developers and industries continue to explore the boundaries and capabilities of smart contracts, the efficiency and functionality of blockchain technology expand correspondingly.

3.9 Introduction to Decentralized Applications (DApps)

Decentralized applications (DApps) represent a pivotal innovation directly stemming from blockchain technology. These applications operate on a decentralized network, underpinned by blockchain, rather than relying on a single computer or server. This section explores the structure, function, and components of DApps, elucidating how they harness the benefits of blockchain technology to offer enhanced security, transparency, and resistance to censorship.

A DApp encompasses three fundamental components: frontend code, smart contracts, and a decentralized datastore. Each of these components plays a critical role in ensuring the autonomous and transparent nature of DApps.

- The frontend code can be written in any language that can make calls to its backend, similar to a traditional app, and often interacts with the blockchain via a web browser extension or library.

- Smart contracts are self-executing contracts with the terms of the agreement directly written into lines of code. They operate as the backend code for DApps, living and running on the blockchain.

- The decentralized datastore refers to the use of blockchain itself for the storage of data, ensuring that data persists across a distributed network to enhance fault tolerance and resistance to tampering.

To understand the operational mechanism of DApps, consider their lifecycle, which typically includes the following steps:

- Development and deployment of smart contracts to the blockchain.

3.9. INTRODUCTION TO DECENTRALIZED APPLICATIONS (DAPPS)

- Interaction by users via the frontend, translated into blockchain operations.

- Validation of operations by the network, ensuring consistency and security through consensus mechanisms.

- Updates to the state of the application stored on the blockchain.

For illustration, a sample DApp code snippet deploying a smart contract and interacting with it through web3.js (a popular JavaScript library to interact with Ethereum blockchains) is provided below:

```
const Web3 = require('web3');
const web3 = new Web3('http://localhost:8545');
const contractABI = [/* ABI Array */];
const contractAddress = '0x123...abc';

const contract = new web3.eth.Contract(contractABI, contractAddress);

// Function to get the stored value
async function getStoredValue() {
    const value = await contract.methods.getValue().call();
    console.log('Stored Value:', value);
}

// Function to set a new value
async function setNewValue(value) {
    const accounts = await web3.eth.getAccounts();
    await contract.methods.setValue(value).send({ from: accounts[0] });
}

// Example Usage
setNewValue(123);
getStoredValue();
```

The getStoredValue() function reads data from the blockchain, and setNewValue() writes data to it, demonstrating basic read/write operations typical of DApps. The output, assumed successful interaction with the blockchain, after setting a new value would look like:

```
Stored Value: 123
```

Deployment and interaction with DApps present various technical challenges and considerations. Transaction speed, cost, user experience, and security are crucial aspects that influence the design and use of DApps. Since these applications are built on blockchain technology, they inherit both the strengths and limitations of the underlying blockchain.

As DApps continue to evolve, industries ranging from finance to supply chain are exploring their potential for creating decentralized, transparent, and secure systems. The inherent benefits of reduced central authority, enhanced security, and potential to operate autonomously position DApps as a significant shift in the landscape of digital applications, poised to impact a broad array of sectors.

3.10 Challenges in Blockchain Development and Maintenance

Developing and maintaining blockchain systems presents a unique set of challenges, primarily because of the technology's decentralized nature, its reliance on consensus mechanisms, and the need for cryptographic security. This section explores the major challenges in blockchain development and maintenance, including scalability, security vulnerabilities, interoperability, and the legal and regulatory implications.

Scalability Challenges

A fundamental issue facing many blockchain implementations, particularly those designed to handle a high volume of transactions, is scalability. This stems from the size constraints of blocks and the interval at which they are added to the blockchain.

- Block Size Limitations: Most blockchains have predefined block size limits, which can restrict the number of transactions processed at a given time. This becomes a bottleneck for networks like Bitcoin where the block size is capped, leading to significant delays and increased transaction fees as the network demand rises.

- Block Creation Time: The interval of block creation can also affect scalability. For instance, Bitcoin blocks are created every 10 minutes. During periods of heavy transaction volumes, this can result in transaction backlogs and prolonged transaction processing times.

Improving scalability can involve methods such as increasing the block size, shortening the block interval, or alternate solutions like the Lightning Network for Bitcoin, which enables off-chain transactions that are later settled on the blockchain.

Security Vulnerabilities

Despite the robust cryptographic techniques that underpin blockchains, security vulnerabilities still pose significant challenges. Common vulnerabilities include the following:

- 51% Attacks: These occur when a single entity gains control of more than half of the total computational power used in mining on the network. This level of control can allow the entity to manipulate block creation, reverse transactions, and double-spend coins.

- Smart Contract Vulnerabilities: Errors in smart contract code can be exploited. For instance, the DAO attack on the Ethereum network occurred due to a flaw in a smart contract, where 50 million in ether was stolen.

- Sybil Attacks: In this type of attack, an attacker subverts the network by creating a large number of pseudonymous entities, allowing them to gain a disproportionate influence.

Addressing security challenges often involves comprehensive code audits, enhanced security protocols, and innovative consensus algorithms that are less susceptible to attacks.

Interoperability Issues

Blockchain interoperability refers to the ability of different blockchain systems to communicate and interact without intermediaries. Current blockchain ecosystems operate largely in isolation, leading to fragmented systems that can undermine the technology's potential benefits. Interoperability issues are addressed through:

- Cross-Chain Technologies: These are specialized protocols designed to facilitate operations between different blockchains. Examples include Polkadot and Cosmos, which enable asset transfers and communication across chains.

- Standardizing Protocols: Advocating for common standards can help ensure that different blockchain networks can communicate seamlessly. Standards such as the Interledger protocol aim to bridge this gap in a secure and scalable manner.

Legal and Regulatory Uncertainties

The decentralized and borderless nature of blockchains often clashes with national regulatory frameworks, leading to uncertainties that can impede adoption.

- Compliance Issues: Blockchain developers must navigate complex and sometimes contradictory regulations concerning securities, data privacy, and anti-money laundering (AML) standards.

- Jurisdictional Challenges: Determining the applicable jurisdiction and legal framework for transactions spanning multiple countries remains problematic.

Efforts to resolve these legal challenges involve engaging with regulators, participating in policy making, and implementing regulatory tech (RegTech) to ensure compliance across various jurisdictions.

Blockchain development and maintenance, thus, require a nuanced understanding of both the technological landscape and the broader economic, legal, and societal factors that influence its evolution. Addressing these challenges is critical not only for the advancement of blockchain technology but also for its integration into the digital fabric of society. The ongoing development of new tools, standards, and practices is essential to harness the full potential of blockchain while mitigating associated risks.

3.11 Evaluating the Scalability, Privacy, and Interoperability in Blockchain

Scalability, privacy, and interoperability represent three critical dimensions in the assessment of blockchain technology's efficacy and suitability for enterprise-grade applications. These aspects not only influence the architecture of blockchain networks but also impact their operational capabilities and the scope of their applications.

Scalability

Scalability in the context of blockchain refers to the capacity of a network to manage an increased throughput of transactions without compromising on performance or security. The challenge of scalability often stands at the forefront of blockchain development because the decentralized nature of blockchain inherently introduces latency and potential bottlenecks in processing transactions.

Blockchains such as Bitcoin and Ethereum initially faced scalability issues primarily due to the size limits of blocks and the frequency with which blocks could be added to the chain. The Bitcoin network, for example, is generally restricted to processing between 3-7 transactions per second (tps), whereas Visa's payment network can handle over 24,000 tps. This contrast underscores a significant scalability challenge.

Improvements and proposals to enhance blockchain scalability encompass several strategies:

- Sharding, which involves dividing the network into smaller pieces or 'shards' that can process transactions in parallel.
- Layer-2 solutions such as the Lightning Network for Bitcoin, that perform transaction processing off the main chain.
- Changes in consensus algorithms, from Proof of Work (PoW) to more efficient systems like Proof of Stake (PoS) or Delegated Proof of Stake (DPoS).

These solutions not only aim at increasing the throughput of the networks but also strive to maintain or improve security and decentralization.

Privacy

Privacy in blockchain systems is another pivotal consideration, especially given the transparent nature of many blockchain implementations, where transaction details are visible to all nodes on the network. This level of transparency, while essential for security and corruption resistance, can be a drawback for businesses that need to protect trade secrets or customer information.

Various approaches have been developed to enhance privacy on blockchains:

- The utilization of zero-knowledge proofs, a method by which one party (the prover) can prove to another party (the verifier) that they know a value, without conveying any information apart from the fact that they know the value.

- Mixing services that combine multiple transactions from multiple users into single transactions to obfuscate the trail back to the transaction's source.

- The deployment of private blockchains where access is restricted to certain nodes, providing confidentiality but potentially at the expense of reduced security and increased centralization.

Interoperability

Interoperability refers to the ability of different blockchain systems to work together seamlessly. In an ideal interoperable blockchain environment, diverse blockchain networks should be able to exchange information, recognize and interact with transactions from other chains, and even share certain operational capacities without needing third-party intermediaries.

Achieving interoperability presents numerous challenges, primarily because different blockchains often have varied protocols, consensus mechanisms, and security practices. Solutions such as blockchain bridges (which allow the transfer of assets and data between different blockchains), sidechains (parallel chains that connect to main blockchains), and layered protocols are all developments aimed at fostering greater interoperability.

Indeed, for blockchains to become pervasive in everyday business processes, they need to operate not in isolation but in ecosystems consisting of multiple blockchain architectures and non-blockchain systems, necessitating robust interoperability.

The ongoing research and development in addressing the scalability, privacy, and interoperability challenges in blockchain technology reflect its evolving nature and the growing understanding of its broader implications in the digital landscape. The balance and trade-offs between these three aspects will significantly determine the architecture choices and the strategic implementation of blockchain technology in enterprise environments.

Chapter 4

Private vs Public Blockchains for Business

This chapter addresses the distinctions, strengths, and limitations of private and public blockchains within a business context, offering insights into how each type serves different business needs. It explores the security implications, scalability, cost efficiency, and regulatory considerations of each blockchain type. By understanding these factors, businesses can make informed decisions about which blockchain configuration best aligns with their strategic and operational goals.

4.1 Defining Private and Public Blockchains

Private and public blockchains represent two distinct types of blockchain architectures, each serving different needs within the business and technology landscapes. To fully understand the subtleties of these blockchain implementations, it is crucial to delve into their foundational characteristics, operational architecture, and inherent access controls.

A public blockchain is a decentralized platform where anyone can join and participate in the core activities of the blockchain, including but not limited to, reading, writing, or auditing the stored data. There is no central authority, and typically, the network is maintained by a protocol agreed upon by the community or network participants. The best-known example of a public blockchain is the Bitcoin blockchain.

Public blockchains maintain security and integrity through cryptographic techniques and consensus algorithms such as Proof of Work (PoW) or Proof of Stake (PoS). Here is an example of a simple transaction verification process in a public blockchain, expressed in pseudocode:

Data: Transaction details, previous block hash
Result: True if valid, False otherwise
1 **begin**
2   calculate hash of incoming transaction;
3   **if** *hash matches expected pattern* **then**
4   broadcast transaction to network for verification;
5   wait for consensus on transaction validity;
6   **if** *consensus achieved* **then**
7   append to blockchain;
8   return True;
9   **else**
10   return False;
11   **end**
12   **else**
13   return False;
14   **end**
15 **end**

Conversely, private blockchains are permissioned environments where participation requires an invitation and subsequent validation by either the network starter or by a set of rules put into place by the network starter. Access control mechanisms are stringent, limiting the visibility of transactions to selected participants. This type of blockchain is often favored by enterprises that require privacy and central control for business operations.

In a private blockchain, read and write permissions can be strictly regulated, and the consensus process might differ significantly from that of public blockchains. Here is an example of a permission verification process in a private blockchain, expressed in pseudocode:

Both types of blockchains leverage cryptographic hashing, digital signatures, and data structuring to form a secure and robust system. How-

```
Data: User credentials, access level request
Result: True if permitted, False otherwise
1  begin
2  |  verify user credentials with central authority;
3  |  if verification successful then
4  |  |  check user access level against requested transaction
       type;
5  |  |  if access level is sufficient then
6  |  |  |  allow transaction processing;
7  |  |  |  return True;
8  |  |  else
9  |  |  |  return False;
10 |  |  end
11 |  else
12 |  |  log unauthorized access attempt;
13 |  |  return False;
14 |  end
15 end
```

ever, the governance model and consensus mechanisms can significantly diverge, which inherently affects the blockchain's usability, efficiency, and security profile. Public blockchains might employ mechanisms like Bitcoin's PoW to secure the network, whereas private blockchains could utilize simpler, less resource-intensive algorithms such as Practical Byzantine Fault Tolerance (PBFT).

Thus, understanding these fundamental differences aids in discerning the suitable blockchain type for specific business requirements, ensuring optimized implementation of this pivotal technology.

4.2 Core Differences between Private and Public Blockchains

The core distinction between private and public blockchains hinges fundamentally on who is allowed to participate in the network and in what capacity. Private blockchains restrict participation whereas public blockchains allow anyone to join.

Access Control: Private blockchains operate on a permissioned basis.

This means that access to the blockchain is restricted to an exclusive group often defined by the organization that owns the blockchain. The entity controlling the private blockchain manages user permissions, deciding who can participate and in what transactions they can engage. For example, in a supply chain management scenario using a private blockchain, specific nodes might be allocated the right to add data whereas others are only allowed permission to read data and verify transactions.

In contrast, public blockchains are permissionless. They enable anyone to interact with the blockchain's data, verifying transactions, and even participating in the consensus process, subject to minimal requirements. The decentralized nature of public blockchains facilitates a higher degree of transparency and openness, exemplified by blockchains like Ethereum and Bitcoin.

- Private Blockchains: Permissioned, limited access.
- Public Blockchains: Permissionless, unrestricted access.

Consensus Mechanisms: The method by which consensus is achieved in blockchain networks varies significantly between private and public blockchains. Private blockchains often employ consensus algorithms like Practical Byzantine Fault Tolerance (PBFT) which rely on a smaller, trusted set of nodes to validate transactions. This can provide efficiencies in terms of transaction speed and scalability.

Public blockchains typically use Proof of Work (PoW) or Proof of Stake (PoS) as a consensus mechanism which involves a competitive validation method ensuring that the person creating a new block is trustworthy. The process is computationally intensive, particularly in the case of PoW, leading to discussions about energy consumption and environmental impact.

- Private Blockchains: Often use faster, more efficient but less decentralized consensus algorithms.
- Public Blockchains: Use decentralized, but resource-intensive consensus mechanisms.

Transaction Speed and Scalability: The controlled access of private blockchains generally allows for faster transaction speeds owing to fewer nodes participating in the consensus process. This presents an advantage in enterprise scenarios where rapid transaction processing is critical. For example, a private blockchain system deployed in financial services can process payments or settle transactions much quicker than traditional banking systems.

Public blockchains, due to their decentralized nature and larger number of nodes verifying transactions, face scalability challenges. The public blockchain's performance can be limited by the size of blocks and the frequency with which they can be created and verified.

```
Private Blockchain: Higher scalability and faster transactions.
Public Blockchain: Lower scalability with slower transaction speeds.
```

Governance: Governance in private blockchains is typically centralized to the blockchain's managing entity. This organization sets policies, updates, and when necessary, rollback changes to the blockchain. This centralization can be beneficial in that it allows for rapid decision-making and concise control over the blockchain's evolution and maintenance.

Public blockchains are governed by a decentralized community where changes require broad consensus from a variety of stakeholders. This can lead to slower evolution but is designed to prevent any single entity from exerting too much influence over the system.

- Private Blockchains: Centralized governance.
- Public Blockchains: Decentralized governance.

The comparative analysis of private versus public blockchains reveals fundamental operational and structural differences that cater to specific business needs and objectives. The choice between these blockchain types should consider factors such as the desired level of accessibility, the criticality of transaction speed, governance preferences, and the trade-offs between efficiency and decentralization.

4.3 Advantages of Private Blockchains for Enterprises

Private blockchains, often referred to as permissioned blockchains, offer specific advantages that are particularly aligned with the needs of enterprise environments where privacy, control, and speed are paramount.

- **Enhanced Privacy and Security:** Private blockchains allow the network participants to maintain complete control over who can access the data recorded on the blockchain. In environments where data sensitivity is a concern, such as in financial services or healthcare, these blockchains provide an environment where transaction details are shared only among permitted users and are hidden from unauthorized parties. This is achieved through rigorous access controls and the use of permissions that dictate who can view and interact with the blockchain.

- **Predictable Performance and Scalability:** Since private blockchains are only accessible to a limited number of users with permissions, they do not face the same performance bottlenecks that public blockchains do, where transaction validation times can vary significantly due to network congestion. The controlled access nature of private blockchains ensures that performance remains stable and predictable, which is crucial for enterprises requiring real-time data processing and transaction handling. Moreover, the scaling processes are more streamlined and can be managed as per the organization's requirements, allowing for more effective handling of growing operational demands.

- **Higher Throughput:** The transaction throughput on a private blockchain can be significantly higher compared to public blockchains. This is due to the lesser number of nodes required to validate transactions, which expedites the consensus process and reduces the time taken for transactions to be finalized. High throughput is essential for industries like banking or manufacturing where a high volume of transactions or data exchanges occur.

- **Customizability and Flexibility:** Enterprises can tailor the architecture and rules of their private blockchain to fit specific business needs and requirements. This includes setting custom transaction validation rules, smart contract functionalities, and consensus protocols that align with the operational objectives of the business. Such flexibility ensures that enterprises are not only able to enforce their governance models but also adapt quickly to regulatory changes or internal policy updates.

- **Reduced Transaction Costs:** Without the necessity to offer incentives to a large group of miners or validators, as is common in public blockchains, private blockchains can operate at a lower cost for transaction processing. This makes them economically viable for enterprises where large-scale routine transactions are common. The cost savings are also evident in the maintenance of the network, which requires fewer resources due to the limited number of participating nodes.

- **Regulatory Compliance:** Private blockchains can be designed to comply with specific regulatory requirements that an enterprise faces. This is particularly important in sectors such as finance, healthcare, and insurance, where data handling and processing are heavily regulated. By configuring the blockchain with compliance embedded in its operation, enterprises can avoid potential legal complications and maintain trust with stakeholders and regulators.

These attributes make private blockchains particularly advantageous for enterprises that prioritize data privacy, require high transaction throughput, seek network performance certainty, and operate under stringent regulatory constraints. As enterprises continue to recognize the value of blockchain technologies, the capability to customize this technology to fit within an organizational context while enhancing internal efficiencies is a significant asset. The choice of blockchain type, therefore, rests on matching the specific operational demands and strategic intentions of the enterprise with the features inherent in a private blockchain setup.

4.4 Use Cases of Public Blockchains in Business

Public blockchains offer transparency, immutability, and widespread accessibility, making them advantageous for various business applications where these attributes are prized. To fully grasp the practical applications, it's imperative to delve into several prominent use cases within the business sphere.

Supply Chain Transparency

In industries like agriculture, manufacturing, and retail, supply chain transparency is critical. Public blockchains can improve visibility throughout the supply chain by providing a decentralized and immutable ledger. For example, suppliers, manufacturers, and consumers can track the origin and handling of products in real-time.

Here's an example of how blockchain technology could be implemented in a supply chain scenario:

```
1  Blockchain supplyChain = new Blockchain();
2  supplyChain.addBlock(new Block("2023-01-01", "{ origin: 'Farm A', product: 'Apples
       ', quantity: 1000 }"));
3  supplyChain.addBlock(new Block("2023-01-02", "{ transport: 'Logistics Co.', route:
       'Route 66', condition: 'Refrigerated' }"));
4  supplyChain.addBlock(new Block("2023-01-03", "{ retailer: 'Supermarket X', received
       : 1000, sellByDate: '2023-02-01' }"));
```

The immutability of blockchain ensures that once data about a product has been uploaded to the blockchain, it cannot be altered, providing a trustworthy record of the product's journey.

Financial Services and Payments

Cryptocurrencies like Bitcoin and Ethereum are underpinned by public blockchains, which facilitate direct peer-to-peer financial transactions without the need for traditional intermediaries such as banks. This feature can be particularly transformative in regions where access to traditional banking is limited. Here, blockchain provides a secure and efficient way to engage in financial transactions and access financial services.

Moreover, the openness of public blockchains enhances financial inclusion by allowing anyone with an internet connection to partake in the global economy.

Smart Contracts for Automated Business Agreements

Smart contracts are perhaps one of the most significant applications of public blockchains in the business domain. These are self-executing contracts with the terms of the agreement directly written into code. When predefined conditions are met, the contract automatically enforces or executes the corresponding agreement.

Consider a simple smart contract that releases payment upon delivery confirmation:

```
1  contract EscrowContract {
2      address payer;
```

```
 3      address payee;
 4      address thirdParty;
 5      uint amount;
 6      bool confirmedDelivery;
 7
 8      constructor(address _payer, address _payee, uint _amount) public {
 9          payer = _payer;
10          payee = _payee;
11          thirdParty = msg.sender;
12          amount = _amount;
13          confirmedDelivery = false;
14      }
15
16      function confirmDelivery() public {
17          require(msg.sender == thirdParty);
18          confirmedDelivery = true;
19      }
20
21      function releaseFunds() public {
22          require(confirmedDelivery);
23          address(payer).transfer(amount);
24      }
25  }
```

This use case underscores how blockchain can automate and secure business processes, reducing dependency on manual processes and neutral third parties.

Voting Systems

Public blockchains are also utilized in creating transparent and tamper-proof voting systems, enhancing the integrity of electoral processes. By recording votes on a blockchain, it becomes virtually impossible to alter votes once they are cast, thereby safeguarding the sanctity of the electoral process.

For instance, a blockchain-based voting system might be implemented as follows:

```
1  Blockchain votingSystem = new Blockchain();
2  votingSystem.addBlock(new Block("2024-11-06", "{ voterId: 'VH674', vote: '
       Candidate_1' }"));
```

Identity Verification and Management

Finally, public blockchains play a crucial role in identity verification and management. Through a decentralized mechanism, individuals can control their digital identities without relying on a central authority. This application is pivotal in mitigating identity theft and fraud.

As seen through these use cases, public blockchains, by virtue of their inherent properties, offer substantial benefits across various business sectors, driving efficiency, transparency, and security.

4.5 Security Aspects: Comparing Private and Public Options

The security attributes of blockchain technologies play a crucial role in determining their suitability for various business applications. This section delves into the security mechanisms inherent in both private and public blockchains and how these influence their reliability and trustworthiness from an enterprise perspective.

Private blockchains are characterized by restricted network access, typically governed by a single organization or a consortium of entities that have mutual interests. The controlled access mechanism significantly reduces the risk of malicious attacks, as all participants are known and vetted entities. In a private blockchain, the consensus process is streamlined since the number of nodes responsible for verifying transactions is smaller. This reduced number of nodes, while beneficial from a throughput perspective, may introduce security concerns such as the risk of collusion or the potential impact of a single point of failure.

```
// Simplified Consensus Mechanism Example in a Private Blockchain
transaction.verifyConsensus(){
    for(int i = 0; i < trustedNodes.length; i++){
        if (!trustedNodes[i].verifyTransaction(transaction)) {
            return false;
        }
    }
    return true;
}
```

Public blockchains, by contrast, permit anyone to participate in the transaction verification process without the need for authorization. This openness increases the potential attack vectors but simultaneously enhances security through decentralization. In public systems, achieving consensus involves sophisticated algorithms which often require substantial computational efforts thus incentivizing honesty and deterring malicious behavior by making attacks economically unfeasible.

```
// Example of a Public Blockchain Consensus Algorithm
block.computeProofOfWork(){
    while(true){
        if (hash(block.header) < targetDifficulty) {
            return true;
```

```
6            }
7            block.nonce++;
8        }
9  }
```

The credibility and security in public blockchains are also bolstered by cryptographic practices like proof-of-work or proof-of-stake. These methods ensure that changing historical data within the blockchain would require enormous amounts of energy and computational power, therefore safeguarding the integrity and immutability of the ledger.

```
Output example from a public blockchain's proof-of-work:
00000000000000000007abd8d2f410c49a63dda5d7c1a8564a8e7417e4bfa5da
```

A critical point of comparison lies in how both blockchain types manage data visibility. Private blockchains can implement stricter privacy controls, enabling highly confidential business operations and reducing exposure to data breaches. Conversely, public blockchains offer transparency as a form of security, allowing activities to be openly audited by anyone, thus enhancing trust through visibility.

From a technical standpoint, security in blockchains is fundamentally about the balance between accessibility and control. Private blockchains offer higher control, which is pivotal for businesses requiring privacy and data control. Public blockchains thrive on wider accessibility, which can lead to a more robust and secure network due to the larger number of nodes involved in maintaining the ledger's integrity.

Both blockchain types embody distinct security frameworks ideal for different business needs. Enterprises must weigh their specific security requirements against the distinct capabilities and potential vulnerabilities of each blockchain type to align with their operational and strategic goals. This decision hinges not merely on the desired level of security but also on the nature of the enterprise's activities, the sensitivity of the recorded data, and the required transparency to stakeholders.

4.6 Cost Implications: Setup and Ongoing Maintenance

Cost implications form a critical determinant in the choice between private and public blockchains for business applications. The setup and ongoing maintenance costs vary significantly between these two types of blockchains due to their underlying architectures, management requirements, and scaling characteristics.

Setup Costs

The initial setup cost of a blockchain system encompasses several components including technological infrastructure, personnel training, and the integration of blockchain with existing systems.

- **Technology Investment**: Private blockchains require substantial investment in setting up the network infrastructure. This involves purchasing physical servers, secure storage solutions, and proprietary software. In contrast, public blockchains are hosted on a distributed ledger through a network of nodes operated by various participants. The reliance on an existing infrastructure significantly reduces the initial capital expenditure for businesses opting for public blockchains.

- **Development and Implementation**: Deploying a private blockchain demands a higher degree of customization to tailor the network's protocol to specific business needs. This typically involves higher costs in software development, testing, and deployment. Public blockchains, however, benefit from the contributions of a wider developer community, potentially reducing the costs associated with development and implementation.

- **Integration Expenses**: Integrating blockchain technology into existing IT systems is a complex task requiring specialized skills. For private blockchains, integration costs can be higher because of the necessity to create bespoke interfaces or modifying existing protocols to ensure compatibility. Public blockchains offer more standardized solutions which may simplify integration but could require additional security measures.

Ongoing Maintenance Costs

Once operational, both private and public blockchains incur ongoing expenses related to their maintenance and operation.

- **Node Management**: In private blockchains, the business is responsible for the continuous operation and maintenance of its nodes. This includes costs for hardware maintenance, electricity consumption, and personnel to manage and secure the infrastructure. Public blockchains, while removing the burden of individual node management from the business, may involve transaction fees which can accumulate significantly with increased activity on the blockchain.

- **Network Security**: Security remains paramount for both types of blockchains, but the approach and associated costs differ. Private blockchains generally require substantial investment in security measures to protect the network from internal and external threats, including advanced cybersecurity solutions and regular audits. In contrast, the security of public blockchains is maintained by the network through cryptographic techniques and consensus algorithms. Business may need to invest in additional layers of security solutions to enhance the protection of sensitive transactions conducted on public blockchains.

- **Software Upgrades and Support**: Both private and public blockchains need regular software updates to address emerging security vulnerabilities, enhance functionalities, or improve performance. Private blockchains might lead to higher costs related to proprietary software licensing for upgrades and technical support. On the other hand, maintenance of public blockchain software may benefit from community-based support and developments, potentially reducing the costs linked to software upkeeps and technical assistance.

Algorithm 4: Cost Management Strategy for Blockchain Deployment

---
1 Initialize projected initial and operational expenditures;
2 Choose blockchain type based on strategic needs;
3 Estimate total cost of ownership over expected lifecycle;
4 Evaluate potential return on investment from blockchain implementation;
5 If private blockchain, plan long-term investment in infrastructure and personnel;
6 If public blockchain, prepare for transaction fees and enhanced security measures;
7 Incorporate flexibility for future scalability and costs;

The decision between deploying a private or a public blockchain comes down to a complex balance between initial and ongoing costs, the scope of the blockchain application, security needs, and potential scalability. Businesses must meticulously calculate total cost of ownership and balance it against the expected benefits to ensure the most cost-effective blockchain solution is chosen. This strategic choice influences not only immediate financial outlays but also long-term innovation and competitive positioning within the industry.

4.7 Regulatory Considerations for Private and Public Blockchains

Navigating through the intricate landscape of regulatory considerations is pivotal when choosing between private and public blockchains for business applications. Regulatory frameworks designed to govern the use of blockchain technology are often influenced by the level of transaction visibility and the governance models adopted by the blockchain. Consequently, understanding these nuances is essential for organizations aiming to comply with laws and regulations while harnessing blockchain capabilities.

Private blockchains offer governance flexibility, typically limited to a predefined group of participants. This select participation factor significantly simplifies regulatory compliance. Organizations can implement robust identity verification processes and can restrict access to sensitive data in alignment with data protection laws such as the General Data Protection Regulation (GDPR) in the European Union or the California Consumer Privacy Act (CCPA) in the United States. Furthermore, the auditability of private blockchains facilitates adherence to industry-specific regulations such as the Health Insurance Portability and Accountability Act (HIPAA) for healthcare data or the Sarbanes-Oxley Act for financial reporting.

- Implement stringent access controls and identity verification to ensure data privacy and protection.
- Utilize the inherent audit capabilities of blockchain to maintain and demonstrate regulatory compliance.
- Tailor the blockchain framework to meet specific industry regulations, enhancing regulatory alignment.

Public blockchains, by contrast, operate under a decentralized model which can present several regulatory challenges, primarily due to the lack of a central authority. The anonymity and borderless nature of public blockchains pose a higher risk of violation of cross-border data transfer laws and anti-money laundering (AML) statutes. Noteworthy is the challenge of complying with the Know Your Customer (KYC) regulations, a critical requirement for financial institutions.

Worldwide regulatory bodies are recognizing these challenges and starting to develop guidelines and frameworks to deal with them. For instance, the Financial Action Task Force (FATF) has issued recommendations on how cryptocurrencies, a prevalent application of public blockchains, should be regulated to prevent their use in money laundering and terrorism financing.

Despite these efforts, the dynamic and evolving nature of public blockchain technologies makes it difficult for regulatory frameworks to keep pace. This scenario often leaves businesses operating in spaces with legal uncertainties or under provisional laws that could be subject to abrupt changes as the understanding and implications of the technology evolve.

- Regularly monitor global regulatory developments as they pertain to public blockchain technologies and applications.
- Implement procedures and systems to maintain compliance with AML and KYC requirements wherever possible.
- Engage with legal experts specialized in blockchain technology to navigate the complex and evolving regulatory landscape.

The decision to opt for a private or public blockchain should be guided, among other factors, by the specific regulatory requirements and the risks a business is prepared to manage. While private blockchains provide greater control and ease in meeting compliance requirements, public blockchains offer broader transparency but come with heightened regulatory scrutiny and compliance complexities. As such, each organization must carefully assess how blockchain technology's characteristics align with their regulatory obligations and strategic goals.

4.8 Performance and Scalability: Which Suits Business Needs?

Performance and scalability are critical factors that influence the suitability of blockchain technologies for business applications. This sec-

CHAPTER 4. PRIVATE VS PUBLIC BLOCKCHAINS FOR BUSINESS

tion explores the distinctions in performance and scalability between private and public blockchains and provides guidance on choosing the appropriate type based on business requirements.

Private blockchains are characterized by their restricted participation, where access is limited to specific entities vetted by the network administrator. This controlled environment typically allows for higher transaction throughput due to the reduced number of nodes that need to reach consensus. For instance, in a private blockchain, transactions can be validated and added to the ledger in milliseconds to seconds, enhancing the performance significantly.

```
// Example of a private blockchain transaction time
TransactionTime privateBlockchain() {
    Instant start = Instant.now();
    // Assume a transaction is processed here
    Instant end = Instant.now();
    return Duration.between(start, end);
}
```

Output: PT0.035S

On the other hand, public blockchains are decentralized with no single entity controlling the network. They allow anyone to participate, which leads to a larger network size. This broader participation enhances security but often at the cost of lowered transaction speeds. Public blockchains like Bitcoin and Ethereum process transactions more slowly, typically taking several minutes to confirm due to the need for widespread agreement across thousands of nodes.

```
// Example of public blockchain transaction time
TransactionTime publicBlockchain() {
    Instant start = Instant.now();
    // Assume a transaction is processed here within a network of 10,000 nodes
    Instant end = Instant.now();
    return Duration.between(start, end);
}
```

Output: PT10M

Scalability in blockchain refers to the ability to handle a growing amount of work or its potential to accommodate growth. Private blockchains offer better scalability by design due to their controlled participation. Networking algorithms like Practical Byzantine Fault Tolerance (PBFT), used by several private blockchain implementations, provide consensus without scaling issues that often plague public blockchains.

- Private blockchains efficiently manage scaling organizational needs, thereby enhancing operational capabilities.

- Public blockchains face significant scalability challenges, mainly when the network grows and transaction volume increases.

Another aspect to consider is the type of consensus mechanism used, which directly impacts both performance and scalability. Public blockchains typically use Proof of Work (PoW) or Proof of Stake (PoS), which, while secure, are slower and less scalable in comparison to the consensus mechanisms used in private blockchains.

```
PBFT

Consensus Mechanisms

PoW, PoS
```

For organizations needing transaction privacy and speed, private blockchains are apt. They can manage higher transaction volumes and rapid processing essential for enterprise operations. However, businesses aiming for transparency, regulatory compliances, and decentralized operations might prioritize public blockchains despite the trade-offs in speed and scalability.

Various business models and requirements will dictate the choice between private and public blockchains. Enterprises must weigh their need for speed and scalability against other priorities such as security, cost, and regulatory compliance to select the most appropriate blockchain technology. The choice determines not only current operational efficiency but also future readiness as business scales and adapts.

4.9 Choosing Between Private and Public Blockchains for Your Business

Deciding whether a private or public blockchain is suitable for a business requires a nuanced understanding of each blockchain type's intrinsic attributes and their alignment with the business's specific needs and constraints. This decision is heavily influenced by factors such as the nature of the business operations, desired levels of security, transparency demands, scalability requirements, and budget constraints. One must also consider the trade-offs between control and trust.

The strategic orientation of a business often informs the choice of blockchain. Companies prioritizing confidentiality, control over operations, and faster transactions may lean towards private blockchains. In contrast, businesses that benefit from decentralized control and greater transparency might opt for public blockchains. This decision impacts business strategy and potential long-term viability in competitive markets.

- **Nature of the Business**: Businesses dealing with sensitive information or those in heavily regulated industries might prefer private blockchains for their better enforcement capabilities and refined access control.

- **Desired Level of Security**: If the paramount concern is security, public blockchains offer advantages due to their robustness against tampering and fraud, reinforced by widespread node distribution.

- **Transparency Requirements**: Industries such as charities or public sectors that require high levels of trust from stakeholders might opt for public blockchains to ensure operations are transparent and accountable.

- **Scalability Needs**: Private blockchains are typically more scalable than public ones, handling more transactions per second due to the controlled node count and optimized consensus algorithms.

- **Budget Constraints**: The cost implications, both initial and ongoing, can be significantly higher for private blockchains due to the requirement for setup, maintenance, and the operation of an owned infrastructure.

We will now explore hypothetical scenarios where businesses chose between private and public blockchains:

1. A pharmaceutical company needing to protect intellectual property and sensitive data during drug trials may choose a private blockchain to control data access and enhance security.
2. A non-profit organization aiming to maintain donor trust and ensure transparency might implement a public blockchain, thereby making all transactions public and easily verifiable.

Each decision relating to blockchain adoption must be preceded by detailed assessments and pilots to determine fit. For instance, a detailed pilot study could reveal unexpected scalability issues or integration challenges with existing IT systems, which can substantially alter the cost-benefit analysis originally envisioned. These experiments are critical in making informed, context-specific decisions that align technical capacities with business objectives.

Ultimately, the choice between a private and public blockchain model should be guided by a clear and strategic assessment of how the specific characteristics of each blockchain type advance a company's business goals while adhering to regulatory and operational constraints, fostering a competitive advantage in an increasingly digital world economy. Thus, enterprises must undertake this choice with keen attention to both current needs and future growth prospects.

4.10 Hybrid Blockchain Models: Combining the Best of Both Worlds

Hybrid blockchains embody a design philosophy that integrates elements of both private and public blockchains, aiming to harness the strengths of each while mitigating their respective weaknesses. This model facilitates controlled access and freedom simultaneously, providing a flexible framework that can be tailored to specific business requirements. In this section, we will explore the architecture of hybrid blockchains, examine their key features, and discuss practical business use cases that demonstrate their unique value proposition.

The architecture of a hybrid blockchain effectively utilizes a controlled access model similar to private blockchains, while still enabling certain data or operations to be exposed publicly, as seen in public blockchains. This is achieved through a layered approach where core ledgers can remain private and only specific subsets of data are shared on a need-to-know basis or according to strategic value.

- The first layer, the private layer, handles the bulk of data processing and is accessible only to authenticated and authorized entities. This layer is optimized for speed and privacy.

- The second layer, or the public layer, includes mechanisms for verifying certain transactions or data integrity without exposing underlying details. It utilizes various consensus mechanisms like Proof of Authority (PoA) which are less energy-intensive than Proof of Work (PoW) used in typical public blockchains.

To illustrate how hybrid blockchains operate, consider code segment handling transaction validation in a hybrid setup:

```
function validateTransaction(transaction) {
    if (isAuthorized(transaction.user)) {
        processPrivateLayer(transaction);
    } else {
        revert("Unauthorized User");
    }
    if (transaction.public) {
        validatePublicLayer(transaction);
    }
}
```

In this example, `validateTransaction` first checks whether a user is authorized in the private layer. Depending on the nature of the transaction (whether it is marked as public), the method `validatePublicLayer` might be called to interact with the public components of the blockchain.

Case studies where hybrid blockchain models have been effectively implemented underscore their practical benefits. One pertinent example is in supply chain management. Businesses can keep sensitive procurement details concealed within the private layer while using the public layer to document transactions verified by external parties like suppliers or customs officials.

Another compelling use case is in the realm of healthcare where patient records are maintained with utmost confidentiality in a private network, but anonymized data can be made available on a public ledger for research purposes. The permissioned nature of private layers ensures that only relevant healthcare professionals or authorized individuals access detailed patient information.

A scenario diagram illustrating data access in a healthcare scenario might look as follows:

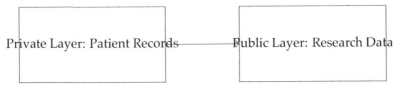

This hybrid approach offers a balance between transparency and privacy, enabling businesses to meet both regulatory and operational demands efficiently. The flexibility to configure the scope of data shared publicly and the conditions under which sharing occurs drastically reduces risks associated with data exposure and malicious activities.

In effect, hybrid blockchains provide a scalable and versatile infrastructure that can support various business applications by offering a customizable solution that does not compromise on the security or accessibility of the data involved. They represent a strategic innovation in blockchain technology, facilitating business models that require both high levels of trust and significant scalability. Through empirical case studies and evolving best practices, hybrid blockchains continue to demonstrate their significant potential in enabling secure, efficient, and transparent business operations across diverse industries.

4.11 Future Outlook: Trends in Blockchain Adoption for Business

As businesses continue to explore and expand their use of blockchain technology, several emerging trends are likely to shape its adoption in the coming years. These trends reflect ongoing developments in technology, shifts in regulatory landscapes, and changing business priorities.

Increased Adoption of Hybrid Blockchains One significant trend is the increasing interest in hybrid blockchains, which combine elements of both private and public blockchain architectures. Hybrid blockchains offer the transaction privacy and access control of private blockchains along with the security and decentralization aspects of public blockchains. This trend is driven by businesses needing to maintain private, internal workflows while also tapping into the broader blockchain network for enhanced security and verifiability.

```
# Example configuration for a hybrid blockchain setup.
Config:
  BlockchainType: Hybrid
  PublicComponents:
    - ConsensusMechanism: ProofOfWork
    - NetworkNodes: PubliclyAccessible
  PrivateComponents:
    - AccessControl: RoleBased
    - DataStorage: EncryptedSharding
```

Integration with Legacy Systems and IoT The integration of blockchain technology with legacy systems and the Internet of Things (IoT) is another burgeoning trend. As blockchain solutions become more robust, businesses are looking for seamless ways to bridge traditional IT infrastructures with modern blockchain networks. Furthermore, with the growth in IoT devices, integrating these devices with blockchain offers enhanced security and tracking of IoT-generated data.

- Integration with ERP systems for automatic ledger updates.

- Use of smart contracts for managing IoT device interactions.

- Implementation of blockchain for secure, scalable IoT data exchanges.

Focus on Programmable Blockchains Blockchains are evolving from simple distributed ledgers to fully programmable environments. Platforms like Ethereum have demonstrated the power of such advanced functionalities with their support for smart contracts. Moving forward, more enterprises might adopt or switch over to blockchains that support complex programming capabilities to automate business processes, enforce compliance, and fuel innovation.

```
Output example:
Transaction successfully executed.
Smart contract conditions met.
```

Heightened Emphasis on Regulatory Compliance Regulatory environments are intensifying scrutiny on blockchain operations, influencing trends in their adoption and utility. Compliance with data protection regulations, like GDPR in the European Union, and financial oversight laws, like the Sarbanes-Oxley Act in the United States, is becoming a priority for businesses using blockchain. Consequently, future blockchain platforms are anticipated to evolve with built-in compliance features to facilitate easier adoption by enterprises.

- Automatic enforcement of data residency regulations via smart contracts.

- Real-time auditing capabilities embedded within blockchain frameworks.

Advancements in Consensus Mechanisms Finally, innovations in consensus mechanisms, crucial for the validation of transactions on blockchain networks, continue to evolve. The shift from energy-intensive mechanisms like Proof of Work (PoW) to more energy-efficient and faster alternatives like Proof of Stake (PoS) or Practical Byzantine Fault Tolerance (PBFT) is ongoing. Such advancements promise to enhance the scalability and environmental sustainability of blockchains, making them more suitable for enterprise applications.

These trends not only highlight the dynamic nature of blockchain technology but also underscore the vast potential it holds for transforming business operations. Businesses willing to adopt and adapt to these changes are likely to find themselves at the forefront of a technological revolution that promises greater efficiency, security, and transparency in their operations.

Chapter 5

Blockchain Security and Encryption Techniques

This chapter delves into the critical security features and encryption methods that underpin blockchain technology's robustness and reliability. It examines various cryptographic techniques, including hashing and digital signatures, which ensure transaction integrity and authentication across blockchain networks. The discussion extends to the specifics of smart contract security and the overarching challenges of maintaining data privacy and security in decentralized systems, providing readers with foundational knowledge to assess and implement secure blockchain solutions.

5.1 Introduction to Security in Blockchain

Blockchain technology fundamentally redefines the approach to data security with its inherent design that is both transparent and resilient to tampering. At its core, blockchain employs a decentralized structure where data is not stored in any single location or controlled by a singular entity, thereby mitigating the risks associated with central points of failure. This section explores the underlying principles that make blockchain a secure technology and the essential security features that are instrumental in maintaining the integrity and confidentiality of blockchain networks.

Blockchain security is implemented through a combination of cryptographic techniques, consensus algorithms, and network protocols. Each block in the blockchain is secured with cryptographic hashes, specifically using the SHA-256 hashing algorithm, which converts input data of any size into a fixed 256-bit hash. This hash function is deterministic, meaning the same input will always produce the same output. The immutability of blockchain arises from these hashes as each block contains the hash of its preceding block, hence creating a chain. Given that any alteration in the input drastically changes the hash, the hashes serve as a powerful deterrent against tampering.

```
# Example of SHA-256 hash function usage in Blockchain
import hashlib

def calculate_hash(data):
    return hashlib.sha256(data.encode()).hexdigest()

# Example data input
block_data = "Block 53: Transactions Data"
block_hash = calculate_hash(block_data)
print("Hash of the block data:", block_hash)
```

Hash of the block data: 836daf...

In addition to hashing, blockchain uses public-key cryptography to ensure the confidentiality and integrity of transactions. Each user on a blockchain network possesses a unique pair of keys: a private key and a public key. The public key is openly shared within the network, while the private key is kept secret by its owner. This mechanism not only helps in encrypting data but also securely associates digital identities with transactions, thereby supporting non-repudiation and user authentication.

```
# Example of signing a transaction with RSA encryption
from Crypto.PublicKey import RSA
from Crypto.Signature import pkcs1_15
from Crypto.Hash import SHA256

# Generating private and public keys
key = RSA.generate(2048)
private_key = key.export_key()
public_key = key.publickey().export_key()

# Signing a transaction
message = 'Transaction: Send 5 BTC to Alice'
digest = SHA256.new(message.encode())
signature = pkcs1_15.new(key).sign(digest)

# The signature can now be verified using the public key
```

Further reinforcing security, blockchain networks utilize consensus mechanisms like Proof of Work (PoW) or Proof of Stake (PoS) to agree on the state of the ledger and to prevent fraudulent activities such as double spending. In PoW, for instance, participants called miners solve complex mathematical problems, and the first to solve and validate the transaction broadcasts it to the network, where others verify its validity before adding it to the blockchain. This not only secures the network but also democratizes the transaction validation process.

```
# Pseudocode representation of Proof of Work mechanism
Initialize (transaction, previousHash)
do {
    nonce = nonce + 1
    hash = calculateHash(transaction + previousHash + nonce)
} while (hash < target)
return nonce, hash
```

Through these integrated security measures, blockchain ensures that each transaction is transparently recorded, cannot be altered or erased, and is verifiable by all network participants. The architecture inherently defends against typical cybersecurity threats and positions blockchain as a suitable technology for applications requiring high levels of security, such as financial transactions, supply chain management, and identity verification. The subsequent sections will delve deeper into each of these cryptographic tools and techniques, exploring their roles in ensuring the robust security of blockchain technology.

5.2 Fundamentals of Cryptography in Blockchain

Cryptography forms the backbone of blockchain technology, providing the necessary mechanisms for data integrity, confidentiality, and authentication. At its core, blockchain cryptography employs a combination of cryptographic techniques, including hash functions, digital signatures, and public-key cryptography.

Hash Functions and Blockchain

Hash functions are a pivotal cryptographic component in blockchain. They convert an input string of any length into a fixed-size string. In the context of blockchain, hash functions enhance data integrity by ensuring that any alteration of transaction data will lead to a completely different hash output. This property is crucial in blockchain operations, as it helps in maintaining an unalterable ledger of transactions.

The most widely used hash algorithm in blockchain is SHA-256, which produces a 256-bit output. Here is a sample application of the SHA-256 algorithm:

```
import hashlib

def hash(input):
    return hashlib.sha256(input.encode()).hexdigest()

# Example of hashing
data = "Blockchain data"
hash_value = hash(data)
print(hash_value)
```

The corresponding output after hashing the data is shown below:

4f8b8a98bde9b2981f5aa292b7c285ca6579e404cb009f3a0f07a00ec9aaa3db

Public Key Cryptography

Public key cryptography, or asymmetric cryptography, is another fundamental aspect of blockchain security. It utilizes a pair of keys—a public key and a private key—for encryption and decryption processes. The public key is shared openly in the network, while the private key remains confidential to the owner.

In blockchain, public key cryptography serves two primary purposes:

- Encrypting data to ensure that only the intended recipient can decrypt it using their private key.

- Creating a digital signature that proves the ownership of data or transactions.

The process of encryption and decryption using public key systems is typically outlined as follows:

For encryption:

```
from cryptography.hazmat.primitives.asymmetric import rsa
from cryptography.hazmat.primitives.asymmetric import padding
from cryptography.hazmat.primitives import hashes
from cryptography.hazmat.primitives import serialization

# Generating keys
private_key = rsa.generate_private_key(
    public_exponent=65537,
    key_size=2048,
)

public_key = private_key.public_key()

# Message to encrypt
```

5.2. FUNDAMENTALS OF CRYPTOGRAPHY IN BLOCKCHAIN

```
15  message = b'Blockchain encrypted message'
16  ciphertext = public_key.encrypt(
17      message,
18      padding.OAEP(
19          mgf=padding.MGF1(algorithm=hashes.SHA256()),
20          algorithm=hashes.SHA256(),
21          label=None
22      )
23  )
24  print(ciphertext)
```

For decryption:

```
1  plaintext = private_key.decrypt(
2      ciphertext,
3      padding.OAEP(
4          mgf=padding.MGF1(algorithm=hashes.SHA256()),
5          algorithm=hashes.SHA256(),
6          label=None
7      )
8  )
9  print(plaintext)
```

Digital Signatures

Digital signatures are crucial for establishing the authenticity and integrity of messages and transactions in a blockchain network. They use a combination of hash functions and public-key cryptography to allow users to sign their transactions digitally. An essential aspect of digital signatures in the blockchain is the ability to verify the signer's identity without revealing sensitive personal information.

The process can be summarized algorithmically as:

Such cryptographic techniques ensure that blockchain technology maintains a high standard of security despite the decentralized nature of its architecture. Cryptography not only secures data but also enables a trustless environment where transactions are verifiable and immutable without the need for central mediation. This cryptographic foundation is what enables blockchains to disrupt traditional mechanisms of transaction and data management across industries.

> **Algorithm 5:** Creating and verifying digital signatures
>
> **Data:** Document to be signed
> **Result:** Signature creation and verification
>
> 1 initialization;
> 2 **Signing Transaction:**;
> 3 Calculate hash of document;
> 4 Use sender's private key to sign hash;
> 5 Append signature to document;
> 6 **Verifying Signature:**;
> 7 Retrieve sender's public key;
> 8 Use public key to verify signature;
> 9 If verified, confirm transaction integrity and authenticity;

5.3 Hashing Algorithms: Ensuring Data Integrity

Within the domain of blockchain security, hashing algorithms stand as the bedrock for ensuring data integrity and the immutability of the blockchain. These algorithms transform an input string of an arbitrary size into a fixed-size string of bytes, typically a digest that represents the original string concisely. Each hash is unique; even the smallest alteration in the input data will yield a significantly different hash.

The key attributes of hashing algorithms used in blockchain technology include:

- **Deterministic:** The same input will always produce the same output.

- **Quick computation:** Hash functions should generate the hash value swiftly, allowing for efficient processing in blockchain operations.

- **Pre-image resistance:** It should be computationally infeasible to reconstruct the original input from its hash output.

- **Small changes in the input produce significant changes:** This characteristic is known as the avalanche effect.

- **Collision-resistant:** Two different input values should not produce the same output hash.

5.3. HASHING ALGORITHMS: ENSURING DATA INTEGRITY

To illustrate how a simple hashing algorithm might function in blockchain contexts, consider the usage of the SHA-256 algorithm, which generates an output of 256 bits. Here's an example using Python to demonstrate SHA-256 hashing:

```
import hashlib

def calculate_hash(input_data):
    return hashlib.sha256(input_data.encode()).hexdigest()

input_data = "Blockchain Technology"
output_hash = calculate_hash(input_data)
print(output_hash)
```

The generated output hash corresponding to "Blockchain Technology" would appear as follows:

```
C7643DF8838B7B80852A84E6CAFAA37BD3A0635656034197CD65B64E2D85743F
```

Each transaction within a blockchain leverages hashing. Transactions are hashed and encoded as leaves in a data structure known as a Merkle tree (or a hash tree). This tree structure allows for efficient and secure verification of the contents of large data structures. The Merkle root, a single hash at the top of the tree, summarizes all the transactions effectively and is stored in the blockchain's header.

Here's a simplified demonstration of how a Merkle tree is constructed and utilized:

```
def hash_pair(hash1, hash2):
    return hashlib.sha256((hash1 + hash2).encode()).hexdigest()

transactions = ['tx1', 'tx2', 'tx3', 'tx4']
transaction_hashes = [calculate_hash(tx) for tx in transactions]

level_1 = [hash_pair(transaction_hashes[i], transaction_hashes[i+1]) for i in range
    (0, len(transaction_hashes), 2)]
root_hash = hash_pair(level_1[0], level_1[1])

print("Merkle Root: ", root_hash)
```

The output, representing the Merkle root for these transactions, would encapsulate the integrity of the entire set of transactions. When any single transaction changes or a fraudulent transaction is inserted, the resulting Merkle root changes, indicating an alteration or a potential security breach.

Understanding the role and mechanics of hashing algorithms is essential because they undergird the entire security architecture of blockchain technology. They ensure that even if an attacker were to gain control over a part of the blockchain network, the immutability of recorded transactions and the integrity of the data could successfully thwart such attempts. Given the evolution in computational power, the continuing evaluation and update of used hashing algorithms is critical to maintain efficacy against potential cryptographic attacks.

5.4 Digital Signatures for Authentication and Non-Repudiation

Digital signatures are a fundamental cryptographic tool used in blockchain technology to ensure both authentication and non-repudiation. These signatures allow participants to verify the origin and integrity of a message, transaction, or document without requiring any central authority, thereby fitting perfectly into the decentralized nature of blockchain.

Operational Mechanism of Digital Signatures

The operational mechanism of digital signatures in blockchain utilizes public key cryptography. Each user in a blockchain network possesses a unique pair of keys: a private key, which is secret, and a public key, which is disseminated across the network. The process of digital signing involves generating a signature from the data to be signed and the signer's private key. This signature is then appended to the data and sent over to the network.

The mathematical relationship between the private and public keys allows the signature to be verified by anyone on the network, using the sender's public key. The primary steps involved in the creation and verification of digital signatures can be formalized as follows:

5.4. DIGITAL SIGNATURES FOR AUTHENTICATION AND NON-REPUDIATION

Algorithm 6: Digital Signature Generation and Verification

Data: Original message M, Private key PK_{pr}, Public key PK_{pu}
Result: Signature S on message M
1 Signature Generation(M, PK_{pr});
2 $S \leftarrow$ Encrypt(M, PK_{pr});
3 send (M, S) to receiver;
4 ;
5 Signature Verification (M, S, PK_{pu});
6 $M' \leftarrow$ Decrypt(S, PK_{pu});
7 **if** $M' == M$ **then**
8 $\quad$ return Valid Signature;
9 **else**
10 $\quad$ return Invalid Signature;
11 **end**

Cryptographic Algorithms Employed

The effectiveness and security of digital signatures depend primarily on the cryptographic algorithm employed. Common algorithms include RSA (Rivest–Shamir–Adleman), ECDSA (Elliptic Curve Digital Signature Algorithm), and EdDSA (Edwards-curve Digital Signature Algorithm). Each has unique properties that affect their performance and security level.

For example, RSA relies on the difficulty of factoring large composite numbers, whereas ECDSA and EdDSA are based on the mathematical challenges of elliptic curves. These differences influence the size of the keys and the overall security, with elliptic curve techniques usually providing high security with shorter key lengths, leading to faster computations and lower power requirements.

Application in Blockchain Transactions

In blockchain systems, every transaction is digitally signed using the private key of the sender. This ensures that transactions are authenticated and cannot be repudiated. Here is a typical example of how digital signatures are integrated into blockchain transactions:

```
1  Transaction: Sender A -> Receiver B, Amount = 100
2
3  // Sender A's public key is known
4  // Sender A encrypts the transaction details using their private key
```

```
 5  Signature = Encrypt("Transaction Details", Sender_A_Private_Key)
 6
 7  // This transaction and its signature are broadcast to all nodes
 8  Broadcast(Transaction + Signature)
 9
10  // Any node can use Sender A's public key to verify the signature
11  VerifySignature("Transaction Details", Signature, Sender_A_Public_Key)
```

Successful verification by any node means the transaction is accepted into the blockchain, after ensuring no double-spend has occurred.

Security Concerns and Limitations

While digital signatures provide robust security features, they are not without limitations. The possibility of a private key being compromised remains the most significant risk. If a private key is stolen or reconstructed through quantum computing attacks, the integrity of the digital signature collapses. To mitigate this risk, regular updating of key pairs and secure key management practices are essential.

Moreover, the advancement in quantum computing poses a threat to current cryptographic standards, including those used in digital signatures. This necessitates ongoing research into quantum-resistant cryptographic algorithms, some of which are already being considered for blockchain implementations.

Digital signatures are indispensable in the context of blockchain security, offering efficiencies in authentication and non-repudiation that are critical in decentralized systems. Their integration into blockchain technology enhances trust and reliability, allowing for secure transactions and data integrity without the need for intermediaries. As the blockchain technology evolves, so will the cryptographic methods ensuring its security, with digital signatures at the heart of this ongoing development.

5.5 Encryption Techniques for Blockchain Data Security

Securing data within a blockchain network requires the utilization of various encryption techniques. These techniques not only protect data at rest but also ensure secure data transmission between parties. This section explores symmetric and asymmetric encryption methods,

5.5. ENCRYPTION TECHNIQUES FOR BLOCKCHAIN DATA SECURITY

alongside the role of secure socket layers (SSL) and transport layer security (TLS) in safeguarding data.

Symmetric encryption, also known as private-key cryptography, uses a single key for both encryption and decryption. The primary advantage of symmetric encryption is its efficiency, which makes it suitable for environments where data volumes are large and performance is a critical factor. The most commonly used symmetric encryption algorithm in blockchain technology is the Advanced Encryption Standard (AES). AES is favored due to its high security and fast performance. Below is an example of AES encryption utilized in a blockchain context:

```
from Crypto.Cipher import AES
import os

def encrypt_data(data):
    key = os.urandom(16)  # Generate a random 16-byte key
    cipher = AES.new(key, AES.MODE_EAX)
    nonce = cipher.nonce
    ciphertext, tag = cipher.encrypt_and_digest(data.encode('utf-8'))

    return (key, nonce, ciphertext, tag)
```

Upon applying AES encryption, the output appears as follows:

```
(Key: b'\xde\x0b\x9a\xf3\x1b\xc8\xd2\xe5\x1e\x0b\xfb\x9f\x8d\xb3\xd8\xb0',
Nonce: b'\xc0Mz\xe5\x12\xe9#|',
Ciphertext: b'\xeb\x9a\x91\xfe...',
Tag: b'\x01\x02\x03...')
```

Asymmetric encryption, or public-key cryptography, involves two keys: a public key and a private key. In blockchain networks, this method is extensively used for data encryption and verification purposes. RSA (Rivest-Shamir-Adleman) is one of the prevalent asymmetric encryption algorithms. It is particularly useful for secure data transmission in decentralized networks where trust establishment is crucial and parties are often unknown to each other.

The following code exemplifies RSA encryption:

```
from Crypto.PublicKey import RSA
from Crypto.Cipher import PKCS1_OAEP

def generate_keys():
    key = RSA.generate(2048)
    private_key = key.export_key()
    public_key = key.publickey().export_key()
    return private_key, public_key

def encrypt_with_public_key(public_key, data):
    public_key = RSA.import_key(public_key)
    cipher = PKCS1_OAEP.new(public_key)
    encrypted_data = cipher.encrypt(data.encode('utf-8'))
    return encrypted_data
```

When data is encrypted using the RSA method, the encrypted data is represented as:

```
Encrypted data: b'\x00\x8d\xbaK\x03\x1d...'
```

In addition to these encryption mechanisms, SSL and TLS play pivotal roles in securing data transmission within a blockchain network. These protocols establish an encrypted link between a web server and a browser, or between two servers, ensuring that all data transmitted remains confidential and protected from interception. These protocols are implemented through a handshake process, involving cipher suite negotiation, key exchange, and mutual authentication using certificates.

To conclude, the careful selection and proper implementation of encryption techniques are fundamental for maintaining the integrity and confidentiality of blockchain data. Whether choosing symmetric encryption for its performance benefits or asymmetric encryption for secure data exchanges, the adequacy of the encryption strategy directly correlates with the assurance level required by the application. Additionally, the reinforcement of data transmissions with SSL or TLS assures a comprehensive security framework that is robust against diverse and evolving threats.

5.6 Smart Contract Security: Best Practices and Common Pitfalls

Smart contracts are autonomous scripts residing on blockchain platforms, executing predefined conditions of an agreement automatically. Due to their self-executing nature and critical role in automating processes, ensuring their security is paramount. This section discusses several best practices for smart contract development and highlights common pitfalls to avoid.

Best Practices for Enhancing Smart Contract Security

1. Comprehensive Testing and Audits:

- Developing a robust testing framework is essential for identifying and rectifying vulnerabilities in smart contracts. Implementing unit tests, integration tests, and end-to-end tests can uncover potential issues at different stages of the development lifecycle.

- Regular audits conducted by external security experts can provide an independent assessment of the smart contracts' security posture. These audits should include both automated tools and manual review to ensure thorough inspection.

2. **Establishing Secure Development Lifecycle (SDLC) Processes:**

- Integrating security into the software development lifecycle is crucial for developing secure smart contracts. This involves adopting security best practices at each stage of development, from planning and design to implementation and maintenance.
- Security should be a continuous consideration, not a one-time check. Regular updates, vulnerability patches, and maintaining awareness of new security threats are integral to the lifecycle.

3. **Utilizing Known Libraries and Inheriting from Established Contracts:**

- Instead of writing code from scratch, using well-vetted libraries and inheriting from contracts that have been extensively tested can reduce the risk of introducing new vulnerabilities.
- Trusted libraries such as OpenZeppelin offer pre-built smart contracts and modules which have undergone rigorous security assessments.

4. **Minimizing Complexity and Modularizing Code:**

- Simplifying the smart contract logic helps avoid security flaws caused by complex and unmanageable code. Breaking down the contract into smaller, manageable, and reusable components can enhance security and maintainability.
- Each module should be responsible for handling a specific functionality. This segregation assists in isolating potential breaches without affecting the entire system.

Common Pitfalls in Smart Contract Development

1. Reentrancy Attacks:

- A Reentrancy attack occurs when a function makes an external call to another untrusted contract before resolving its effects. Attackers can exploit these calls to reenter and disrupt the initial function.

- The famous DAO attack is a prime example of a Reentrancy attack. Preventing such attacks involves ensuring that all state changes occur before calling external contracts or using reentrancy guards.

2. Overflow and Underflow:

- Integer overflow and underflow can occur when arithmetic operations reach the maximum or minimum limits of the storage size. These bugs can lead to unexpected behavior and vulnerabilities.

- Safe arithmetic operations should be mandated by using libraries such as SafeMath from OpenZeppelin, which contain built-in checks to prevent these issues.

3. Fallback Function Vulnerabilities:

- Improper implementation of fallback functions can lead to loss of ETH or cause the contract to execute unintended actions. Fallback functions are triggered when a contract receives a transaction with no calldata.

- Ensuring that fallback functions are well-designed and only minimally implemented is crucial for preventing unintended interactions with the contract.

4. Gas Limit and Loops:

- Contracts with loops that execute an unpredictable number of iterations can potentially run out of gas, causing transactions to fail. This not only disrupts contract functions but also can lead to denial of service attacks.

- Avoiding unbounded loops and instead implementing fixed-run or capped iterations can mitigate the risks associated with such infinite loops.

Ensuring the security of smart contracts requires a proactive, thorough, and strategic approach. By adhering to best practices such as employing matured libraries, simplifying code, auditing consistently, and understanding the common pitfalls, developers can significantly enhance the reliability and security of smart contracts. These measures not only prevent potential financial losses but also build trust in the blockchain platforms that host these contracts.

5.7 Security Challenges in Decentralized Networks

Decentralized networks, by their very nature, pose unique security challenges. These challenges stem from the lack of a central authority, the intrinsic openness of the system, and the reliance on consensus mechanisms for network governance. This section explores several key security vulnerabilities inherent in decentralized networks and discusses the implications of these vulnerabilities on blockchain technology.

Sybil Attacks

One of the primary security concerns in any decentralized network is the Sybil attack. In this attack, a single actor gains disproportionate influence in the network by creating a large number of pseudonymous entities. This can lead to the attacker disrupting or manipulating network operations through these fake identities.

In the context of blockchain, a Sybil attack could potentially endanger the integrity of the consensus process. For instance, in networks utilizing a Proof-of-Work (PoW) consensus mechanism, an attacker could control enough computational power to influence the blockchain ledger. This form of attack is often referred to as a 51% attack.

Routing Attacks

Decentralized networks heavily rely on the internet for message passing between nodes. During a routing attack, an attacker can intercept and manipulate the data packets en route. This manipulation could involve altering, delaying, or dropping the packets. The consequences of such attacks in blockchain include delayed transaction confirmations or even double-spending, where the same digital token is spent multiple times.

End-point Security Vulnerabilities

The security of a decentralized network is not solely dependent on the network architecture but also on the security of the individual nodes or end-points. These nodes, typically user-controlled computers or devices, are vulnerable to malware and phishing attacks. If an attacker gains control over a user's private keys through such methods, they can execute unauthorized transactions on the user's behalf.

Smart Contract Vulnerabilities

Smart contracts are autonomous scripts that reside on the blockchain. However, they can contain vulnerabilities, either in their design or implementation. Such vulnerabilities may be exploited to alter the intended behavior of the contract, leading to loss of funds or unexpected contract behaviors.

For instance, the DAO attack on the Ethereum blockchain in 2016 exploited a recursive calling vulnerability in a smart contract, leading to a significant financial loss.

51% Attack

As previously mentioned under Sybil attacks, the 51% attack represents a significant threat to blockchains using PoW consensus mechanisms. If an attacker controls more than half of the network's hashing power, they can manipulate the blockchain's state. This could involve reversing transactions or preventing new transactions from gaining confirmations, thereby undermining the blockchain's reliability and trustworthiness.

Network Partitioning (Eclipse Attacks)

In an eclipse attack, an attacker takes control of all the peer connections of a node, effectively isolating it from other honest nodes. This isolation can trick the affected node into accepting an attacker's alternative blockchain reality, or it can be used to stage further attacks such as double spending.

An effective mitigation strategy involves implementing robust peer discovery and connection management protocols that resist monopolization by potential attackers.

The decentralized nature of blockchain networks offers numerous benefits in terms of redundancy, transparency, and resistance to censorship. However, it also introduces a variety of security challenges that need to be meticulously managed. Addressing these challenges is crucial to the successful deployment and operational stability of blockchain systems. Continuous improvements in cryptographic techniques, consensus algorithms, and network protocols are imperative to safeguard these digital ecosystems against evolving security threats. Thus, maintaining and enhancing security in decentralized networks is not only a technical necessity but also a critical ongoing task that ensures trust and integrity within the blockchain infrastructure.

5.8 Quantum Resistance: Future-proofing Blockchain Security

The rapid advancements in quantum computing pose significant risks to the cryptographic underpinnings of traditional blockchain technologies. Current cryptographic practices, such as RSA and ECC (Elliptic Curve Cryptography), which are fundamentally dependent on factorization and discrete logarithm problems, could potentially be compromised by quantum computational abilities. This section examines the principles of quantum resistance and evaluates methodologies that can be integrated into blockchain systems to mitigate these risks.

The core vulnerability arises from quantum algorithms like Shor's algorithm, which can efficiently solve integer factorization and discrete logarithm problems, and Grover's algorithm, which provides a quadratic speedup for searching unsorted databases. These capabilities enable quantum computers to break the cryptographic security that protects blockchain.

To counteract these threats, blockchain systems must evolve towards quantum-resistant cryptographic algorithms. These are often referred to as post-quantum cryptography (PQC). The main classes of PQC that are currently considered to be promising for blockchain integration include:

- Hash-based cryptography
- Lattice-based cryptography
- Multivariate polynomial cryptography
- Code-based cryptography

Hash-based cryptography is particularly noteworthy for its simplicity and high speed, with the security based on the well-understood assumption of the hardness of finding collisions in hash functions. This characteristic makes it a strong candidate for securing blockchain transactions even in a post-quantum world.

Lattice-based cryptography is another leading choice. It is based on the hardness of lattice problems like the Shortest Vector Problem (SVP) and the Closest Vector Problem (CVP), which are believed to be resistant to both classical and quantum attacks. An example of a lattice-based cryptographic algorithm is NTRU, which combines both encryption and digital signatures functionalities and is known for its efficiency in terms of computational and communication overhead.

Multivariate polynomial cryptography and code-based cryptography are less explored but provide feasible alternatives due to their resistance against quantum attacks. The security of multivariate polynomial cryptography is derived from the complexity of solving systems of multivariate quadratic equations, while code-based cryptography builds on the difficulty of decoding a general linear code.

Implementing these quantum-resistant algorithms into blockchain infrastructure involves several considerations:

- **Key Size and Transaction Overhead**: Increased key sizes can lead to bigger blocks and, consequently, increased processing times and storage requirements.
- **Compatibility**: Ensuring that new cryptographic algorithms operate seamlessly with existing blockchain protocols without compromising on functionality or security.
- **Regulation and Standardization**: Engaging with ongoing efforts by bodies such as the National Institute of Standards and Technology (NIST) to standardize post-quantum cryptographic techniques.

The transition to quantum-resistant blockchains not only involves upgrading cryptographic protocols but also necessitates comprehensive audits and updates to the entire blockchain ecosystem, including smart contracts and decentralized applications (dApps).

Listing 5.1: Example Implementation of Hash-based Signature Algorithm

```
# Example Python implementation using hash-based signatures for Post-Quantum
    Security

import hashlib

def create_hash(input_data):
    return hashlib.sha256(input_data.encode()).hexdigest()

def generate_signature(private_key, data):
    hash_data = create_hash(data)
    # Signature generation logic using the private key and the hash
    signature = hash_data # Simplified for illustration
    return signature

data = "Blockchain transaction data"
private_key = "private_key_example"
signature = generate_signature(private_key, data)
print("Signature:", signature)
```

Signature: 5f16f4c9f91b8ce688b041b2ccf9187e2a6f2456753igf461bfb46fd8725bf92

In deploying quantum-resistant technologies, blockchain platforms not only shield against emerging quantum threats but also reinforce their position as tamper-proof and secure infrastructures in the face of rapidly evolving computational powers. The proactive incorporation of PQC ensures the longevity and security of blockchain systems against the conceivable future scenario of a quantum-enabled world capable of breaking current encryption models.

5.9 Security Tools and Protocols for Blockchain Environments

The field of blockchain security is multifaceted, involving both proactive and reactive measures to protect data integrity, ensure transaction confidentiality, and maintain user privacy. This section explores the primary tools and protocols necessary to safeguard blockchain environments from common threats and vulnerabilities.

Cryptography Libraries and Development Kits

To start, cryptographic libraries and development kits form the foundational layer for implementing robust security in blockchain applications. These libraries provide well-tested functionalities that prevent common errors associated with custom cryptographic implementations. Popular libraries such as OpenSSL and Bouncy Castle offer a comprehensive suite of cryptographic algorithms that are critical in blockchain applications, including encryption, hashing, and digital signatures.

```
# Example of using the Bouncy Castle library in a blockchain application
from org.bouncycastle.jce.provider.BouncyCastleProvider import Security

# Adding the Bouncy Castle provider
Security.addProvider(BouncyCastleProvider())
# Example usage: Encrypting data using AES algorithm
cipher = Cipher.getInstance("AES/GCM/NoPadding", "BC")
```

Using these libraries ensures compliance with current cryptographic standards, minimizing the risk of vulnerabilities due to outdated or flawed implementations.

Secure Wallet Protocols

Blockchain wallets are essential for managing cryptocurrencies and digital assets securely. Wallet software generally utilizes a combination of public-key cryptography and secure key management protocols to ensure that only legitimate users can access and transact with their assets. Protocols such as WalletConnect and hardware wallets like Ledger Nano X enhance security by facilitating blockchain interactions in a more secure and user-friendly manner.

```
# Connecting a DApp to a mobile wallet using WalletConnect
import WalletConnect from "@walletconnect/client";
import QRCodeModal from "@walletconnect/qrcode-modal";

const walletConnector = new WalletConnect({
  bridge: "https://bridge.walletconnect.org",
  qrcodeModal: QRCodeModal,
});

walletConnector.createSession();
```

These tools enable secure, multi-platform interactions between blockchain applications and users' wallets, incorporating measures like two-factor authentication and air-gapped operations to mitigate the risks of cyber attacks and unauthorized access.

Smart Contract Auditing Tools

Smart contract vulnerabilities pose significant risks, including financial losses due to exploits in contract logic. Automated tools and platforms such as MythX, Slither, and Etherscan provide security auditing services that detect vulnerabilities and code smells in smart contracts. Moreover, these tools assist developers in adhering to best practices and avoiding common pitfalls in smart contract programming.

```
# Basic usage of the Slither tool for analyzing a smart contract
slither MySmartContract.sol --print human-summary
```

```
+------------------+-------+
|      Issue       | Count |
+------------------+-------+
| Reentrancy       |   2   |
| Unchecked Calls  |   5   |
| Outdated Compiler|   1   |
+------------------+-------+
```

Contracts that undergo rigorous auditing are less likely to contain severe security flaws, giving confidence to developers and stakeholders in the platform's security.

Consensus Mechanisms Enhancements

Protecting the integrity of the consensus mechanism is essential for preventing attacks such as double-spending and majority attacks. Recent developments in consensus algorithms, including Proof of Stake (PoS), Delegated Proof of Stake (DPoS), and practical Byzantine fault tolerance (PBFT), provide alternatives to the traditional Proof of Work (PoW) mechanism, reducing the risk of 51% attacks while enhancing scalability and energy efficiency.

```
# Example of a basic PBFT consensus mechanism implementation
for node in network.nodes:
    if node.state == VALIDATE:
        if consesus.is_reached():
            commit_block(block)
            break
```

Implementing these advanced consensus protocols reduces the overall security risks for blockchain networks, especially those prone to specific attacks related to their less robust consensus mechanisms.

Each tool and protocol discussed here contributes uniquely to securing blockchain environments. By employing a combination of these methods, developers can substantially mitigate the risks associated with decentralized technologies. This combination of strategies ensures that blockchain applications remain secure, reliable, and ready to handle diverse and challenging operational environments.

5.10 Implementing Multi-layer Security in Blockchain Systems

Implementing multi-layer security in blockchain systems is paramount to ensuring the resilience and trustworthiness of blockchain technology. Security in this context spans several layers, each addressing different threats and vulnerabilities prevalent in a decentralized environment. This section will cover the integration of multiple security measures at various layers: network, consensus, transaction, and application.

At the network layer, it is crucial to prevent potential attacks such as Sybil or Eclipse attacks that can compromise the entire network. Network security can be enhanced by implementing a robust peer-to-peer (P2P) protocol configuration that includes node identity management through cryptographic techniques. Generating and verifying node identities using Public Key Infrastructure (PKI) ensures that only authenticated nodes participate in the network. The following code snippet exemplifies the implementation of node authentication:

```
from Crypto.PublicKey import RSA

# Generate RSA key pair
key = RSA.generate(2048)

# Node identity
public_key = key.publickey().exportKey()
private_key = key.exportKey()

def authenticate_node(node_public_key):
    # Assume a function that verifies node's public key against a CA
    is_authenticated = verify_certificate(node_public_key)
    return is_authenticated
```

In terms of consensus layer security, enhancing the resilience against attacks, such as the 51% attack, involves not only the choice of a robust consensus algorithm but also monitoring and timely response mechanisms. For blockchains utilizing Proof of Work (PoW), choosing an appropriate difficulty target and adjusting it periodically can prevent monopolization of the mining process. Furthermore, for blockchains based on Proof of Stake (PoS) protocols, measures like penalizing malicious validators and incorporating multi-factor authentication mechanisms to verify stake ownership can be helpful.

At the transaction layer, ensuring the integrity and non-repudiation of transactions is crucial. Digital signatures, serving as proof of consent from the sender, play a critical role here. More so, implementing robust input validation and transaction propagation policies can prevent various transaction-based attacks such as double-spending. Below is a code example on how digital signatures might be utilized:

```
from Crypto.Signature import pkcs1_15
from Crypto.Hash import SHA256

message = b'Transaction content'
digest = SHA256.new(message)

# Sender signs the transaction
signature = pkcs1_15.new(private_key).sign(digest)

# Verifying the signature
def verify_transaction_signature(public_key, message, signature):
    digest = SHA256.new(message)
    try:
        pkcs1_15.new(public_key).verify(digest, signature)
        return True
    except (ValueError, TypeError):
        return False
```

The application layer encompasses smart contracts and decentralized applications (dApps). It is vital to adopt best practices in coding, conduct thorough audits using both automated tools and manual inspections, and implement strict access controls. Observance of established security patterns, coupled with proactive vulnerability assessments, ensures the resilience of application-layer entities against execution flaws such as reentrancy and integer overflow vulnerabilities.

Considering the heterogeneity and complexity of blockchain systems, a one-size-fits-all approach to security does not suffice. Blockchain platforms must therefore implement a flexible, yet rigorous multi-layered security strategy that adapts to their specific operational models and threat landscapes. By meticulously adopting appropriate security measures at each layer, blockchain systems can ensure that they are not only robust against isolated threats but also have the resilience to withstand sophisticated, multi-vector attacks that target multiple layers simultaneously. The integration of advanced cryptographic mechanisms and continuous monitoring further enhances the security posture, thereby maintaining the integrity and trust that are fundamental to blockchain technology.

5.11 Auditing and Monitoring for Enhanced Blockchain Security

Blockchain auditing involves systematically reviewing and verifying a blockchain's operations, including its smart contracts and transaction records, to ensure security and compliance with established protocols. Monitoring, on the other hand, is a continuous process of overseeing the blockchain network to detect and respond to real-time security threats and anomalies.

Effective auditing in blockchain involves comprehensive inspections of smart contract code. Moreover, transaction histories across the blockchain must be thoroughly examined to detect any discrepancies or anomalous patterns that might suggest malicious activities or misconfigurations.

```solidity
// Example of a basic smart contract audit code snippet in Solidity
pragma solidity ^0.5.0;

contract AuditExample {
    uint public transactionsCount;

    // Modifiers to check transaction integrity
    modifier validTransaction() {
        require(transactionsCount < 1000, "Transaction limit reached");
        _;
    }

    function addTransaction() public validTransaction {
        transactionsCount++;
    }
}
```

The above Solidity code demonstrates a preliminary check where transactions are capped at a maximum, ensuring that no overflow or other types of attack can exploit the contract once this set limit is reached.

Auditing tools and frameworks play a crucial role in ensuring the integrity and security of blockchain applications. Tools such as Mythril, Slither, and Oyente automatically analyze smart contracts to detect vulnerabilities like reentrancy, integer underflows, and out-of-bounds access. Outputs from these tools often include critical information, such as:

Vulnerability	Contract	Severity
Reentrancy	AuditExample	High
Integer Overflow	AuditExample	Medium

Monitoring blockchain networks involves deploying tools that track changes to the ledger in real time, monitor pool sizes, transaction rates, and validate consensus activity. Nodes within the network can be scrutinized to ensure they haven't been compromised by examining incoming and outgoing connections and transaction patterns.

The implementation of Intrusion Detection Systems (IDS) and Intrusion Prevention Systems (IPS) is paramount in a robust blockchain security strategy. These systems analyze network traffic to detect patterns that deviate from the norm, intervening before potential breaches exploit vulnerabilities.

- Continuous monitoring analyzes network packets, flagging data that might indicate a security breach.

- Alerts are generated in real-time, facilitating swift corrective actions to mitigate potential threats.

- Transaction audits are periodically conducted to ensure all recorded transactions are valid and tamper-proof.

As blockchain platforms evolve, the interaction between these security measures intensifies. Future blockchain implementations must consider advanced, AI-based security systems capable of adapting to new threats dynamically.

The integration of auditing and monitoring processes forms a defensive duet that is crucial for maintaining the security vitality of blockchain infrastructures. Through diligent auditing complemented by vigilant monitoring, blockchain systems can uphold robust security standards that are essential in the revolutionary aim of blockchain technology.

5.12 Conclusion: The Importance of Robust Security in Blockchain Implementations

The preceding discussions have elaborated the various facets of security within blockchain technology, underpinning the necessity of integrating robust cryptographic mechanisms to uphold integrity, confidentiality, and availability in digital transactions. Through an examination of hashing algorithms, digital signatures, and encryption techniques, the inherent security features of blockchain have been thoroughly explored, providing a vital foundation for trust in decentralized systems.

A critical insight emerged from the analysis of hashing algorithms, highlighted by their indispensable role in guaranteeing data integrity. The application of functions like SHA-256 ensures that even minuscule alterations in input data produce unrecognizably different hashes, safeguarding against unauthorized data modifications. Secure hashing offers the blockade that prevents adversaries from compromising the transaction records encapsulated within blockchain blocks, an assurance delineated through the application of Merkle trees to enhance data verifiability without excessive overhead.

Moreover, the utilization of digital signatures manifests as a profound bolstering of both authentication and non-repudiation. Enabled through cryptographic keys, signatures ensure that transactions are both attributable and irreversible once appended to the blockchain. This mechanism not only fortifies transaction security but also instills confidence among users regarding the immutability of the ledger.

Encryption techniques further augment blockchain security by provisioning for data confidentiality—a pivotal aspect particularly in scenarios where transaction data may involve sensitive information. Techniques such as public key encryption facilitate a secure exchange of data on an otherwise transparent network, reaffirming the adaptable nature of blockchain security to diverse application needs.

In addressing the complexities of smart contract security, it has been acknowledged that while they allow for unprecedented applications, they are also susceptible to specific vulnerabilities such as reentrancy attacks and issues stemming from programming oversights. The development and incorporation of best practices and robust development frameworks are therefore imperative to mitigate such risks.

The overarching challenges in decentralized networks also necessitate a nuanced understanding of network-specific threats and the adoption of specialized security measures. As examined, the aspects of consensus algorithms and network partitioning articulate significant roles in sustaining the operational and security standards required by blockchain systems.

As blockchain technologies evolve, the emergence of advanced computational capabilities such as quantum computing posits potential disruptions to current cryptographic standards. Proactive measures,

5.12. CONCLUSION: THE IMPORTANCE OF ROBUST SECURITY IN BLOCKCHAIN IMPLEMENTATIONS

focused on quantum resistance, are not just optional but necessary to future-proof blockchain technologies against upcoming shifts in computational paradigms.

Undeniably, the multiplicity of security tools and protocols tailored for blockchain environments, as well as methodologies for auditing and monitoring, consolidate the layers of security essential for robust blockchain implementations. Implementing a multi-layer security strategy, as discussed, plays an essential role in not just defending against, but also anticipating, a variety of sophisticated threats.

This comprehensive appraisal of blockchain security underscores the imperative of maintaining high security standards. Each layer of security from cryptographic primitives to the protocols and tools designed for blockchain, collectively contributes to a resilient ecosystem. Therefore, enterprises and individuals alike must stay abreast with the evolving security landscape, ensuring diligent, ongoing assessments and enhancements to their blockchain implementations to foster trust, reliability, and scalability.

The journey through various security dimensions within this discourse thrusts forward a clear message: the integrity and success of blockchain implementations are inexorably tied to the rigor of their security measures. As blockchain technology continues to refine and integrate into global infrastructures, the commitment to stringent, rigorously tested security practices will remain central to its effectiveness and acceptance.

Chapter 6

Smart Contracts and Their Applications

This chapter explores the concept of smart contracts, programmable agreements that automatically execute conditions on the blockchain. It covers the technical foundation, deployment, and practical uses of smart contracts across various industries. By examining case studies and current implementations, the discussion highlights the benefits these contracts offer, such as increased transparency and reduced operational costs, while also considering the technical and legal challenges involved.

6.1 Introduction to Smart Contracts

Smart contracts represent a transformative technology that fundamentally alters the landscape of agreements and transactions. By embedding contractual clauses within the protocol of decentralized networks, such as those found in blockchain technology, these contracts execute automatically based on the fulfillment of predefined conditions.

A smart contract is essentially a program stored on a blockchain that runs when predetermined conditions are met. They are typically coded in high-level programming languages that are suited for blockchain environments, such as Solidity in the Ethereum network. The automation and decentralization aspects lead to a reduction in operational inefficiencies and remove the need for intermediaries, streamlining business processes significantly.

At its core, a smart contract includes three main elements: the agreement terms encoded as functionalities in the smart contract code, trigger events recognized by the blockchain network that determine when the smart contract executes, and the execution that manages the transfer of currencies or assets following the prescribed agreement logic. The immutability and security of blockchains ensure that the contracts are resistant to tampering, thus increasing trust among parties.

To begin with, one must understand the distinction between traditional contracts and smart contracts. Traditional contracts involve manual interventions for execution and often require third-party intermediaries such as lawyers or escrow services to ensure compliance and execute the terms. In contrast, smart contracts automate execution and facilitate transaction transparency. This is exemplified in the code below:

```
//Pseudocode example of a simple smart contract
contract PaymentContract {
    address public payer;
    address payable public payee;
    uint public paymentAmount;
    bool public paid;

    constructor(address _payer, address payable _payee, uint _paymentAmount) {
        payer = _payer;
        payee = _payee;
        paymentAmount = _paymentAmount;
        paid = false;
    }

    function executePayment() public {
        require(msg.sender == payer);
        require(address(this).balance >= paymentAmount);
        payee.transfer(paymentAmount);
        paid = true;
    }

    function deposit() payable public {}
}
```

The smart contract designed in the above example, when deployed to a blockchain, ensures that the payment from a payer to a payee can only occur if the payer initiates the payment and there are sufficient funds to cover the transaction. This prevents potential disputes and delays associated with conventional payment processes.

The deployment of these contracts begins with writing the contract code, followed by testing for vulnerabilities and finally deploying it on a blockchain network. This deployment process is crucial and error-prone but ensures that once deployed, the contract behaves exactly as specified without alterations.

Smart contracts enable numerous applications across various sectors. Their potential extends beyond simple transactions and into complex, multi-party agreements, supply chain management, financial services, and beyond. By transforming contract management and engagement, they offer significant advantages over traditional contract law, particularly in enforcing agreements and reducing potential conflicts.

Having laid the groundwork in this section, the subsequent parts of this chapter delve deeper into how smart contracts operate, including their programming, deployment, and integration into business processes across industries. The automation of agreement execution and the self-enforcing nature of smart contracts not only ensure compliance but also significantly enhance operational efficiency. Furthermore, the inherently secure architecture of blockchain provides robust protection against fraud and unauthorized modifications. This sets the stage for exploring the technical layers and components that facilitate such capabilities in following sections.

6.2 How Smart Contracts Work: A Technical Overview

Smart contracts are self-executing contracts with the terms of the agreement directly written into lines of code. The code and the agreements contained therein exist across a distributed, decentralized blockchain network. The code controls the execution, and transactions are trackable and irreversible.

Smart contracts follow a simple principle: *if* predefined rules are met, *then* certain actions are automatically executed. These contracts run on blockchain technology, ensuring that all participants know the outcome immediately without any intermediator or time delay.

Lifecycle of a Smart Contract

The lifecycle of a smart contract generally involves the following steps:

- **Authoring:** The contract is written using a specific programming language. Popular languages for writing smart contracts include Solidity, Vyper, and Chaincode.

- **Testing:** Before deployment, the contract must be thoroughly tested to ensure that it functions as expected. This step helps in identifying and fixing bugs.
- **Deployment:** Once tested, the contract is deployed to the blockchain. It becomes immutable and can be interacted with by users or other contracts.
- **Execution:** When predefined conditions are met, the smart contract automatically executes the agreed-upon actions.
- **Termination:** Depending on the design, a contract may have conditions upon which it can terminate or it might continue indefinitely.

Execution Environment

Smart contracts operate in a highly deterministic, transaction-based state machine. This environment is part of blockchain technology. Within this framework:

- Every transaction is submitted by an externally owned account, initiated by a signature corresponding to the account's private key.
- State transitions occur by executing the transactions on all nodes of the network. Each node updates its copy of the state of the blockchain.

The Ethereum Virtual Machine (EVM) is a prominent example of such an execution environment. It is designed to serve as a runtime environment for smart contracts based on Ethereum. It provides a sandboxed virtual stack embedded within each full Ethereum node, capable of executing contract bytecode, which is compiled from high-level languages, such as Solidity.

Transactions and Gas

Executing actions on smart contracts requires a fee, known as "gas", which compensates for the computing energy required to process and validate transactions on the blockchain. A transaction in a smart contract typically includes the following elements:

- `nonce` – a counter used to ensure that each transaction can only be processed once.

- `gasPrice` – the amount of Ether the sender is willing to pay per unit of gas for the transaction.

- `gasLimit` – the maximum amount of gas the sender is willing to use for the transaction.

- `to` – the address of the recipient, which could be another user or a smart contract.

- `value` – amount of Ether to transfer from the sender to the recipient.

- `v, r, s` – components of the transaction signature.

The smart contract cannot initiate transactions on its own. It only executes in response to transactions initiated by others.

Through well-defined states and the deterministic nature of the execution environment, smart contracts ensure that all participants have confidence in the automatic, visible performance of agreed terms, without requiring any intermediary. The security and reliability of this setup depend heavily on the underlying blockchain architecture and the precision of the original coding of the contract. All interactions are audited and replicated across each node in the blockchain, leading to unquestionable transaction integrity. Engaging with these contracts, businesses can look forward to more streamlined processes, thereby reducing operational costs and enhancing service delivery.

6.3 Programming Languages for Smart Contracts

The selection of a programming language for developing smart contracts is pivotal, influencing not only the functionality and efficiency of the contracts but also their reliability and security. Three primary languages widely used in this domain are Solidity, Vyper, and Chaincode. Each language has been designed with specific use cases and security features in mind, reflecting the diverse ecosystem of blockchain technologies.

Solidity is arguably the most prominent language used for Ethereum smart contracts. Developed by Ethereum's original contributors, it was designed to be both accessible to those familiar with JavaScript and robust enough to handle complex operations on the Ethereum Virtual Machine (EVM). Solidity is object-oriented and statically typed, offering constructs similar to those found in C++, Python, and JavaScript.

```solidity
1   // Example of a simple Solidity Smart Contract
2   pragma solidity ^0.5.0;
3
4   contract Purchase {
5       uint public value;
6       address payable public seller;
7       address payable public buyer;
8
9       enum State { Created, Locked, Release, Inactive }
10      State public state;
11
12      constructor() public payable {
13          seller = msg.sender;
14          value = msg.value / 2;
15          require((2 * value) == msg.value, "Value has to be even.");
16      }
17
18      function confirmPurchase() public payable {
19          require(msg.sender != seller, "Seller cannot confirm the purchase.");
20          require(state == State.Created, "Contract already processed.");
21          buyer = msg.sender;
22          state = State.Locked;
23      }
24  }
```

Vyper, on the other hand, was developed to produce more auditable code. It has deliberately removed some of the complex features found in Solidity, such as modifiers and class inheritance, to simplify and enhance the security of the codebase. Vyper aims for a minimalistic approach, encouraging developers to write straightforward, transparent contracts.

```python
1   # Example of a basic Vyper Smart Contract
2   @public
3   def __init__():
4       self.owner = msg.sender
5
6   @public
7   @payable
8   def buy():
9       assert msg.value >= 1 ether, "Insufficient funds sent."
10      self.owner.send(self.balance)
```

Chaincode is used in Hyperledger Fabric, an enterprise-focused blockchain. Unlike Ethereum, Hyperledger does not have a cryptocurrency native to its platform and does not require a fuel such as 'gas' for contract execution. Chaincode is written in Go, and more recently,

6.3. PROGRAMMING LANGUAGES FOR SMART CONTRACTS

support for JavaScript and Java has been added, making it versatile across different use cases in the business environment.

```go
// Example of a basic Chaincode Smart Contract in Go
package main

import (
    "fmt"
    "github.com/hyperledger/fabric/core/chaincode/shim"
    pb "github.com/hyperledger/fabric/protos/peer"
)

type SimpleChaincode struct {
}

func (t *SimpleChaincode) Init(stub shim.ChaincodeStubInterface) pb.Response {
    return shim.Success(nil)
}

func (t *SimpleChaincode) Invoke(stub shim.ChaincodeStubInterface) pb.Response {
    function, _ := stub.GetFunctionAndParameters()
    if function == "invoke" {
        // Business logic
    }

    return shim.Error("Invalid invoke function name.")
}
```

Each language offers specific advantages depending on the requirements and constraints of the blockchain application. Solidity, with its vast community support and extensive documentation, remains the popular choice for applications requiring Turing-complete scripts. Vyper, with its focus on security and simplicity, presents an excellent alternative for projects where contract transparency and auditability are paramount. Meanwhile, Chaincode provides a robust environment for enterprise applications, exhibiting integration with traditional data systems and flexible transaction agreements.

Choosing the right programming language for smart contracts requires a careful analysis of the project's needs regarding security, complexity, and the blockchain environment. Whether developing for a public blockchain like Ethereum or a permissioned ledger like Hyperledger Fabric, the language chosen can significantly impact the functionality and security of the deployed smart contracts. Moreover, developers must stay informed about updates and new developments in these languages to ensure optimal performance and compliance with evolving security standards.

6.4 Benefits of Using Smart Contracts in Business

Smart contracts, by employing the immutable and distributed nature of blockchain technology, present substantial benefits for business applications across various sectors. This section delves into the array of advantages these digital contracts offer, such as cost reduction, increased speed and efficiency, improved transparency, enhanced security, error reduction, and trust minimization.

Cost Reduction

Deploying smart contracts in business operations significantly lowers the expenses associated with traditional contract execution. These costs include paperwork, administrative overhead, and the need for intermediaries such as lawyers and brokers. Smart contracts automate many of these processes, allowing for direct transactions between parties. For instance, in the real estate sector, property sales can be executed on a blockchain, automating deed transfers in response to payments, thus bypassing traditional costly and time-consuming legal processes.

```
// Smart Contract Example: Real Estate Transaction
contract RealEstate {
    address public seller;
    address public buyer;
    uint public price;

    constructor(address _seller, address _buyer, uint _price) {
        seller = _seller;
        buyer = _buyer;
        price = _price;
    }

    function finalizeSale() public payable {
        require(msg.sender == buyer, "Only buyer can finalize the sale");
        require(msg.value == price, "Payment must be exact price");
        // Ownership transfer logic here
    }
}
```

Increased Speed and Efficiency

Smart contracts automate and streamline complex processes leading to increased speed and efficiency in transactions. By executing predefined rules automatically, these contracts eliminate delays inherent in manual processing, such as wait times for approvals and error checking. For example, smart contracts in supply chain management can automatically release payments upon the receipt and verification of goods, thus speeding up the entire supply chain process.

```
Transaction processed in: 0.35 seconds
Previous manual processing time: 5-7 business days
```

Improved Transparency

Transparency is a core advantage of smart contracts facilitated by blockchain technology. All parties involved in a contract have access to the same version of the contract terms and the execution history, which is recorded immutably on the blockchain. This level of transparency ensures that all parties are aware of contract conditions and outcomes, reducing the potential for disputes.

```
// Sample visibility in a Smart Contract
contract PurchaseOrder {
    string public terms;
    uint public deliveryDate;

    constructor(string memory _terms, uint _deliveryDate) {
        terms = _terms;
        deliveryDate = _deliveryDate;
    }
}
```

Enhanced Security

Security is inherently increased as smart contracts leverage the cryptographic protection mechanisms of blockchain technology. Unauthorized access and fraud are minimized since altering the data recorded on a blockchain requires consensus from the network majority. Moreover, the deterministic nature of smart contracts can prevent unauthorized transactions which do not meet the required contract conditions.

Error Reduction

The automation of contract execution and management reduces human intervention, which, in turn, minimizes errors. Once a smart contract is deployed on the blockchain, it will execute exactly as it is programmed when trigger conditions are met. This precise operation ensures that contractual obligations are fulfilled without the manual errors that can occur in traditional contracts.

Trust Minimization

Smart contracts provide an environment where trust is placed in code rather than in any single party involved in the contract. The trust is shifted towards the blockchain technology and the network of participants that validate the blockchain's integrity, reducing the risk of bias or malicious intent. This feature is particularly crucial in environments where parties do not have a pre-existing trust relationship.

- Reduced need for trust in business relationships
- Reliance on the cryptographic security of blockchains
- Dependence on the impartial execution of contract terms

These benefits collectively enhance business processes by making them more efficient, transparent, and secure. They mark a substantial shift in how contractual relationships can be managed and executed within various industries. The adoption of smart contracts stands to revolutionize traditional business operations, aligning them with the new digital and automated business environment. As such, they hold the potential to significantly impact how business is conducted, offering a competitive edge to early adopters.

6.5 Smart Contract Deployment: Steps and Best Practices

Deploying a smart contract involves several critical steps that ensure its reliable operation and security on the blockchain network. This section delineates the standardized deployment process and recommends best practices to minimize risks and optimize performance.

Environment Setup

Before deploying a smart contract, developers must set up a suitable development environment. The choice of blockchain, such as Ethereum,

6.5. SMART CONTRACT DEPLOYMENT: STEPS AND BEST PRACTICES

and tools like Truffle or Remix, depends on the requirements and complexity of the project.

- Installing necessary development tools and libraries (e.g., Node.js, Web3.js).
- Setting up a blockchain test network (testnet) like Rinkeby or Ganache for simulating transactions without real assets.

Smart Contract Coding

The coding phase is critical in defining the behavior and capabilities of the smart contract. Using programming languages such as Solidity or Vyper, the code must be thoroughly commented and adhere to the latest standards.

```solidity
pragma solidity ^0.6.0;

contract Voting {
    mapping(address => uint) public votesReceived;

    function vote(address candidate) public {
        votesReceived[candidate] += 1;
    }
}
```

This rudimentary code snippet highlights a simple voting mechanism where the function vote increments votes for specific candidates.

Code Review and Auditing

Once the contract is developed, it undergoes a series of reviews and audits:

- Peer review of the smart contract by other developers for logic errors or security vulnerabilities.
- Formal auditing processes carried out by professional auditing firms to ensure adherence to security practices.

Testing

Thorough testing is crucial for the integrity and security of smart contracts. This involves:

- Unit testing individual functions using frameworks like Mocha or Jasmine.

- Integration testing to ensure components work harmoniously.

- Stress testing under high load to verify contract performance and stability.

An example test using Truffle might look like:

```
const Voting = artifacts.require("Voting");

contract("Voting", function(accounts) {
   it("allows a user to cast a vote", async function() {
      let instance = await Voting.deployed();
      await instance.vote(accounts[0]);
      let votes = await instance.votesReceived(accounts[0]);

      assert.equal(votes, 1, "votes should be 1");
   });
});
```

Deployment to a Test Network

Deploying to a testnet allows developers to understand how the contract performs in a blockchain environment.

```
Deploying 'Voting'
---------------------
> transaction hash:    0x123..
> Blocks: 2            Seconds: 17
> contract address:    0x345...
```

Mainnet Deployment

After thorough testing, the smart contract is deployed to the mainnet. This is a critical step requiring:

- Verification of the contract's bytecode on the blockchain.

- Comprehensive monitoring of transaction activities once live.

Bringing together best practices involves ensuring accurate coding, rigorous testing, and secure deployment strategies. By adhering to these practices, developers can mitigate risks associated with smart contracts and leverage the full potential of the blockchain technology. This meticulous adherence to protocol not only enhances the trustworthiness of deployed contracts but also fortifies the foundation of enterprise blockchain applications.

Through such meticulous and structured deployment processes, businesses can effectively utilize smart contracts to automate processes, enhance transparency, and optimize operational efficiency.

6.6 Verification and Testing of Smart Contracts

Ensuring the trustworthiness and reliability of smart contracts is critical given their autonomous execution and potential impact on financial and data transactions. The verification and testing of smart contracts involve rigorous methodologies and tools to detect vulnerabilities, prevent failures, and guarantee that the contract behaves as intended under varied circumstances.

Static Analysis: One fundamental approach in the smart contract verification process is static analysis. This technique examines the contract's code without executing it, aiming to uncover issues such as security vulnerabilities, coding errors, and deviations from coding standards. Tools like Solium and Mythril are popular in the Ethereum development ecosystem, providing static analysis to identify common security weaknesses and non-compliance with established best practices.

The application of static analysis can be exemplified by examining reentrancy attacks, where recursive calls can drain funds from a contract. The tool performs a syntactic analysis to identify patterns that match known reentrancy signatures. By flagging these potentialities, developers can restructure the contract's functions or implement additional checks to mitigate such risks.

Formal Verification: Beyond static analysis, formal verification constructs mathematical models to prove or disprove the correctness of algorithms underlying the smart contracts. This method uses logic and computational theories to ensure that the contract will operate as intended under every conceivable scenario. Tools like the KEVM (a formal model of Ethereum's EVM) allows developers to validate smart contracts against formal specifications. A noteworthy feature of KEVM is its capacity to ensure complete adherence to the smart contract's operational semantics, thus providing a high degree of assurance regarding contract reliability.

An instance of formal verification would be verifying a smart contract governing an escrow arrangement. Here, the KEVM tool can verify properties like "funds can only be released if all parties agree" or "funds will return to the payer if conditions are not met within a specified time."

Unit Testing: Practical and hands-on, unit testing involves writing test cases for various functions within the smart contract to guarantee their correct behavior individually. Frameworks such as Truffle in the Ethereum ecosystem enable developers to write and run unit tests written in JavaScript. This method helps to ensure functional correctness and detect inconsistencies or logical errors at the function level.

Here is an example of a unit test written using the Truffle framework, which checks whether a transaction updates the state as expected:

```
 1  const EscrowContract = artifacts.require("Escrow");
 2
 3  contract('TestEscrow', function(accounts) {
 4    it('should release funds correctly', async () => {
 5      const escrow = await EscrowContract.deployed();
 6      await escrow.deposit({ from: accounts[0], value: 1000 });
 7      await escrow.release(accounts[1], 500);
 8      assert.equal(await web3.eth.getBalance(escrow.address), 500, "Balance did
            not update correctly");
 9    });
10  });
```

Integration Testing: Unlike unit testing that focuses on individual components, integration testing assesses how different parts of the smart contract interact with each other and with external systems such as oracles or other contracts. This type of testing is crucial for detecting issues related to interfacing and data exchanges that might not be evident from unit testing alone.

Simulation and Testnets: Before deploying on the main network, conducting simulations or using Ethereum testnets (Ropsten, Kovan, etc.) allows developers to execute the contract in an environment that mimics the main blockchain. These testnets provide invaluable real-world insights without risking actual funds and allow for load testing and stress testing under near-real conditions.

Each of these methods plays a critical role in a comprehensive testing strategy necessary to ensure the effective performance and secure operation of smart contracts. As the technology evolves, the nature of these testing methodologies will also need to adapt to accommodate new challenges and innovations in smart contract development. Thus, the continuous enhancement of testing tools, coupled with a thorough understanding of the inherent characteristics of blockchain environments, remains pivotal in deploying robust and reliable smart contracts.

6.7 Common Use Cases for Smart Contracts

Smart contracts have revolutionized various sectors by offering a self-executing and decentralized method of agreement. The applications are numerous, ranging from finance to healthcare, and provide significant improvements in efficiency and security. This section will delve into the most common use cases where smart contracts have been effectively applied.

Automated Insurance Payouts

Insurance is an industry ripe for disruption by smart contracts due to the frequent discrepancies and delays in claims processing. Smart contracts can automate the evaluation and payout process, decreasing the possibility for fraud and error, and significantly speeding up transactions.

For instance, consider a flight insurance scenario, where a smart contract automatically issues refunds based on real-time flight data. The pseudocode for such an insurance smart contract could be:

Algorithm 7: Automated Flight Insurance Refund

Data: Flight status data feed
Result: Customer refund

1 **if** *flight is canceled* **then**
2 | Send refund to customer wallet
3 **else**
4 | No action required

The simplicity and effectiveness of this automatic transaction show why the insurance sector is seeking more extensive integration of smart contracts in their processes.

Supply Chain Management

In the context of supply chains, smart contracts provide an irrefutable record of transactions and ensure compliance with contracts from all parties involved. They enable real-time, automated interactions across the logistics process, which reduces discrepancies and improves supply chain transparency.

Take a batch of produce shipped from a supplier to a retailer as an example. A smart contract can automate release of payments to the supplier only when a set of predetermined conditions (like time, temperature conditions throughout the transport, and delivery confirmation) are met. This is further exemplified by the following code snippet:

```
contract SupplyChain {
    function confirmDelivery() external {
        if (deliveryConditionsMet()) {
            releaseFunds();
        }
    }

    function deliveryConditionsMet() private returns (bool) {
        // Checks related to delivery conditions
    }
}
```

This approach not only streamlines the operations but also reduces the need for manual oversight and audits, cutting down operational costs considerably.

Real Estate Transactions

Real estate transactions are typically complex, involving multiple parties and requiring significant oversight. Smart contracts can simplify these transactions by automating property sales, lease management, and record keeping.

For example, a smart contract for a rental agreement might automatically transfer the security deposit to the landlord and grant digital access to the tenant upon the fulfillment of the contract's start date and payment conditions. Such automation not only simplifies the management but also provides a transparent and immutable log of all interactions and transaction histories related to a property.

The following code snippet could represent part of a smart contract for rental management:

```
contract RentalAgreement {
    address payable public landlord;
    address public tenant;
    uint public rent;
    uint public securityDeposit;
    uint256 public startDate;
```

```
 8     function checkInTenant() external payable {
 9         require(block.timestamp >= startDate, "Lease has not started");
10         require(msg.value == rent + securityDeposit, "Insufficient funds transferred
               ");
11
12         // Code to grant access to tenant goes here
13         landlord.transfer(securityDeposit + rent);
14     }
15 }
```

By ensuring that the terms of the agreement are adhered to strictly, smart contracts adjacent to real estate dealings have greatly enhanced the trust and efficiency in the sector.

Through these diverse applications—from insurance claims and supply chain logistics to real estate management—smart contracts demonstrate a robust utility across different fields. Their ability to enforce contract conditions automatically provides a heightened level of security and efficiency, promising to be pivotal in the continuous evolution of digital transactions and record-keeping. The adaptability of smart contracts to cater to different industry needs while providing transparency and reducing administrative burdens underscores their transformative potential.

6.8 Smart Contracts in Financial Services

Smart contracts, by automating contractual obligations through code, have introduced a paradigm shift in how financial services manage agreements and execute transactions. The inherent characteristic of blockchain technology as an immutable ledger with timestamping capabilities allows smart contracts to provide enhanced security and transparency. In the financial sector, this translates to a significant reduction in operating costs and fraud, while increasing the speed of transaction processing and the reliability of compliance checks.

One profound application of smart contracts within financial services is in the domain of payments and remittances. Through the use of blockchain-based smart contracts, these services can bypass traditional banking intermediaries, thus expediting cross-border transactions and reducing the associated fees. For instance, a smart contract can be programmed to automatically transfer funds from one party to another upon the fulfillment of specified conditions, without the need for manual processing or verification by banks. The code can be set to execute only when certain conditions, such as verification of the sender's and recipient's account details and sufficiency of funds, are met.

```
function transferFunds(address recipient, uint amount) public {
    require(balanceOf[msg.sender] >= amount);
    require(msg.sender != recipient);
    balanceOf[msg.sender] -= amount;
    balanceOf[recipient] += amount;
    emit Transfer(msg.sender, recipient, amount);
}
```

The above smart contract code snippet illustrates a basic fund transfer function in a financial application. Here, require statements function as safeguards that check if the sender has sufficient balance before permitting the transaction and ensure that the sender and recipient are not the same entity.

- Reduction in processing time: Transactions are settled in real-time or within a few minutes.

- Decrease in operational costs: Eliminates the fees usually paid to intermediaries.

- Increase in reliability: Transactions are immutable and only executed after all conditions are met, reducing the risk of fraud.

Another crucial application is in the trading of financial instruments, such as bonds, stocks, and derivatives. Smart contracts offer the possibility of tokenization of these instruments, making the assets easier to divide and trade on digital platforms. This tokenization enhances liquidity and market efficiency. Smart contracts automate the execution of trades and settlements, which minimizes the potential for errors and the need for reconciliations.

```
contract ShareTrading {
    struct Share {
        uint256 shareID;
        address owner;
        uint256 price;
    }

    Share[] public sharesAvailable;

    function buyShare(uint256 _shareID) public payable {
        Share memory share = sharesAvailable[_shareID];
        require(msg.value == share.price, "Incorrect amount transferred");
        require(share.owner != msg.sender, "Seller cannot be the buyer");

        share.owner.transfer(msg.value);
        sharesAvailable[_shareID].owner = msg.sender;
        emit SharePurchased(_shareID, msg.sender, share.price);
    }
}
```

In the trading contract example, smart contracts enforce trading terms directly within the blockchain protocol. Such automation ensures the accuracy of ownership recording and payment transfers based on mutually agreed-upon rules encoded within the contract.

Furthermore, the use of smart contracts extends into compliance and regulatory reporting. Financial institutions operate under strict regulatory frameworks requiring them to report various operations to governing bodies. Blockchain smart contracts can facilitate real-time auditing and ensure ongoing compliance by automatically generating reports and sending them to regulators as transactions occur.

As financial institutions continue to adopt smart contracts, the industry sees a potential shift in how trust and transparency are perceived within the sector. Although transformational, the adoption is also met with challenges including aligning existing systems and standards with new blockchain functionalities. However, the strategic deployment of smart contracts in financial services promises a future where efficiency, security, and compliance are greatly enhanced by technological advancement. This progression towards integrating technology starkly contrasts with traditional financial models, offering a compelling insight into the benefits that innovation brings to financial ecosystems.

6.9 Smart Contracts in Supply Chain Management

In the landscape of global commerce, supply chain management is crucial. It encompasses the oversight of materials, information, and finances as they move from supplier to manufacturer to wholesaler to retailer to consumer. Blockchain-based smart contracts offer revolutionary solutions in this domain, providing mechanisms that contribute significantly to the efficiency, transparency, and security of supply chains.

Smart contracts are autonomous programs that execute predefined conditions in a supply chain. These immutable and distributed agreements record and verify each transaction that takes place within the blockchain, enabling a trustless, transparent, and tamper-proof ecosystem. Their implementation in supply chain management streamlines processes, eliminating many of the current challenges, such as manual paperwork and coordination failures, which are oftentimes susceptible to human error and fraud.

The typical use case for smart contracts in a supply chain begins with the automated execution of contracts when certain conditions are met. For instance, a smart contract could automatically release payments to a supplier only when a shipping company confirms that goods have been delivered. This is achieved through the integration of digital sensors and RFID tags that provide real-time data directly to the blockchain.

Here's a detailed example demonstrating the implementation of a smart contract within a supply chain at a technical level:

```solidity
pragma solidity ^0.5.0;

contract SupplyChain {
    address owner;
    uint productCount = 0;
    mapping(uint => Product) products;

    struct Product {
        uint id;
        string name;
        uint price;
        address payable owner;
        bool purchased;
    }

    event ProductCreated(
        uint id,
        string name,
        uint price,
        address payable owner,
        bool purchased
    );

    event ProductPurchased(
        uint id,
        uint price,
        address payable owner,
        bool purchased
    );

    constructor() public {
        owner = msg.sender;
    }

    function createProduct(string memory _name, uint _price) public {
        // Require a valid name and price
        require(bytes(_name).length > 0);
        require(_price > 0);
        // Increment product count
        productCount ++;
        // Create the product
        products[productCount] = Product(productCount, _name, _price, msg.sender, false);
        // Trigger an event
        emit ProductCreated(productCount, _name, _price, msg.sender, false);
    }

    function purchaseProduct(uint _id) public payable {
```

```solidity
        // Fetch the product
        Product memory _product = products[_id];
        // Validate the product
        require(_product.id > 0 && _product.id <= productCount);
        require(!_product.purchased);
        require(msg.value >= _product.price);
        require(_product.owner != msg.sender);
        // Mark as purchased
        _product.owner.transfer(msg.value);
        _product.purchased = true;
        products[_id] = _product;
        // Trigger an event
        emit ProductPurchased(_id, _product.price, msg.sender, true);
    }
}
```

The code listing above illustrates a simplified smart contract using Solidity, deployed on the Ethereum blockchain. This contract facilitates the creation and purchase of products within a supply chain environment. The inherent transparency and security provided through such smart contracts bolster trust among parties, as all transactions are verified and recorded across multiple nodes on the blockchain.

For this reason, using smart contracts in supply chain management not only simplifies processes but also provides an audit trail that is often legally compliant and adherent to industry standards, thereby reducing complexity and increasing operational efficiency across the board. Moreover, by minimizing manual oversight, it allows for cost-effective management of supply chains.

Efficient integration of IoT devices also enables the incorporation of real-time data tracking and management, enhancing the ability to monitor the condition of goods, the authenticity of products, and the compliance of supply chains with regulatory standards.

Therefore, it is evident that smart contracts are transforming supply chain management by improving workflows, reducing discrepancies, ensuring product quality, and strengthening trust. The exemplary benefits noted across various case studies underscore their potential to significantly improve how supply chains operate worldwide, providing all stakeholders with a more reliable, efficient, and secure system.

6.10 Integrating Smart Contracts with IoT

The integration of smart contracts with the Internet of Things (IoT) represents a significant evolution in automating device-driven transactions and data exchange across various sectors. IoT devices, which are often deployed to monitor processes and environments, can trigger actions based on the data they collect. When these devices are linked with smart contracts, the actions become instantaneous, autonomous, and fully documented on a blockchain, thereby enhancing efficiency and transparency.

The Conceptual Framework

To understand the integration of smart contracts with IoT, it is pivotal to examine the architecture typically employed. An IoT device equipped with sensors collects real-time data from its environment. This data could range from temperature metrics in a cold chain logistics scenario to occupancy information in smart real estate applications. Once data is collected, it is transmitted through a secure, connected infrastructure to the blockchain system where smart contracts are deployed.

Upon receipt of the data, the predefined conditions within the smart contracts are evaluated. If the conditions are met, the smart contract automatically executes the associated actions, which may include releasing payments, sending notifications, or adjusting parameters on other IoT devices without further human intervention.

```
// Example of a Smart Contract Integrated with IoT
contract IoTMonitoring {
    function executeAction(uint _sensorData) external {
        if (_sensorData exceeds threshold) {
            // Code to execute action
        }
    }
}
```

For instance, in an industrial application, sensors monitoring machine temperatures can activate a contract to halt operations if the machine overheats, thereby preventing damage or potential hazards.

Technical Implementations

Achieving a seamless integration necessitates several critical technical implementations:

- **Secure Communication**: The data transfer between IoT devices and the blockchain must be secured to prevent tampering or data breaches. Techniques like TLS/SSL can be employed for this.

- **Efficient Data Handling**: Given the potential volume of data from multiple IoT devices, the system must handle large data influxes efficiently. Data minimization strategies where only necessary data is sent and processed can alleviate congestion on the network.

- **Scalability**: The blockchain infrastructure must be scalable enough to accommodate the growth in IoT device integrations without significant losses in performance.

- **Interoperability**: Devices and the blockchain must support interoperable protocols to ensure that different devices from various manufacturers can communicate with the smart contract effectively.

Case Study: Smart Logistics

A practical application of integrating smart contracts with IoT is in the logistics industry. Consider a scenario where goods that are sensitive to environmental conditions, like pharmaceuticals, are being transported across multiple jurisdictions.

IoT sensors monitor the conditions inside the transportation vehicles in real-time, sending data to a blockchain network. Smart contracts in this network are set to automatically initiate preventive actions or alert relevant parties if the conditions deviate from the agreed standards, ensuring compliance and quality assurance throughout the journey. This not only dramatically reduces the risks of spoilage but also enforces accountability through an immutable record of the conditions maintained during shipping.

Concluding Insights

Given the practical examples and methodologies discussed, it is clear that integrating smart contracts with IoT extends the capabilities of autonomous system handling and inter-device communication. This convergence not only aids in individual device management but also reshapes entire operational frameworks within industries, making processes more agile, secure, and transparent. Thus, as we continue to advance towards more interconnected environments, the importance of robust, scalable smart contract solutions in the IoT space will undoubtedly increase, catalyzing further innovations in this field.

6.11 Challenges and Limitations of Smart Contracts

Smart contracts are a transformative technology with potential to revolutionize various sectors by automating processes, minimizing fraud, and reducing administrative costs. However, despite their benefits, they are not without challenges and limitations. This section discusses technical vulnerabilities, scalability issues, legal ambiguity, and integration complexities that currently limit the wider adoption of smart contracts.

Technical Vulnerabilities

Smart contracts are executable codes that run on a blockchain platform, and like any software, they are prone to bugs and vulnerabilities. The immutable nature of blockchain means that once a smart contract is deployed, it can be challenging to modify or correct it. This immutability, while ensuring security and trust, can become an issue if bugs are discovered post-deployment. A notorious example highlighting this problem is the DAO hack on the Ethereum platform, where approximately $50 million worth of Ether were siphoned off due to a re-entrancy bug in a smart contract.

To address and minimize such vulnerabilities, it is imperative to conduct comprehensive testing and auditing of smart contracts before deployment. The following listings provide an example of a vulnerable contract and demonstrate how unintended actions can occur.

```
pragma solidity ^0.6.6;

contract VulnerableContract {
    mapping(address => uint) private userBalances;

    function withdrawBalance() public {
        uint amountToWithdraw = userBalances[msg.sender];
        require(msg.sender.call.value(amountToWithdraw)(""));
        userBalances[msg.sender] = 0;
    }
}
```

6.11. CHALLENGES AND LIMITATIONS OF SMART CONTRACTS

The above contract intends to allow users to withdraw their assigned balance. However, the `require` statement calling an external address can be exploited to re-enter the `withdrawBalance` function, allowing a malicious user to withdraw more than their balance.

Scalability Issues

Blockchain platforms, especially those supporting smart contracts like Ethereum, can face significant scalability issues. The throughput of transactions is limited by the size and frequency of blocks. During periods of high demand, transaction backlogs can occur, leading to delays and increased costs for executing smart contracts.

Scalability enhancements are crucial for smart contracts to be viable on a large scale. Various solutions, such as layer two protocols and sharding, are in development to address these issues, but they have yet to be proven at scale.

Legal Ambiguity

The integration of smart contracts into existing legal frameworks presents its own set of challenges. One key issue is the interpretation and enforcement of contract terms encoded into a smart contract. Because smart contracts are written in code, there can be discrepancies between the legal intent of the contract and how it is executed by the code.

This legal uncertainty makes it difficult for businesses to fully rely on smart contracts, especially in transactions involving large amounts or significant legal consequences. Ensuring that smart contracts comply with the relevant laws and regulations is critical but currently lacks standardization and clear guidance.

Integration Complexities

Integrating smart contracts with traditional business systems poses significant technical and managerial challenges. Many enterprises rely on legacy systems that do not easily interface with blockchain technologies. The lack of interoperability between various blockchain platforms and existing IT infrastructure makes the integration process cumbersome and often costly.

Moreover, the need for a cultural shift within organizations and the training of staff to understand and manage blockchain and smart contracts cannot be underestimated. Companies must invest in education and change management to successfully implement this technology.

Despite these challenges, the ongoing developments and improvements in smart contracts technology hold promise for addressing these limitations. Continuous research, technological advancement, and more defined regulatory frameworks may eventually pave the way for broader adoption and more effective applications of smart contracts across industries.

6.12 Future Developments in Smart Contracts Technology

As smart contract technology matures, anticipated developments are poised to enhance its efficiency, security, and widespread application. These technological advancements will not only refine the capabilities of smart contracts but will also expand their usability across more industries, fueling further innovation in blockchain technology.

Scalability Enhancements: One of the primary focus areas is enhancing the scalability of networks that host smart contracts. High throughput, low latency, and reduced transaction costs are critical for enterprise-scale applications. Currently, platforms like Ethereum are transitioning to proof-of-stake algorithms (Ethereum 2.0) which promises significant throughput improvements and lower gas fees.

```
1  Upgrade Initiation:
2  - Transition from PoW to PoS
3  - Implementation of sharding mechanisms
4  - Rollup integration for compressing transactions
```

Privacy Enhancements: Privacy remains a key concern, particularly for businesses that handle sensitive data. Techniques such as zero-knowledge proofs (ZKPs) offer the potential to execute contracts without revealing underlying data. Enhanced privacy features will be integral in promoting smart contract adoption in fields requiring data confidentiality, such as in healthcare and finance.

```
1  Privacy Improvement Technique:
2  - Implementation of Zero-Knowledge Proofs to ensure data privacy while maintaining
      trust
```

6.12. FUTURE DEVELOPMENTS IN SMART CONTRACTS TECHNOLOGY

Interoperability Between Blockchains: Future developments are likely to stress the importance of cross-chain interoperability. This would enable smart contracts to operate across different blockchain networks, broadening their applicability and efficiency. Protocols like Polkadot and Cosmos are leading this area with promises of enabling cross-chain transactions and contract executions.

- Development of cross-chain communication protocols.
- Implementation of atomic swaps.
- Creation of bridge services for asset transfers.

AI Integration: The integration of Artificial Intelligence (AI) with smart contracts could lead to more dynamic contracts that can make autonomous decisions based on external data inputs and machine learning models. This could profoundly shift how contracts are executed, making them more responsive to real-time data and events.

```
1  AI-Enhanced Smart Contract Example:
2  - Input: Real-time market data
3  - Process: AI-driven decision making
4  - Output: Contract adjustment based on predictive analytics
```

Regulatory Compliance Automation: As regulatory frameworks around smart contracts mature, there will be a greater need for built-in compliance checks within the contract logic itself. This would automate many aspects of compliance, reducing the administrative burden on businesses and decreasing the risk of non-compliance.

```
Compliance Check:
"IF regulatory_condition THEN execute compliance_action"
```

Enhancement of Development Tools: Improvements in the tools available for creating, testing, and deploying smart contracts will lower the entry barrier for developers new to blockchain development and enhance the security and reliability of contracts through better testing frameworks and deployment practices.

- Development of integrated development environments (IDEs) tailored for smart contract creation.
- Enhancement of debugging tools specifically designed for blockchain.
- Creation of more comprehensive and automated testing frameworks.

As these enhancements are progressively realized, they promise to solve many of the current limitations of smart contracts, promoting wider adoption and more innovative applications. The continuous collaboration between developers, researchers, businesses, and regulatory bodies is crucial to address these challenges and to unlock the full potential of smart contracts in the digital economy.

Chapter 7

Blockchain in Supply Chain Management

This chapter investigates the application of blockchain technology in supply chain management, emphasizing its potential to revolutionize transparency and efficiency in tracking goods and services. It explores how blockchain facilitates real-time, immutable tracking of products from origin to consumer, potentially reducing fraud and errors. The chapter also discusses the integration challenges and the impact of blockchain on reducing costs and improving compliance across global supply chains.

7.1 Overview of Supply Chain Management

Supply Chain Management (SCM) encompasses the broad range of activities required to plan, control, and execute a product's flow, from acquiring raw materials and production through distribution to the final customer, in the most streamlined and cost-effective way possible. SCM integrates supply and demand management within and across companies. More than just a business function, it is a complex network of business relationships, logistical planning, and execution of processes, and it is pivotal in securing competitive advantage and customer satisfaction.

Central to SCM is the notion of value creation. The fundamental objective is to synchronize the supply functions with customer demand, not only within a company but also across companies that are involved in the fulfillment process on both a local and global scale. This alignment is crucial because it affects all aspects of a business, from the creation of the product to its delivery to the end-user.

The management of a supply chain involves various entities such as suppliers, manufacturers, and retailers. Operations range from order generation through product delivery, and include managing their respective interdependencies in a strategic manner. The efficiency of these operations is often enhanced through the use of technology that provides automated systems and tools for things like inventory management, order processing, and shipment tracking.

Inventory management is a pivotal aspect of SCM, where the strategic placement of stock can significantly affect the responsiveness and efficiency of the supply chain. Effective inventory management considers both demand forecasting and the economics of inventory costs, balancing the amount of stock kept on hand to meet the needs of customers with the cost of maintaining that inventory.

The logistics component of SCM is concerned with the transportation, storage, and distribution of goods. Transportation management seeks to maximize service levels to the customer while minimizing costs through optimized route planning, load planning, and delivery scheduling. Storage and handling of goods is another crucial factor where the type of warehousing solution depends on the nature of the products, volume, and frequency of the demand.

Another critical area in SCM is procurement, which involves the selection, negotiation, and acquisition of goods or services from external sources. Effective procurement directly contributes to an organization's competitive positioning. It requires partaking in ethical sourcing practices, vendor management, and cost control, ensuring that all procured goods and services meet the necessary quality standards and compliance requirements.

SCM is also increasingly driven by data and analytics, providing insights that lead to better demand forecasting, supply chain optimization, and customer satisfaction. Advanced analytics can improve operational efficiencies, mitigate risks by managing supply chain vulnerabilities, and optimize logistics costs.

Moreover, as globalization continues to expand, SCM has become more intricate. Companies must manage their supply chain operations across diverse regulatory environments and cultural landscapes, often dealing with issues around tariffs, international logistics, and varying standards for quality and compliance.

Managing a supply chain effectively requires continual reassessment of internal and external environments and the adoption of new methodologies and technologies. The emergence of digital technologies such as blockchain, the Internet of Things (IoT), and artificial intelligence (AI) has begun to transform traditional supply chains, making them smarter, more agile, and more customer-focused. Through such innovations, supply chains can achieve unprecedented integration and cooperation among all stakeholders involved.

This overview sets the stage for understanding the intricacies and dynamics of SCM and paves the way to delve into the transformative potential of blockchain within this domain.

7.2 The Role of Blockchain in Enhancing Supply Chain Transparency

Transparency in supply chain management refers to the visibility and clarity of information pertaining to the processes and transactions within the supply chain, from origin to consummation. In traditional supply chain models, this transparency is often compromised due to the disparate systems and limited data sharing between stakeholders. Blockchain technology, however, introduces a paradigm shift in how information is recorded, stored, and shared across a supply chain network.

Blockchain technology provides an immutable, decentralized ledger for recording transactions in a chronologically timestamped manner. Every transaction on this ledger is accessible for all participants in the network, which enhances transparency significantly. Implementation of blockchain enables all parties—from suppliers to consumers—to access the same information, thereby reducing discrepancies and fostering a climate of trust.

To illustrate, consider a simple supply chain network involving producers, logistics providers, intermediaries, retailers, and consumers. We set up a blockchain where each transaction or movement of goods is recorded as a blockchain transaction. Below is an example of how a transaction might be recorded:

CHAPTER 7. BLOCKCHAIN IN SUPPLY CHAIN MANAGEMENT

```
1  INSERT INTO blockchain (transaction_id, from_id, to_id, product_id, timestamp)
2  VALUES ('123', 'ProducerA', 'LogisticsB', 'ProductX', '2021-07-21T13:45:00Z');
```

The effect of recording transactions in such a manner is profound. Each transaction includes the sender, receiver, product, and timestamp details, which ensures that every stakeholder has the complete history of the product's journey at their fingertips.

By utilizing smart contracts, blockchain enhances this transparency further. Smart contracts are self-executing contracts where the terms are directly written into code. When certain conditions are met, the contract executes the corresponding contractual clause. Below is a pseudocode example of a smart contract in use:

```
1  contract ProductTransfer{
2  function executeTransfer(string memory from_id, string
     memory to_id, string memory product_id) public{
3  if(verifyConditions(from_id, to_id, product_id)){
     transferProduct(from_id, to_id, product_id); emit
     TransferComplete(from_id, to_id, product_id); }
4  else{ revert("Transfer conditions not met."); } } }
```

Here, 'verifyConditions' might check that all regulatory and compliance checks are passed, ensuring that goods are transferred only when all stipulated conditions are fully satisfied. This not only streamlines operations but also ensures compliance is met at each stage of the supply chain.

Furthermore, transaction data stored on blockchain can be leveraged to generate real-time reports and visual dashboards, providing stakeholders with up-to-date information about the supply chain status. This capability can be demonstrated using the following simple diagram created with TikZ:

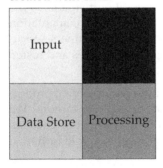

Every box represents a logical component of the dashboard system, from data input and storage to processing and final output, illustrating at a high level how data from the blockchain might be manipulated and displayed.

The role of blockchain is thus integral in enhancing transparency in supply chain management. Not only does it provide a tamper-evident register of all transactions, but it also offers mechanisms like smart contracts for automated enforcement and operational compliance, alongside tools for real-time data visualization. These capabilities collectively contribute to an unprecedented level of clarity and trust between all parties in the supply chain.

7.3 Blockchain for Traceability in Supply Chains

The implementation of blockchain technology in supply chain traceability represents a transformative advancement towards achieving unparalleled visibility and accountability in the movement and authentication of products across the globe. Traceability refers to the ability to track every product from the source to the customer through the recording of detailed transaction and movement at each phase of the supply chain.

To begin with, the genesis of blockchain-enabled traceability lies in the inherent characteristics of blockchain technology—decentralization, immutability, and transparency. Each transaction in a blockchain is recorded as a block of data, which includes the nature of the transaction, timestamps, and participating entities. Once a transaction is validated by consensus among participants in the network, it is chronologically added to the chain of previous transactions. Due to its cryptographic sealing, each block is tamper-evident, promoting a secure and unalterable record of product journey which is critical for traceability.

Given the complexity and scope of modern supply chains, the integration of blockchain facilitates a streamlined approach to tracing the origins and touchpoints of products. This is especially pertinent in industries like pharmaceuticals and food and beverages where safety compliance and authenticity are of utmost importance. For instance, in order to trace a product in a blockchain-based system, stakeholders such as manufacturers, logistics providers, and distributors engage by entering their transactional data into the blockchain. This continuous, sequential documentation creates a permanent history of a product's journey that can be easily audited by authorized parties.

To make these benefits tangible, consider the following code representation of a blockchain transaction in a supply chain:

```
class Block:
    def __init__(self, timestamp, transactions, previous_hash):
        self.timestamp = timestamp
        self.transactions = transactions
        self.previous_hash = previous_hash
        self.hash = self.calculate_hash()

    def calculate_hash(self):
        initial_data = str(self.timestamp) + str(self.transactions) + self.previous_hash
        return hashlib.sha256(initial_data.encode()).hexdigest()
```

This simplistic model captures the essence of how blockchain can securely and transparently facilitate traceability in supply chains by creating blocks that consist of critical transaction details.

Furthermore, implementing traceability through blockchain not only assists in authentication of product provenance but also significantly reduces the risks associated with fraudulent activities and counterfeiting. A clear, immutable trail of records helps in identifying discrepancies at any point in the supply chain, thereby allowing for timely corrective measures. The following is a pseudocode that illustrates the process of verification of a product's origin in the blockchain:

Data: Blockchain
Result: Verification of Product Origin

1 **foreach** *block in Blockchain* **do**
2   **if** *block.transactions.contains('Product ID')* **then**
3   **if** *block.previous_hash matches expected* **then**
4   print 'Product trace verified to this point'
5   **else**
6   print 'Discrepancy found in product trace'
7   break

The efficiency and effectiveness of blockchain in enhancing traceability in supply chains are contingent upon the collaborative participation of all stakeholders and the integrity of the data provided. As the technology and adoption mature, blockchain is poised to be an indispensable tool for ensuring transparency and trust in increasingly complex global supply chains, ultimately allowing consumers and businesses to decisively and confidently trace the origin and authenticity of their products without excessive regulatory burden or reliance on intermediaries.

7.4 Improving Efficiency in Supply Chains through Blockchain

Blockchain technology stands to significantly enhance efficiency within supply chain management. This enhancement stems from blockchain's inherent characteristics: decentralization, transparency, and immutability. By leveraging blockchain, supply chain operations can realize not only enhanced transparency but also substantial improvements in operational efficiencies, which are pivotal for achieving competitive advantage.

Tracking and documentation in traditional supply chains often involve substantial paperwork and processes that can be prone to human error and inefficiency. Blockchain offers a streamlined approach by enabling the digitization of these processes. Each transaction and its associated details are recorded on a blockchain, allowing for a single, immutable version of truth that is visible to all participants. This setup minimizes discrepancies and reduces the time spent reconciling them, thus simplifying operations.

- `Order fulfillment` becomes faster and more accurate as blockchain allows for real-time tracking and automated triggering of subsequent actions in the supply chain process, based on predetermined conditions being met.

- `Inventory management` is improved as entities across the supply chain have the same view of stock levels in real time, thanks to blockchain-based systems. This shared visibility helps prevent overstocking and stockouts, leading to a more balanced and cost-effective inventory management.

- `Audit processes` are streamlined and less resource-intensive. With blockchain, every transaction is recorded with an indelible timestamp and is readily verifiable against the blockchain, thus facilitating quicker and more efficient audits.

Additionally, the deployment of blockchain greatly reduces the need for intermediaries typically involved in confirming, authenticating, and reconciling transactions within supply chains. By decreasing the dependency on middlemen, blockchain reduces potential points of failure, accelerates processes, and curtails costs. These efficiencies streamline interactions between goods and service providers, distributors, consumers, and regulators.

Blockchain also enables stronger collaborative practices among supply chain stakeholders without compromising security or privacy. For instance, smart contracts can autonomously execute commercial actions under certain conditions, such as issuing payments or restocking orders once delivery confirmation is blockchain-verified. This automated mechanism enhances operational speed and reduces bottlenecks.

```solidity
// Example of a smart contract for automated payment upon delivery
pragma solidity ^0.5.0;

contract PaymentUponDelivery {
    address payable public seller;
    address payable public buyer;
    uint public price;

    constructor(address payable _seller, address payable _buyer, uint _price)
        public {
        seller = _seller;
        buyer = _buyer;
        price = _price;
    }

    function confirmDelivery() external payable {
        require(msg.sender == buyer, "Only buyer can confirm");
        require(address(this).balance >= price, "Insufficient balance");

        seller.transfer(price);
    }

    function pay() external payable {
        require(msg.sender == buyer, "Only buyer can pay");
        require(msg.value == price, "Incorrect amount transferred");
    }
}
```

These programmed transactions ensure that compliance and obligations are maintained without continuous human monitoring, thus fostering an environment of trust and accountability.

Moreover, the use of blockchain can significantly mitigate delays caused by documentation errors, fraud, or mismanagement. Every ledger entry on a blockchain is cryptographically linked to the preceding transaction, which provides no room for after-the-fact alterations without consensus from the network. This characteristic inherently protects against fraud and enhances the overall security of supply chain transactions.

Blockchain technology, when appropriately implemented, acts as a pivotal enabler of efficiency in supply chain management. The transformation from traditional methods to a blockchain-based system not only expedites processes but also embeds a higher degree of accuracy and reliability, necessary for modern supply chains facing complex global demands.

7.5 Reducing Costs with Blockchain in Supply Chain Management

The implementation of blockchain technology in supply chain management can substantially reduce operational costs by increasing efficiency, eliminating redundancies, and reducing the incidence of fraud and errors. This section explores these cost-saving mechanisms specific to blockchain application in supply chains.

Streamlining Processes Blockchain technology offers an immutable and transparent ledger, ideal for streamlining supply chain processes. Typically, conventional supply chain activities are burdened with multiple layers of bureaucracy and paperwork, which not only delay operations but also increase the risk of human errors. By digitizing the entire process on a blockchain platform, firms can drastically reduce the need for repetitive manual processes and eliminate the requirement for intermediaries. The reduction of intermediary involvement directly translates to lower transaction costs. For instance, automating the verification of transactions and the execution of agreements through smart contracts bypasses the need for manual intervention, consequently reducing the cost associated with labor.

Improving Inventory Management Efficient inventory management is crucial to reducing costs within supply chains. The traditional methods often involve various forms of estimation and uncertainty, leading to either surplus or shortage, both expensive to manage. With blockchain, all entities involved in the supply chain gain visibility into real-time data updates, which include inventory levels, transportation progress, and demand forecasts. This precise tracking helps in minimizing excess inventory and reducing shortages, thus optimizing the inventory holding costs.

```
// Example of a blockchain transaction updating inventory data
transaction InventoryUpdate {
    string productID;
    int updatedQuantity;
    DateTime timeStamp;
}
```

Reducing Fraud and Errors The immutable nature of blockchain ensures that once a record has been added to the ledger, it cannot be altered retrospectively without detection. This characteristic notably enhances the security of data, significantly reducing the potential for fraud and clerical errors. In scenarios where goods are transferred across multiple checkpoints, blockchain's tamper-proof architecture helps in maintaining an accurate trail of product origins and transaction histories. This accountability helps in minimizing losses from counterfeit goods and unauthorized selling, thereby safeguarding revenue.

Enhancing Compliance and Reducing Related Costs Compliance with regulatory standards can be both challenging and expensive. Blockchain facilitates enhanced compliance with trade regulations and standards across different geographies by providing auditable trails of information. Smart contracts embedded in the blockchain can automatically execute transactions based on predefined legal and compliance guidelines. Compliance costs are further reduced through improved reporting mechanisms, as blockchain systems can be designed to automatically compile and verify necessary compliance data, thereby reducing the workload on human resources.

Fostering Collaborative Cost Reduction Blockchain fosters an ecosystem where multiple participants in the supply chain can collaborate more effectively. By providing a single source of truth, it eliminates discrepancies and disputes that often arise due to the inaccuracies in individual record-keeping systems. The synchronization of data across participants reduces delays and speeds up resolution times for discrepancies and disputes, which in turn decreases the associated administrative costs.

Moreover, by utilizing tokenization, which is the process of substituting sensitive data with a non-sensitive equivalent, often referred to as a token, that has no extrinsic or exploitable meaning or value, blockchain can incentivize various stakeholders in the supply chain, including suppliers, manufacturers, and consumers to participate actively in the cost reduction initiatives.

Overall, the implementation of blockchain technology in supply chain management is not merely about adopting a new technology; it is about redefining the traditional cost structures associated with multi-step global supply chains. The reduction in administrative burdens, the mitigation of risks, and the improved effectiveness of compliance practices all contribute significantly to the overarching goal of cost reduction.

7.6 Ensuring Product Authenticity and Compliance

Ensuring product authenticity and compliance in supply chain management is critical to maintaining brand reputation, adhering to regulatory standards, and providing consumer safety. Blockchain technology offers a robust mechanism for bolstering these aspects through its properties of decentralization, immutability, and transparency.

Each transaction in a blockchain is recorded as a block of data, which includes information about product origin, batch numbers, factory and processing details, expiration dates, and shipping history. This data is recorded on a ledger that is distributed across multiple nodes, ensuring that no single entity controls the entire dataset. As a result, this significantly enhances the security and authenticity of the data recorded.

Product Authentication via Blockchain

To authenticate a product using blockchain, a unique digital identifier is assigned to each product or batch at the point of origin. This identifier can take various forms, such as a QR code or RFID tag, which is scanned at each checkpoint in the supply chain. Each scan is recorded as a transaction on the blockchain, creating a traceable history of the product's journey from production to sale.

```
// Example of assigning a digital identifier to a product
productID = generateUniqueID(productDetails);
blockchain.recordTransaction(productID, originDetails);
```

As products move through the supply chain, stakeholders can scan the identifier to verify the authenticity and compliance of the product against the immutable blockchain records. This process effectively deters counterfeiting and unauthorized distribution, as altering the blockchain would require consensus from all participants in the network.

Ensuring Compliance

Blockchain's capacity to store detailed data provides an auditable trail of compliance with applicable regulations and standards. For example, in the pharmaceutical industry, drug safety is paramount, and blockchain can help ensure that all handling and transportation processes meet strict regulations.

```
// Recording compliance data in the blockchain
blockchain.recordTransaction(productID, complianceData);
```

Regulatory bodies can be granted access to the blockchain, allowing for real-time auditing of compliance data. This facilitates quicker certification processes and faster response times in the event of an issue.

Integration with IoT Devices

Integration of blockchain with Internet of Things (IoT) devices further enhances product authentication and compliance. IoT devices can automatically record data to the blockchain at each stage of the supply chain—such as temperature control, humidity levels, and geolocation—ensuring that all products meet the required standards for storage and transportation.

```
// Example of IoT device recording temperature data to blockchain
IoTDevice.captureData(sensorData);
blockchain.recordTransaction(productID, sensorData);
```

This integration provides a higher degree of precision in monitoring, significantly reducing human error, and increasing the granularity of data available for ensuring compliance with environmental and safety standards.

The implementation of blockchain for ensuring product authenticity and compliance in supply chain processes offers significant advantages. These include reduced risk of counterfeit products, increased consumer trust, and streamlined compliance monitoring. However, the adoption also requires rigorous planning, stakeholder collaboration, and continued technological refinement to address scalability and interoperability challenges. Through such efforts, the benefits of blockchain can be effectively harnessed to foster an environment of trust and reliability in supply chains.

7.7 Integration Challenges: Blockchain and Existing SCM Systems

The integration of blockchain technology into existing supply chain management (SCM) systems presents a unique set of challenges. These challenges stem primarily from the technological, organizational, and operational differences between traditional SCM systems and blockchain-based systems.

Firstly, one of the principal technological challenges is the issue of interoperability. Existing SCM systems are often built on heterogeneous platforms and standards, making it difficult to achieve seamless communication between these systems and new blockchain solutions. For effective integration, there must be a standardized protocol that allows data exchange across different platforms without loss of fidelity or functionality. To this end, developers can utilize APIs that facilitate data sharing and interaction between blockchain networks and traditional SCM software.

```
// Example API usage in a blockchain-integrated SCM system
BlockchainAPI.connectToSCMSystem({
    systemId: "legacy_scm_platform_001",
    credentials: {
        user: "api_user",
        password: "api_password"
    },
    onDataReceived: (data) => {
        BlockchainAPI.recordTransaction(data);
    }
});
```

Secondly, the challenge of data consistency and accuracy must be addressed. Blockchain technology inherently ensures data immutability and transparency. However, the data fed into the blockchain network from legacy SCM systems might not always meet these standards. This inconsistency can be mitigated by implementing robust data validation mechanisms before the data entry into the blockchain ledger.

```
Data verified successfully:
Transaction Record: {
    ProductID: 12345,
    Timestamp: 1617125123,
    Origin: "Factory 9",
    Destination: "Warehouse 5",
    Status: "In Transit"
}
```

Thirdly, scalability is a considerable concern when integrating blockchain into existing SCM systems. Blockchain networks, particularly those utilizing proof-of-work consensus mechanisms, can suffer from low transaction throughput, which might not be suitable for high-volume, fast-paced supply chain operations. Solutions such as adopting more scalable consensus mechanisms like proof-of-stake or implementing sharding techniques can help overcome these limitations.

Algorithm 8: Algorithm for processing transactions in a scalable blockchain

Input: Transactions to be processed, T
Output: Block of transactions

1 **begin**
2     $Block \leftarrow empty$
3   **for** $t \in T$ **do**
4   **if** $isValidTransaction(t)$ **then**
5           $Block.addTransaction(t)$
6     $return\ Block$

Organizational challenges also play a critical role. The adoption of blockchain technology in supply chains requires significant change management efforts. The workforce needs to be trained not only on the use and maintenance of the new system but also on the underlying principles of blockchain technology. Additionally, there may be resistance from stakeholders who are accustomed to the existing workflows and systems.

Lastly, regulatory and compliance issues pose significant integration challenges. The decentralized and immutable nature of blockchain may conflict with regulations around data privacy and international trade. This discrepancy requires a careful redesign of blockchain systems to comply with such legal frameworks while retaining the benefits of the technology.

To summarize, various challenges hinder the straightforward integration of blockchain technology into established SCM systems. Addressing these challenges requires a thorough understanding of both blockchain technology and the specific characteristics of current SCM systems. Equipped with this knowledge, developers, and business leaders can tailor blockchain solutions that harmoniously integrate with, and enhance, existing supply chain processes.

7.8 Blockchain-Powered Smart Contracts in Supply Chains

The advent of smart contracts on blockchain platforms represents a transformative shift in conducting business transactions within supply chains. A smart contract is an executable code that automatically enforces, executes, and manages the terms and conditions laid out in a contract. In the domain of supply chain management, these digital contracts facilitate streamlined operations, enhanced security, and automated compliance with trading standards.

Smart contracts are deployed on the blockchain, ensuring that the rules embedded in the contract are immutable and transparent to all parties involved. This section elucidates the role of blockchain-powered smart contracts in supply chains, detailing their operational dynamics, benefits, and practical applications.

Operational Dynamics of Smart Contracts in Supply Chains

Smart contracts utilize the decentralized and tamper-resistant ledger of a blockchain to execute predefined conditions upon achieving certain triggers or milestones within the supply chain. For instance, when a product moves from manufacturing to logistics, a smart contract automatically releases payment to the supplier.

Example of a Smart Contract in Supply Chain:

```
pragma solidity ^0.5.0;

contract SupplyChain {
    address public owner = msg.sender;
    mapping (address => uint) public payments;

    constructor() public payable {
        owner = msg.sender;
    }

    function releasePayment(address payable supplier, uint amount) public
```

```
12          require(msg.sender == owner, "Only the owner can release
        payments.");
13          require(payments[supplier] == 0, "Payment already made.");
14
15          supplier.transfer(amount);
16          payments[supplier] = amount;
17      }
18  }
```

In the above example, the `releasePayment` function gets called when a product passes quality inspection. It ensures that only the owner of the contract (typically the buyer in the supply chain) can release payment, and that each supplier receives payment only once for their service.

Benefits of Using Smart Contracts in Supply Chains

- **Automation of Processes**: Smart contracts automate various supply chain operations such as payments, receipts, and shipments, thereby reducing dependency on manual processes and decreasing the scope for human errors.

- **Increased Transparency**: All transactions and their statuses are recorded on the blockchain, visible to all participants, but immutable and unchangeable once recorded.

- **Enhanced Security**: The decentralized nature of the blockchain enhances security, as data is not held in a single location and thus, is less susceptible to tampering and cyber threats.

- **Reduced Costs**: By automating tasks that were traditionally handled by middlemen or third parties, smart contracts reduce administrative and operational costs.

- **Compliance and Traceability**: They ensure compliance with contractual obligations automatically and provide an accurate, real-time traceability of goods.

Practical Applications of Smart Contracts in Supply Chains

Several industries have witnessed the deployment of blockchain-powered smart contracts to address specific challenges inherent in their supply chain processes. Pharmaceuticals, agriculture, electronics manufacturers, and the automotive sector are among those reaping the benefits of this technology.

For example, in pharmaceuticals, smart contracts are used to ensure the integrity of drug shipments, controlling storage conditions like temperature and humidity to comply with safety standards. Each sensor reading can trigger a relevant action within the smart contract, such as notifications to relevant parties or conditional release of payments, upon satisfying the shipment criteria.

The integration of smart contracts in supply chain management has not only proven beneficial in terms of operational efficiency but also in establishing trust and accountability among parties. The adoption of this technology continues to grow as businesses recognize its potential to address long-standing challenges within the industry.

7.9 Case Studies: Blockchain Implementations in Supply Chain

The following subsections detail specific case studies where blockchain technology has been implemented within supply chain management processes, highlighting the successes and unique applications in varied industries.

Walmart and IBM for Food Traceability

One of the most cited case studies in blockchain supply chain management is the collaboration between Walmart and IBM on the Food Trust blockchain project. Walmart, needing a more robust method to track food items to ensure safety and reduce waste, leveraged IBM's blockchain technology to enhance transparency and efficiency in its massive supply chain.

Initially, the project focused on tracing back the source of sliced mangos. Walmart conducted a traceability test in its stores. Using traditional methods, it took approximately seven days to track the origin of the fruits. However, with the blockchain implemented, the information was available in mere seconds.

Here is a simplified example of how data is entered into the blockchain:

```
1  BlockChain blockchain = new BlockChain();
2  Product mango = new Product("Mango", "1234", "Mexico");
3  blockchain.addBlock(mango.toBlock());
```

The outcome of this implementation in operational term was fascinating:

CHAPTER 7. BLOCKCHAIN IN SUPPLY CHAIN MANAGEMENT

```
Block 2:
Product Name: Mango
Product ID: 1234
Origin: Mexico
Time-stamp: 2023-03-01 12:00:00
```

This practical application clearly displays the transformative effects of real-time data retrieval in food safety and efficiency.

Maersk and IBM's TradeLens Platform

Another significant implementation of blockchain in supply chains is the TradeLens platform, developed jointly by Maersk, the world's largest container shipping company, and IBM. This platform is built on the IBM Blockchain, aimed at applying the ledger technology to the global supply chain. TradeLens functions by providing an immutable record of transactions, shipping documents, and other shipping data accessible by various stakeholders in the supply chain.

Through the use of TradeLens, the involved parties can access real-time shipping data which reduces delays and conflicts over custody and ownership. As a case in point, during a pilot test of TradeLens:

```
1  TradeLens trace = new TradeLens();
2  Container container = new Container("Container001", "China", "Germany");
3  trace.addContainerJourney(container.toJourney());
```

The resulting data access shows:

```
Journey Record:
Container ID: Container001
Origin: China
Destination: Germany
Status: In Transit
Time-stamp: 2023-03-05 09:30:00
```

This case study demonstrates the crucial role of blockchain technology in improving the transparency and efficiency of international shipping operations.

De Beers and Diamond Traceability

De Beers, the famous diamond company, implemented a blockchain-based initiative named Tracr. The principal aim was to track the entire journey of a diamond, from the mine to the retail market, ensuring that the diamonds are ethically sourced and conflict-free.

The system operates by creating a digital certificate for each diamond, which records key attributes such as carat, color, and clarity alongside the journey through the supply chain. This certificate is updated at every transaction:

```
1  Tracr platform = new Tracr();
```

```
2   Diamond diamond = new Diamond("Diamond001", "2.5", "VS1");
3   platform.recordDiamond(diamond.createCertificate());
```

Verification of this certificate provides:
```
Certificate for Diamond001:
Carat: 2.5
Clarity: VS1
Current Holder: Retailer X
Location: London
Time-stamp: 2023-03-10 15:00:00
```

By implementing this system, De Beers ensures that each stone is traceable, combatting the prevalent issues of diamond mislabelling and improving consumer trust.

Summary of Impacts

These case studies exemplify the powerful impact of blockchain on improving transparency, efficiency, and trust in supply chain management. Each example, from food safety, international shipping to luxury goods, reflects significant advancements in tracking and verification processes. As businesses continue to develop and integrate such blockchain systems, the potential to further optimize supply chain operations is immense. The continued success stories further highlight blockchain's capability to revolutionize traditional supply chain management frameworks, stepping towards a more transparent, efficient, and secure global trading environment.

7.10 Future Trends: Blockchain Technology in Supply Chain Management

Blockchain technology has already started to reshape the landscape of supply chain management with its ability to offer unprecedented levels of transparency, security, and efficiency. As we look towards the future, several key trends are emerging that could further enhance the applicability and effectiveness of blockchain in this field.

Increased Adoption of Blockchain-as-a-Service (BaaS): One significant trend is the growth of Blockchain-as-a-Service offerings. These services, provided by major tech companies like IBM, Amazon, and Microsoft, enable businesses to implement blockchain technology without the need to develop their own infrastructure. The convenience and reduced upfront costs of BaaS models encourage more businesses, especially small to medium-sized enterprises (SMEs), to adopt blockchain within their supply chains.

- Streamlining setup processes
- Decreasing the necessity for in-house expertise
- Offering scalability as per business needs

Integration of IoT with Blockchain: The convergence of blockchain technology with the Internet of Things (IoT) is set to further drive innovation within supply chains. IoT devices can continuously send real-time data directly to a blockchain network, enabling automatic updates and triggering actions on smart contracts. This integration can lead to:

- Greater data accuracy through automated data capture
- Enhanced traceability of goods from production to delivery
- Increased efficiency by minimizing manual interventions

Sensitive industries, such as pharmaceuticals and perishable goods, could profoundly benefit from these advancements.

Advancements in Smart Contract Usability: Smart contracts are poised to become more accessible and widely used in supply chain management. With ongoing advancements in programming languages and tools designed specifically for blockchain frameworks, businesses can more easily implement complex contracts that automatically enforce, execute, and manage terms agreed upon by various participants in the supply chain. Here, we observe:

- Development of more user-friendly smart contract development tools
- Enhancements in the security auditing processes for smart contracts
- Increasing legal clarity and standards around smart contracts

Rise of Sustainable and Ethical Supply Chains: As consumers grow increasingly aware of and concerned about the ethical aspects of production, blockchain is enabling more transparent supply chains that promote sustainability. Blockchain's ability to provide a tamper-evident record of product history from origin to retailer makes it easier for companies to prove the ethical integrity of their products. Future blockchain enhancements will likely focus on:

- Recording and verifying sustainable practices
- Ensuring fair labor practices and compliance with regulations
- Enhancing consumer trust through greater transparency

Government Regulations and Standardizations: Looking ahead, the role of government in regulating and facilitating blockchain adoption in supply chain management will be crucial. Regulation could help establish standards that ensure the interoperability of blockchain systems across borders and industries, which is essential for the global nature of modern supply chains. Possible government actions might include:

- Development of standard protocols for blockchain in supply chains
- Implementation of legal frameworks that recognize blockchain transactions
- Support for blockchain innovation through subsidies or tax incentives

Each of these trends not only demonstrates the continuing evolution of blockchain technology but also highlights the shifts in the broader economic, technological, and regulatory landscapes that businesses must navigate. As these trends progress, they promise to enhance the capabilities of supply chains but they require businesses to remain adaptable and forward-thinking in their strategies. The dynamic interplay between technological advancements and business adaptation will likely define the transformative journey of blockchain in supply chain management over the coming years.

7.11 Conclusion: The Impact of Blockchain on Supply Chain Operations

The deployment of blockchain technology within supply chain management has demonstrated substantial improvements in transparency, efficiency, and trust among all stakeholders. By anchoring every transaction within an immutable ledger, blockchain provides a verifiable and tamper-evident record system. This transformation addresses many classical supply chain challenges, reshuffling the foundations of how goods are tracked and managed from source to consumer.

One of the most distinguishable impacts of blockchain technology is the enhancement of transparency. By allowing every participant in the supply chain to view the progress and history of a product, blockchain drastically reduces the opacity that has been typical in traditional supply chains. This increased visibility helps prevent theft, loss, and counterfeiting, contributing positively to overall security and authenticity across the board.

The ability of blockchain to improve operational efficiency is reflected in reduced reconciliation times and lower costs associated with labor and error management. Automated processes, undergirded by smart contracts, expedite transactions that traditionally took days to complete. For instance, remittances and payment clearances between manufacturers and suppliers or retailers and suppliers are expedited, optimizing the entire cash flow cycle within the supply chains.

Cost reduction emerges not merely from streamlined processes but also from the significant diminishment of fraud and error rates. The enhanced validation mechanisms inherent in blockchain platforms ensure that all entries are authentic and unchanged. This aspect alone mitigates the risk exposures related to financial overheads, including insurance and warranty claims which traditionally form a substantial part of the operational costs.

In regard to compliance, blockchain introduces an easier methodology for maintaining and demonstrating adherence to legal and regulatory standards. Compliance logs, maintained on a blockchain, can be instantaneously audited and verified without the possibility of unauthorized alterations. This feature is particularly beneficial in industries with heavy regulatory burdens such as pharmaceuticals, food and beverages, and aerospace.

However, the introduction of blockchain into existing supply chain systems is not devoid of challenges. The integration with traditional SCM technologies requires meticulous planning, a robust technological infrastructure, and a willingness to adopt a new operational ethos. Additionally, the shift in paradigm from centralized systems to decentralized networks requires an overhaul of governance structures, posing a significant barrier to adoption.

Despite these challenges, the future trends of blockchain in supply chain promise further enhancements as the technology matures and becomes more widely understood. Continued advancements in blockchain technology are expected to lead to more sophisticated integrations, addressing current limitations and expanding the potential applications within supply chains.

Reflecting on all these impacts, it becomes evident that blockchain's role in supply chains serves as a cornerstone for a new era of digital transformation in the industry. The converging effect of efficiency, cost reduction, enhanced transparency, and improved compliance foster a model that not only boosts profitability but also assures more sustainable business practices. As we move forward, continuous exploration and adoption of blockchain will likely set a new standard in supply chain management, shaping the global trade frameworks of tomorrow.

CHAPTER 7. BLOCKCHAIN IN SUPPLY CHAIN MANAGEMENT

Chapter 8

Blockchain for Finance and Banking

in enhancing transaction efficiencies, security, and transparency. It discusses the deployment of blockchain for various financial processes including payments, settlements, and compliance operations. The chapter also addresses challenges specific to banking such as integration with existing systems and regulatory concerns, providing detailed insights into how financial institutions can leverage blockchain to innovate and streamline operations.

8.1 Introduction to Blockchain in Finance and Banking

The financial sector is witnessing a significant transformation with the integration of blockchain technology, which has begun to redefine transactions, security, and confidentiality in profound ways. Blockchain stands as a decentralized ledger technology (DLT), which records transactions across several computers such that the included records cannot be altered retroactively, without the alteration of all subsequent blocks. This foundational property of blockchain ensures the integrity and veracity of the financial data it holds, which is imperative in a sector where trust and accountability are paramount.

Finance and banking involve the orchestration of numerous complex transactions, including but not limited to transfers of funds, securing of loans, issuance, and trading of securities, compliance with regulatory requirements, and management of financial risk. Each of these operations requires an ecosystem that can provide seamless, transparent, and secure processing. Blockchain offers such an ecosystem, fundamentally through its attributes of decentralization, immutability, and transparency.

Decentralization in the context of blockchain mitigates the risks associated with centralized processing systems. In traditional financial systems, central points of control can lead to inefficiencies, such as time delays for cross-border payments and vulnerabilities in security. Blockchain eliminates the need for a central control point, thereby distributing the processing across a network of nodes. This not only speeds up transaction processing due to the elimination of intermediary validations but also significantly increases the system's resistance to fraud and cyber-attacks.

The immutability characteristic of blockchain comes from the use of cryptographic hashing and consensus mechanisms. When a transaction is recorded on a blockchain, it is secured by cryptographic algorithms that ensure the data cannot be changed without changing all subsequent blocks and without the network consensus. This makes blockchain an exceptionally secure platform for financial transactions, where records once written into the blockchain become unalterable and permanent.

Transparency, another key feature of blockchain, ensures that all transactions are visible to all participants in the network while safeguarding user privacy through the use of pseudonyms. This level of transparency is vital in regulatory compliance and financial auditing processes, enabling regulators to efficiently monitor financial activities without compromising individual privacy and security.

Beyond these foundational advantages, blockchain introduces new capabilities in financial operations, involving smart contracts and automated compliance. Smart contracts are self-executing contracts where the terms of the agreement between buyer and seller are written into lines of code. These contracts execute automatically when predefined conditions are met, reducing the need for manual intervention and thereby enhancing the efficiency of contractual transactions in finance.

To integrate blockchain into the financial and banking sectors, however, is not devoid of challenges. The adaptation of existing systems, alignment with financial regulations, scalability of the technology, and the establishment of a new operational paradigm need considerable strategic planning and implementation. Nevertheless, the continuous advancements in blockchain technology are systematically addressing these issues, paving the way for more robust financial systems.

This section laid a foundation for understanding the pivotal role blockchain technology plays in shaping the modern financial and banking industries. It also set the stage for a deeper exploration of specific applications and challenges in subsequent sections.

8.2 Benefits of Blockchain in Financial Services

The adoption of blockchain technology in financial services offers a myriad of benefits, primarily enhancing the efficiency, security, and transparency of transactions. The following detailed discussion delves into these advantages, elucidating how they translate into tangible improvements in various financial operations.

First, blockchain technology introduces an unprecedented level of transparency that benefits financial institutions and their clients alike. Each transaction on a blockchain is recorded on a distributed ledger that is accessible to all network participants, while maintaining the confidentiality of the parties involved. This transparency helps in reducing fraud and corruption, a significant concern in financial transactions. For instance, the finality and immutability of blockchain records make it virtually impossible to alter any details of transactions after they are executed and recorded. This characteristic ensures a higher degree of accuracy and trustworthiness in financial reporting and auditing processes.

Second, the operational efficiency of financial services is considerably enhanced through the elimination of intermediaries typically required in traditional banking systems. By leveraging smart contracts on blockchain platforms, tasks that previously required manual intervention and verification, such as loan approval or international money transfers, can be automated. Smart contracts execute automatically based on predefined criteria and conditions, significantly speeding up transaction times and reducing potential errors. The following code snippet demonstrates a simplified example of a smart contract used for releasing payment upon delivering a service:

```solidity
pragma solidity ^0.5.0;

contract PaymentContract {
    address payable public serviceProvider;
    address public client;
    uint public paymentAmount;

    constructor(address payable _serviceProvider, uint _paymentAmount) public {
        serviceProvider = _serviceProvider;
        paymentAmount = _paymentAmount;
        client = msg.sender;
    }

    function releasePayment() public {
        require(msg.sender == client, "Only the client can release the payment.");
        serviceProvider.transfer(paymentAmount);
    }
}
```

Furthermore, blockchain facilitates improved compliance mechanisms for financial institutions. Regulatory compliance can be programmed into blockchain networks through smart contracts, which help in enforcing and monitoring compliance in real-time. This automated compliance not only reduces the cost associated with regulatory adherence but also minimizes human errors. The consequent operational records generated are useful during audits and for regulatory reviews.

Cost reduction is another significant advantage offered by blockchain in financial services. The technology reduces costs associated with transaction processing and the need for reconciliation since the transaction records are unified and consistent across all parties. Moreover, the maintenance of a decentralized ledger eliminates the expenses typically incurred in managing centralized databases, not to mention reducing costs related to data breaches which are more common in traditional financial systems.

Enhanced security is also a critical benefit. Blockchain's use of advanced cryptography ensures that information is securely stored and transmitted. Every transaction is encrypted and linked to the previous transaction, forming a chain that is extremely difficult to alter. This aspect is particularly crucial in mitigating the risks associated with cyber threats, which are increasingly becoming sophisticated.

Lastly, the inherently decentralized nature of blockchain guarantees better resistance to systemic failures. Unlike centralized systems where a single point of failure can affect the entire network, blockchain distributes operational risks across a wide array of nodes making it more resilient to attacks and operational errors.

The integration of blockchain into financial services not only streamlines operations by making them more efficient, secure, and transparent but also catalyzes the transformation of financial institutions into more agile entities capable of adapting to new market demands and regulatory requirements.

8.3 Blockchain for Payment Systems and Money Transfers

The deployment of blockchain technology in payment systems and money transfers is transforming the landscape of financial transactions globally. This transformation is primarily driven by blockchain's inherent properties such as decentralization, transparency, and immutability. These attributes enhance the efficiency, security, and reliability of payment processes.

Blockchain technology operates on a distributed ledger system, where each transaction gets recorded across multiple nodes. This distribution ensures that no single point of failure can affect the entire network, markedly enhancing the resilience and reliability of payment systems. For instance, in traditional payment channels, transactions often rely on a central authority for processing and validation, which can be a bottleneck and a vulnerability point. In contrast, blockchain enables a peer-to-peer (P2P) transaction model that eliminates the need for intermediaries, thereby reducing costs and processing time.

```
// Example of a P2P blockchain transaction process
Transaction transaction = new Transaction(senderPublicKey, receiverPublicKey,
    amount);
transaction.addSignature(senderPrivateKey);
block.addTransaction(transaction);
blockchain.addBlock(block);
```

Upon submission of a transaction, it undergoes verification by multiple participants in the blockchain, commonly referred to as nodes. Each node validates the transaction against a specific set of criteria to ascertain its legitimacy. Post-validation, the transaction is added to a new block, which is then linked to the chain of previous blocks. Due to the cryptographic connection between blocks, the alteration of a single block's data retroactively in the blockchain is practically infeasible without alerting the system.

```
Block 7897:
{
  Transactions: [..., "TXN6789054"]
  PreviousHash: "0000AEFC987..."
  Hash: "0000XYZ7890..."
  Nonce: 56002
}
```

One paramount advantage of utilizing blockchain in payment systems is the transparent nature of transactions. Each transaction is logged and visible to all network participants, fostering increased trust and verifiability in financial transactions. Moreover, this transparency also aids in anti-money laundering (AML) and combating the financing of terrorism (CFT) by making transaction trails readily available and auditable by regulatory entities without compromising customer confidentiality.

- Reduction in transaction costs by removing intermediaries.
- Settlement of transactions in real-time.
- Enhancement in the security of transactions through cryptographic techniques.
- Provision of a transparent, auditable transaction ledger.

Settlement speed is another crucial factor where blockchain shows significant promise. Traditional banking systems typically take several business days to settle transactions, especially in cross-border payments. Blockchain technology can drastically reduce this duration to minutes or even seconds, permitting near-instantaneous global financial transactions.

An example of this is Ripple, a blockchain-based digital payment protocol; it enhances worldwide money transfers by connecting banks, payment providers, and digital asset exchanges through a unified network.

```
1  // Ripple transaction example
2  const rippleAPI = new RippleAPI({server: 'wss://s1.ripple.com'});
3  await rippleAPI.connect();
4  await rippleAPI.preparePayment(...)
```

The integration of smart contracts in blockchain payment systems further extends the use cases into areas like conditional transactions where payments are automatically processed upon meeting pre-defined conditions, thereby saving time and reducing the administrative burden associated with manual processing.

Despite these advantages, the implementation of blockchain in payment systems prevents specific challenges around scalability, interoperability with existing banking infrastructures, and regulatory acceptance. Efforts such as adapting blockchain designs to suit different scalability requirements and working with regulatory bodies to frame acceptable operational guidelines are active areas of development that seek to address these challenges.

By fine-tuning the underlying technology and fostering a cooperative regulatory environment, blockchain can significantly optimize traditional payment systems, making financial transactions more streamlined, cost-effective, and secure. This optimization not only benefits the financial sector but also promises a more inclusive global financial system where barriers to access and high transaction fees are decisively reduced.

8.4 Enhancing Loan and Credit Processing through Blockchain

The application of blockchain technology in loan and credit processing comprehensively alters traditional methods, addressing issues like transparency, efficiency, and security. Within the context of the financial services sector, the implementation of blockchain for these purposes not only speeds up the processing time but also reduces the potential for fraud, and significantly diminishes overhead costs associated with these banking services.

Traditionally, the loan and credit approval processes are dependent on the assessment of client data, which includes identity verification, credit history, income, and debt-to-income ratio. This evaluation is time-consuming, labor-intensive, and susceptible to human error. By integrating blockchain into these processes, financial institutions are enabled to streamline operations by leveraging the inherent properties of blockchain technology - decentralization, immutability, and transparency.

Firstly, blockchain facilitates an enhanced verification system. By storing the KYC (Know Your Customer) data on a blockchain, the information becomes verifiable across multiple parties without the need for repeated checks. Each entry on a blockchain is time-stamped and linked to previous entries, making the data innate secure and immutable. This deters data tampering and prevents fraud. For example, consider how a decentralized ledger can be used to maintain an immutable record of a client's financial transactions and interactions:

```
BlockchainLedger.addRecord(previousHash, transactionDetails, timestamp);
```

This code snippet represents a simplified function to add a new record into a blockchain ledger. By encapsulating the previous hash, the transaction details, and the timestamp, each record securely connects to its predecessor, hence maintaining a continuum of data integrity.

Secondly, smart contracts automate and enforce contract terms and conditions, mitigating the potential for disputes and the need for manual intervention. These digital contracts execute automatically when predefined conditions are met. In the context of loan agreements, smart contracts facilitate:

- Automatic credit checks and approvals based on predetermined criteria,
- Disbursement of funds upon approval,
- Collection and recording of repayments,
- Implementation of penalties for late payments or defaults.

Consider the implementation of a smart contract in a loan approval process:

```
if (applicant.creditScore > 700 && applicant.debtToIncomeRatio < 0.4) {
    BlockchainContract.approveLoan(amount);
    disburseFunds();
}
```

This pseudocode outlines the conditions under which a loan approval and disbursement might be processed automatically within a blockchain network.

Moreover, blockchain supports greater transparency and auditability in loan and credit services. Every transaction processed on a blockchain is recorded, and each entry is accessible to authorized parties, which significantly hampers the concealment of information and aids in regulatory compliance and audit processes. This feature not only fortifies the trust relationship between clients and financial institutions but also simplifies compliance with financial regulations.

However, while blockchain presents several benefits, its implementation in the banking sector requires institutional will, technical adaptability, and regulatory support. The transformation involves not only technology overhaul but also a paradigm shift in the operational and regulatory frameworks of financial institutions.

Efforts in international cooperation and technology standardization might further pave the way for widespread adoption of blockchain in enhancing loan and credit processes across the globe, dramatically reshaping how traditional banking operates in the borrowing and lending markets.

8.5 Blockchain Solutions for Securities Settlements

The traditional securities settlement process often involves multiple intermediaries, including custodians, clearinghouses, and central securities depositories. These entities manage the transfer of ownership records, ensure the availability of funds, and reconcile transactions over a period that can extend to several days. This section examines the transformative role blockchain technology can play in reshaping the securities settlement landscape, drastically reducing settlement times and associated costs, while enhancing security and transparency.

Blockchain technology introduces a decentralized ledger that provides a single, immutable record of ownership and transaction history. This feature is pivotal in the context of securities settlements, where the accuracy and reliability of transaction records are paramount. Implementing blockchain in securities settlements not only simplifies the complex web of interactions but also provides real-time transaction visibility to all parties involved.

- **Reduction in Settlement Time**: By enabling peer-to-peer transfers, blockchain technology can eliminate the need for intermediaries, thereby significantly reducing the settlement time from T+2 or T+3 days (transaction day plus two or three) to near real-time.

- **Lower Transaction Costs**: The disintermediation achieved by using blockchain reduces the fees associated with multiple parties and infrastructures, lowering overall transaction costs.

- **Increased Transparency and Auditability**: Every transaction on a blockchain is recorded on a ledger that is accessible by all market participants, increasing transparency. Additionally, the immutability of the blockchain ensures that records cannot be altered, enhancing audit trails.

- **Improved Security**: The cryptographic nature of blockchain significantly heightens security against fraud and unauthorized activities.

- **Enhanced Liquidity**: Faster settlements could improve the liquidity of assets by speeding up the process of freeing capital tied up during the settlement period.

To illustrate how blockchain can be integrated into the securities settlement process, consider the following hypothetical implementation:

```
Day 1: A buyer and seller agree on a securities transaction.
Day 1: The transaction details are recorded on the blockchain, triggering the settlement process.
Day 1: Cryptographic proofs verify the transaction.
Day 1: Securities and cash are swapped simultaneously via blockchain smart contracts, concluding the settlement instantly.
```

The above process contrasts sharply with the existing system, where the actual transfer of securities and cash involves several steps, reliant on different systems and checks that can extend over multiple days.

However, integrating blockchain into existing financial systems is not devoid of challenges. These include scalability concerns, as the current technology may not be able to handle the high volume of transactions typical to major securities markets. Additionally, regulatory acceptance is crucial, as the technology must be compliant with the existing legal and regulatory framework governing securities transactions.

Major financial regulators and institutions have started experimenting with blockchain for securities settlements. Notable among these initiatives is the blockchain project operated by the Australian Securities Exchange, which aims to replace its current clearing and settlement system with a blockchain-based system. This move signals a significant endorsement of blockchain's potential in securities settlements.

The application of blockchain in this domain is still at a nascent stage but is poised to grow as technological and regulatory frameworks mature. The inherent characteristics of blockchain could potentially turn it into a foundational technology for the securities industry, similar to how the internet revolutionized communication.

By addressing the inefficiencies of the traditional securities settlement process, blockchain stands ready to redefine the landscape, promising more streamlined, cost-effective, and transparent operations. As these potentials are progressively realized, financial markets may witness a substantial shift in how securities transactions are processed, delivering benefits to all stakeholders involved.

8.6 Use of Smart Contracts in Financial Products

Smart contracts are self-executing contracts with the terms of the agreement directly written into lines of code. In the context of financial services, these contracts automatically enforce, execute, and manage the terms agreed upon by all parties, without the need for intermediaries. This section explores the use of smart contracts in various financial products, detailing their implementation, benefits, and operational mechanisms.

The advent of smart contracts in financial products primarily targets areas such as derivatives, bonds, and insurance, where complex arrangements and multiple stakeholders are common. The inherent features of blockchain-based smart contracts, such as immutability, transparency, and security, align well with the requirements of these financial services.

Derivatives: Smart contracts automate many aspects of derivatives trading, from execution to clearing, and settlement. For instance, a derivative contract can be programmed so that it executes automatically when certain market conditions are met. This eliminates the need for manual intervention, reduces errors, and enhances market efficiency. Consider the following example implemented on an Ethereum-based platform:

```solidity
pragma solidity ^0.5.0;

contract DerivativeContract {
    uint public value;
    address payable public investor;
    address payable public issuer;
    uint public maturityDate;
    bool public contractSettled;

    constructor(uint initialValue, address payable contractIssuer, uint maturity) public {
        value = initialValue;
        investor = msg.sender;
        issuer = contractIssuer;
        maturityDate = now + maturity;
        contractSettled = false;
    }

    function executeContract() public {
        require(now >= maturityDate);
        require(msg.sender == investor);
        issuer.transfer(value);
        contractSettled = true;
    }
}
```

This example shakes off the traditional complexity and introduces a streamlined approach where the contractual obligations, once triggered, lead to automatic value transfer.

Bonds: Blockchain enhances the issuance and administration of bonds through smart contracts by automating coupon payments and principal repayment on maturity dates. This use case not only simplifies management but also provides regulators and investors with greater transparency regarding the state and performance of the bond.

Insurance: In the insurance sector, smart contracts can be used to manage and automate claims processing. For instance, in the event of a valid claim condition being met (e.g., data from flight trackers confirming flight cancellation), the smart contract can instantly process the claim without waiting for manual claim handling. Below is a pseudocode example illustrating this:

Algorithm 9: Automated Insurance Claim Processing

Data: Flight status data
Result: Claim processed if conditions met
1 initialization;
2 **while** *insurance contract is active* **do**
3   check flight status;
4   **if** *flight is canceled* **then**
5   verify claim validity;
6   process payment to insured party;
7   terminate contract;

This reduces the likelihood of fraudulent claims and increases customer satisfaction by ensuring immediate payout after the triggering event, maintaining high transparency in contract enforcement.

- Immutability guarantees that once a contract is deployed, its conditions cannot be altered, preventing any post-agreement tampering or fraud.

- Transparency allows all parties to view the terms and current state of the contract, fostering trust and confidence among participants.

- Security practices within blockchain networks protect against data breaches and unauthorized access, crucial for maintaining sensitive financial data.

Employing smart contracts in the financial domain offers transformative potential. It reduces operational risks and administrative burdens, enhances compliance monitoring, and revolutionizes traditional financial operations. The illustrated examples across derivatives, bonds, and insurance demonstrate the robustness, efficacy, and versatility of smart contracts. This technology supports a shift toward more transparent, efficient, and secure financial services, although it requires a well-calibrated regulatory framework to fully realize its potential within the financial landscape.

8.7 Regulatory Compliance and Reporting with Blockchain

Regulatory compliance presents a significant challenge for financial institutions, heavily impacting resource allocation and operational efficiency. The adoption of blockchain technology offers a promising avenue for simplifying compliance processes and ensuring transparency, thereby easing the burden on banks and financial entities. Blockchain's intrinsic characteristics, such as immutability and decentralized verification, naturally align with regulatory demands for accuracy, auditability, and security in financial reporting.

The application of blockchain in regulatory compliance and reporting can be analyzed through several key functionalities: decentralized data management, automation of compliance processes, and improved auditability. Each of these aspects plays a vital role in streamlining compliance operations, reducing errors, and safeguarding data integrity.

Decentralized Data Management

In traditional financial systems, data management involves central authorities and multiple intermediaries, which often leads to inefficiencies and increased opportunities for data tampering. Blockchain introduces a decentralized ledger technology where all transaction records are distributed across a network, enhancing data consistency and transparency. This decentralized nature of blockchain means that once a transaction is recorded on the ledger, it becomes nearly immutable. This feature is particularly beneficial for compliance officers who require a reliable and unalterable record of transactions to ensure adherence to financial regulations.

```
// Example of a simple blockchain ledger entry
block = {
   index: 1,
   timestamp: 1633036800,
   transactions: [
      {
         from: "bankA",
         to: "bankB",
         amount: 100000,
         currency: "USD",
         message: "Loan payment"
      }
   ],
   prev_hash: "91a73664b0085d...",
   hash: "ec3a0eaeb2239..."
}
```

Transaction entries such as the one shown above are permanently written, providing an exact, timestamped record of financial movements.

Automation of Compliance Processes

Blockchain can significantly enhance regulatory compliance by automating many of the processes involved. Smart contracts, which are self-executing contracts with the terms directly written into code, can be employed to automate compliance tasks. For instance, a smart contract could automatically execute transactions according to pre-defined regulatory standards, or flag transactions that do not comply with those standards.

```
// Example of a smart contract for compliance
pragma solidity ^0.4.24;

contract ComplianceContract {
   // Define parameters and compliance rules
   uint public constant minTransactionValue = 50000;
   uint public constant maxTransactionValue = 1000000;

   function checkCompliance(uint transactionValue) public pure returns (bool) {
      if(transactionValue < minTransactionValue || transactionValue > maxTransactionValue) {
         return false; // Non-compliant transaction
      }
      return true; // Compliant transaction
   }
}
```

Automating these processes not only speeds up transactions but also minimizes human errors and the associated risks of non-compliance.

Improved Auditability

The immutable and chronological nature of blockchain's distributed ledger provides a highly effective framework for auditing. Regulators can access a secure, verifiable, and complete history of all financial transactions at any point. This capability is critical where financial institutions are required to undergo frequent audits to ensure compliance with strict regulatory frameworks.

```
Output example for an audit query:
- Transaction ID: TXN12345
- Date: 2023-09-15
- From: Bank A
- To: Client C
- Amount: $75,000
- Status: Compliant
```

Such clarity and ease of access considerably reduce the time and cost associated with audits, facilitating more frequent and thorough examinations without disrupting daily operations.

The integration of blockchain into regulatory compliance and reporting represents a transformative approach that can fundamentally enhance the structure and efficiency of financial governance. By ensuring data integrity, automating compliance, and improving audit processes, blockchain technology not only supports financial institutions in meeting strict regulatory requirements but also enhances operational efficiencies enabling a sharper focus on their core business activities. With ongoing advancements in blockchain technology, the potential for its application within financial compliance continues to expand, promising even greater efficiency and security in the management and reporting of financial data.

8.8 Security and Fraud Prevention in Banking using Blockchain

Blockchain technology, by design, offers several inherent characteristics that make it an exceptional foundation for enhancing security protocols and mechanisms in the banking sector. The immutable nature of transaction records and the decentralized architecture are the primary attributes that drive security in blockchain applications.

Immutability and Security: By virtue of blockchain's data integrity features, once a transaction is recorded on a blockchain, it cannot be altered or deleted by any single actor. This immutability ensures that all transaction records are permanent and tamper-evident. For banking, this means that fraudulent activities such as transaction reversal and double-spending can be effectively countered.

Consider an instance where a transaction record on the blockchain has the following basic structure in pseudo code:

```
Transaction {
    string fromAddress;
    string toAddress;
    float value;
    string transactionHash;
}
```

A transaction initialized and recorded in such a structure will carry its own unique hash, which is recalculated every time any transaction data is altered. Consequently, any attempt to change a transaction detail after it has been recorded will result in a different hash, making tampering evident.

Decentralized Ledger Technology (DLT): Traditional banking systems are often centralized, which presents single points of failure that malicious entities might exploit. Blockchain technology employs DLT, which distributes the ledger across multiple nodes. This means that there isn't a central point to attack, significantly enhancing the system's resilience to fraudulent activities and cyberattacks.

A key aspect of blockchain's DLT is the consensus mechanism. In a banking blockchain, every transaction must be verified and agreed upon by a majority of nodes based on predetermined rules set in the system. The consensus process could be illustrated as follows:

Algorithm 10: Blockchain consensus mechanism

Input: A list of new transactions
Output: A confirmed block added to the blockchain

1 **while** *Transactions are being generated* **do**
2   Gather transactions into a new block
3   Broadcast the block to all nodes
4   Each node checks validity of transactions
5   Nodes vote on the veracity of the block
6   **if** *Majority votes YES* **then**
7   Add block to the blockchain

This mechanism not only prevents fraud but ensures all participating nodes store a verified copy of the truth which reflects all transactions as they are authorized.

Use of Cryptography: Blockchain utilizes cryptographic practices such as hashing and public-private key encryption to secure transactions. Each transaction is signed using the private key of the sender, assuring non-repudiation and integrity. The public key of the sender can be used by the receiver and other participants to validate the authenticity of the transaction. Here's how a transaction digital signature might be verified:

```
VerifyTransactionSignature(transaction, publicKey) {
    return verifySignature(transaction.hash, transaction.signature, publicKey);
}
```

This function verifies that the transaction has not been tampered with and was indeed initiated by the holder of the private key corresponding to the publicly known sender address.

Enhanced Transparency and Auditability: Although the term transparency might seem contradictory to privacy, blockchain provides a controlled transparency where access to data can be meticulously managed through permissions and smart contracts. This level of transparency ensures that audits can be conducted more efficiently and with less effort. The immutable and decentralized nature of the block means that each entry can be traced back to its origin, enabling easy identification of discrepancies.

The combination of these features culminates in a potent application of blockchain technology that can significantly mitigate the risks of security breaches and fraud within the banking sector. This is achieved not only through technological mechanisms but also by reinventing the underlying processes and interactions within the banking industry. Thus, it becomes evident that blockchain is not just a technological improvement but a strategic asset in the quest for fortified security and integrity in banking transactions.

8.9 Challenges of Implementing Blockchain in Financial Institutions

Integration with Existing Legacy Systems

One significant challenge that financial institutions face when adopting blockchain technology is the integration with existing legacy systems. These legacy systems are often deeply entrenched within the institution's infrastructure, making integration complex. Below are specific aspects that tend to present challenges:

- `Data Format Discrepancy` - Traditional systems and blockchain technologies often use fundamentally different data formats, requiring robust transformation tools to map and convert data accurately.

- `System Interoperability` - Achieving a seamless operational flow between blockchain platforms and traditional banking systems requires significant modifications, often involving both software and hardware upgrades.

- `Transaction Speed` - While blockchain offers improvements in security and transparency, the transaction speed can be lower compared to conventional high-speed transaction systems.

Integration not only demands substantial initial investment but also a high level of technical expertise to ensure that new and old systems work synchronously without compromising performance or security.

Scalability Issues

Blockchain scalability is another considerable concern. Financial institutions process thousands of transactions per second, and the blockchain platforms must be capable of handling such volumes efficiently. Current blockchain solutions often struggle with scalability due to:

- `Network Size` - As more nodes join the blockchain, the complexity of managing and verifying transactions increases, often leading to a bottleneck.

- `Consensus Mechanisms` - Mechanisms like Proof of Work are secure but slow. Alternatives like Proof of Stake or Delegated Proof of Stake are faster but still under investigation for potential security risks in a financial context.

- `Block Size Limit` - Current block size limits may throttle the number of transactions that can be processed at a given time, impacting transaction throughput.

In addressing these issues, financial institutions may consider hybrid solutions that combine traditional databases with blockchain's decentralized features to strike a balance between efficiency and the benefits offered by blockchain technologies.

Regulatory Challenges

Regulatory compliance presents an ongoing challenge given the evolving nature of blockchain technology. Several factors contribute to the complexity of complying with legal and regulatory standards:

- Lack of Standardization - The absence of a unified global standard for blockchain technology means that compliance requirements can vary significantly between jurisdictions.

- Data Privacy Laws - Institutions must navigate the compliance of blockchain's transparency with strict data protection regulations such as GDPR in Europe or CCPA in California.

- Reporting Obligations - Blockchain can complicate traditional reporting mechanisms to financial authorities, particularly when looking at cross-border transactions and differing national laws.

Financial institutions must work closely with regulatory bodies, possibly influencing policy-making processes, to ensure that any blockchain implementation aligns with current and prospective regulatory demands.

Cultural and Organizational Resistance

Apart from technical and regulatory challenges, cultural and organizational resistance within institutions can impede blockchain implementation. This resistance typically stems from:

- Lack of Blockchain Understanding - A general lack of understanding of blockchain's potential benefits and operation among key stakeholders can lead to resistance towards its adoption.

- Fear of Job Displacement - Employees may fear that the automation and efficiency brought by blockchain technologies could lead to job reductions or significant shifts in job roles.

- Change Management - Introducing a radical technological shift requires effective change management strategies, adjusting organizational structures, and aligning the strategic direction towards innovation.

Ensuring adequate training programs and maintaining clear communication about the benefits and changes introduced by blockchain can play a critical role in mitigating such resistance.

By addressing these challenges through a combination of strategic planning, collaboration with technology experts, and regulatory bodies, financial institutions can harness the full potential of blockchain technology. This process entails not only overcoming technical and regulatory hurdles but also reshaping organizational culture and expectations to pave the way for innovative future banking solutions.

8.10 Case Studies: Successful Blockchain Adoption in Finance

The finance sector has witnessed several prominent applications of blockchain technology, showcasing substantial benefits across various operations. This section delves into detailed case studies of successful blockchain implementations in financial services, focusing on different aspects such as payments, securities, compliance, and more.

JPMorgan Chase: JPM Coin and the Interbank Information Network

JPMorgan Chase, one of the world's leading financial services firms, launched the JPM Coin and the Interbank Information Network (IIN). The JPM Coin is a digital coin designed to make instant payments using blockchain technology.

```
1  // Example of transaction using JPM Coin
2  BlockchainTransaction transaction = new BlockchainTransaction();
3  transaction.setAmount(100);
4  transaction.setCurrency("JPM Coin");
5  transaction.setToAccountId("12345");
6  transaction.setFromAccountId("67890");
7  transaction.execute();
```

The implementation allowed JPMorgan to enhance the speed at which payments were processed between institutional accounts. Moreover, the IIN helped in resolving discrepancies in cross-border payments at a much faster rate than traditional banking networks.

```
Transaction successful: 100 JPM Coins transferred from 67890 to 12345
```

The network grew to over 400 participant banks, illustrating significant efficiency gains and cost reductions in interbank transactions.

Santander: Blockchain-based Bond Issuance

Santander became the first bank to issue an end-to-end blockchain bond. The bank used Ethereum blockchain to issue $20 million in bonds, with the entire issuance process occurring on the blockchain, including cash management, maturity, and coupon payments.

```
// Bond issuance on Ethereum
function issueBond(address investor, uint amount) public {
    Bond bond = new Bond(amount);
    bond.issueTo(investor);
    emit BondIssued(investor, amount);
}
```

This blockchain approach not only simplified the process by reducing the number of intermediaries involved but also ensured transparency and security in the issuance process.

```
BondIssued: Investor 0x123abc, Amount $20,000,000
```

HSBC: HSBC FX Everywhere

HSBC developed "HSBC FX Everywhere," a blockchain-based system used to handle foreign exchange transactions. The system has processed more than $250 billion worth of transactions, leveraging blockchain to make internal cash flows more efficient.

```
// Simplified pseudocode of HSBC FX transaction on blockchain
transaction = createTransaction(fromAccount, toAccount, amount, currency);
blockchain.post(transaction);
```

This technology allowed the bank to ensure better regulatory compliance, reduce operational risks, and improve the speed of foreign exchange transactions.

```
FX transaction completed: $1,000,000 from USD to EUR
```

Through these case studies, it is evident that blockchain technology offers significant advances in operational efficiency and security for financial transactions. Each of these institutions has not only innovated their own processes but also laid down a blueprint for further adoption in the industry, propagating a move towards more transparent, secure, and efficient banking systems. The implications for future applications in banking continue to be promising as these technologies mature and more institutions join the blockchain movement.

8.11 The Future of Blockchain in the Financial Industry

The trajectory of blockchain technology in the financial sector is marked by evolving regulatory frameworks, advances in technology, and shifts in business strategies. As we look forward into the future, several key developments can be anticipated that will further define this path.

The first significant development will be the broader integration of blockchain technology into mainstream financial services. Traditionally, the use of blockchain was primarily experimental, relegated to specific use cases such as cryptocurrency transactions and smart contracts. However, moving forward, we will see a more comprehensive adoption as financial institutions start leveraging blockchain for a wider array of products and services. This includes utilizing blockchain for enhanced credit scoring systems by pulling decentralized data, thereby offering a more holistic view of a borrower's creditworthiness.

```
chaincode_registerCreditScoring -> {
    invoke_decentralizedCreditDatabase();
    update_scoringModel();
    return_newCreditScore();
}
```

The potential for blockchain to facilitate real-time transaction settlements will drive another major evolutionary step. Real-time gross settlement systems, which currently face delays due to inter-bank processing and time-zone differences, will greatly benefit. Blockchain could offer a unified, instantaneous transaction layer for banks globally.

```
Transaction settled in 0.215 seconds using Blockchain-based RTGS.
```

Growth in quantum computing and advancements in cryptographic techniques will also precipitate significant changes. These technological advancements will necessitate the development of quantum-resistant blockchains. Financial institutions will likely invest in upgrad-

8.11. THE FUTURE OF BLOCKCHAIN IN THE FINANCIAL INDUSTRY

ing their blockchain infrastructures to protect against quantum computing threats which can compromise traditional cryptographic systems.

- Enhance cryptographic algorithms.

- Implement quantum-resistant ledger technology.

- Regularly update security protocols in response to advancements in quantum computing.

Regulatory compliance and transparency are areas ripe for blockchain's impact. Global regulatory bodies are currently formulating frameworks to accommodate and govern blockchain applications in banking. Future collaborations between regulatory entities and financial institutions will likely produce standardized procedures and guidelines for blockchain integration, focusing on compliance, auditability, and consumer protection.

Algorithm 11: Blockchain-based Regulatory Compliance Algorithm

Data: Blockchain transactions
Result: Compliance report
1 initialization;
2 **while** *Transaction* **do**
3   check_regulatory_requirements();
4   validate_transaction();
5   log_transaction_for_audit();
6   generate_compliance_report();
7 **end**

Advancements in blockchain interoperability will facilitate smoother cross-chain transactions and interactions between different blockchain protocols. This will enable a more cohesive network of financial services that can seamlessly operate across various blockchain platforms, thereby enhancing the user experience and expanding the service capabilities of financial institutions.

```
crossChain_transfer -> {
    connect_toTargetBlockchain(protocolIdentifier);
    validate_interchainTransaction();
    execute_transfer();
}
```

Finally, customer adoption will play a crucial role in shaping the use of blockchain in financial services. As more clients become accustomed to and trust blockchain-powered solutions, financial institutions will likely see a significant shift in the deployment strategy, focusing primarily on user-centric services.

The future of blockchain in the financial industry remains promising. With continued technological advancements, increased regulatory clarity, and widespread adoption, blockchain is poised to redefine how financial operations are conducted, ultimately leading to a more efficient, transparent, and secure financial ecosystem.

Chapter 9

Blockchain in Healthcare

This chapter explores the transformative potential of blockchain technology in the healthcare industry, focusing on enhancing data security, patient privacy, and interoperability of health records. It discusses how blockchain can streamline processes, from managing patient records and controlling pharmaceutical supply chains to ensuring the integrity of clinical trials. The benefits are balanced with a look at the challenges of implementing blockchain solutions in healthcare, such as compliance with stringent regulatory environments and the need for significant infrastructure changes.

9.1 Overview of Blockchain Application in Healthcare

Blockchain technology has emerged as a revolutionary force across various industries, and healthcare is no exception. Its inherent characteristics such as decentralization, immutability, and transparency offer substantial benefits to the healthcare sector, especially in addressing longstanding issues like data security, privacy, and interoperability.

The decentralization aspect of blockchain inherently prevents any single entity from taking complete control of the data, thus democratizing the data management and ensuring a more collaborative environment. This is particularly important in healthcare, where patient data comes from various sources including hospitals, clinics, and laboratories. By using blockchain, these entities can contribute to a comprehensive health record that is not owned by a single party but shared across a network with clear audit trails.

- Ensuring the immutability of records is another foundational benefit provided by blockchain. Once a transaction (e.g., a health record entry) is recorded on a blockchain, it becomes nearly impossible to alter. This is critical in a field where the integrity of medical data can directly impact patient care and outcomes.

- Transparency, facilitated by blockchain, allows for a transparent audit of data transactions. This feature is instrumental in building trust among all stakeholders, including patients, healthcare providers, and regulatory bodies. Transparency is also crucial for compliance with healthcare regulations and for facilitating healthcare audits.

Blockchain application in healthcare is not limited to the management of patient records but extends to other domains such as pharmaceutical supply chain, clinical trials, and health insurance. The pharmaceutical supply chain, for example, benefits from blockchain through enhanced traceability of drugs from manufacturer to end-user, combating issues like counterfeiting and unauthorized distribution.

```
Example: A typical transaction on a healthcare blockchain may look like this:
{
    "TransactionId": "1234",
    "PatientId": "ABCD1234XYZ",
    "Operation": "Add",
    "Data": {
      "Date": "2023-01-25",
      "HealthInfo": {
         "Diagnosis": "Type 2 Diabetes",
         "Treatment": "Metformin 500mg",
         "PrescribingDoctor": "Dr. Jane Doe"
      }
    },
    "Timestamp": "2023-01-25T14:30:00Z",
    "AuthorizedBy": "Hospital A"
}
```

Such detailed and unalterable records enhance the credibility and utility of medical information across the continuum of care and beyond.

Investigating the technical side, blockchain empowers smart contracts, which can automatically enforce contracts and policies. For instance, these smart contracts can automate the claiming processes in insurance agreements ensuring that claims are transparent and settled in accordance with predefined rules, reducing fraud, and increasing efficiency.

```
1  Smart contract example for automated health insurance claims:
2  function claimInsurance(patientId, treatmentId, claimAmount) {
3    if (verifyTreatment(patientId, treatmentId) && verifyCoverage(patientId,
          claimAmount)) {
4      processClaim(patientId, claimAmount);
5      return true;
6    }
7    return false;
8  }
```

Each step forward in adopting blockchain reflects a move towards a more integrated, transparent, and secure healthcare system that significantly reduces administrative burdens and costs, while enhancing patient care and data fidelity. This establishes a foundation not only for better healthcare delivery but also for innovations that can spring from reliably interconnected data.

9.2 Challenges in Healthcare Data Management

Healthcare data management faces multifaceted challenges, primarily revolving around the volumes of data generated, the sensitivity of the data, and the stringent regulatory frameworks governing its use and dissemination. Each aspect presents unique issues that can impede the effective delivery of healthcare services unless adequately addressed.

Volume and Variety of Data

The healthcare industry generates vast amounts of data daily from various sources, including electronic health records (EHRs), medical imaging, genomic data, and information from wearable health devices. Managing these data types entails not only significant storage capacities but also sophisticated systems to ensure their availability, integrity, and confidentiality.

The variety of data, ranging from structured formats in databases to unstructured notes in medical transcripts, necessitates robust data management systems capable of handling this diversity efficiently. These systems must also support rapid retrieval and processing to meet clinical needs in real-time.

Data Privacy and Security Concerns

Given the highly personal nature of medical data, ensuring its privacy and security is paramount. Healthcare organizations are frequently targeted by cyberattacks, which can lead to breaches with severe consequences for patient privacy and institutional integrity.

The Healthcare Insurance Portability and Accountability Act (HIPAA) in the United States and the General Data Protection Regulation (GDPR) in the European Union set out stringent compliance requirements for the handling of personal health information. These regulations require that healthcare providers and their associated entities adopt comprehensive security measures to protect patient data against unauthorized access and breaches.

Implementing suitable encryption practices and ensuring that only authorized personnel have access to sensitive data are among the tactics used to uphold data security. This, however, increases the complexity of data management systems, potentially reducing operational efficiency unless carefully managed.

Interoperability Issues

Interoperability across different healthcare systems and platforms is essential to ensure seamless patient care and efficient data use across multiple healthcare providers. However, disparate systems often do not share a common standard, leading to compatibility issues and data silos. These silos prevent the effective sharing of information, thus slowing diagnosis and treatment processes and increasing healthcare costs due to redundant tests and procedures.

Efforts are being made to adopt universal data standards such as Health Level 7 (HL7) and Fast Healthcare Interoperability Resources (FHIR), but integration is slow, and many legacy systems still require considerable customization or upgrades to comply with these standards.

Data Accuracy and Quality

Data accuracy is a significant challenge in healthcare data management. Inaccurate data can result from human error during data entry, errors in data transmission, or mismatches in data capture formats. High-quality data is critical for effective decision-making in healthcare, particularly in areas such as personalized medicine and predictive analytics.

Ongoing efforts to improve data quality involve implementing more robust data validation checks, improving user interfaces to reduce human error, and increasing the use of automated systems for data capture and entry. However, these measures can be resource-intensive and require ongoing maintenance and oversight.

The challenges in healthcare data management are considerable, yet addressing them is essential for improving the efficiency, security, and quality of healthcare services. Blockchain technology offers potential solutions to many of these issues, particularly through its capabilities for secure, transparent, and immutable data transactions that can enhance data security, improve interoperability, and ensure high data quality and integrity. As healthcare systems continue to evolve, leveraging advanced technologies such as blockchain will be crucial in overcoming these data management challenges and achieving a more integrated, reliable, and patient-centered healthcare system.

9.3 Blockchain for Medical Records and Patient Data Security

The criticality of maintaining the confidentiality and security of medical records cannot be overstated. Medical data is sensitive by nature, containing detailed personal health information that must be protected under laws such as HIPAA (Health Insurance Portability and Accountability Act) in the United States and GDPR (General Data Protection Regulation) in the European Union. Traditional electronic health record (EHR) systems, while beneficial in digitizing and centralizing patient records, present substantial challenges in terms of data security, privacy protection, and vulnerability to cyberattacks.

Blockchain technology offers a promising solution to these challenges by leveraging its inherent characteristics: decentralization, immutability, and encryption. Decentralization reduces the reliance on a single point of failure, which can mitigate the risks of data breaches. Immutability ensures that once a record is entered into the blockchain, it cannot be altered or deleted, safeguarding the integrity of the medical data. Moreover, the use of cryptographic techniques secures the data against unauthorized access and tampering.

Implementing blockchain in the healthcare sector specifically for managing medical records involves several key technical considerations. Each block in the blockchain can serve as a secure container for transactions, which, in this context, could be individual entries of patient data or medical actions. When a medical record is created or updated, the transaction is encrypted and a unique hash is generated. This hash, as well as the hash of the previous block, is included in the new block, which is then appended to the chain after the required consensus is achieved.

```
1  function addMedicalRecord(string memory _patientId, string memory _record) public {
2      uint _recordId = records.length + 1;
3      records.push(Record(_recordId, _patientId, _record, now));
4      emit RecordAdded(_recordId, _patientId, now);
5  }
```

In the above sample smart contract written in Solidity, every time a new medical record is added, the 'addMedicalRecord' function takes as inputs the patient ID and the record details. It generates a unique record ID based on the length of the existing records array and pushes a new record into the blockchain. It also emits an event 'RecordAdded', which can be used to alert systems or interfaces that a new record has been created.

To ensure data accuracy and restrict unauthorised access, blockchain-based systems can implement role-based access controls. This means that the access to medical records is controlled based on the role of the user (e.g., doctor, nurse, administrative staff, or patient). Only authorized personnel are able to access and perform functions on the blockchain network, thus maintaining compliance with privacy regulations and ensuring patient data security.

```
Access Log:
    Time: 1625541122
    AccessorID: DOC12345
    PatientID: PAT67890
    AccessGranted: Yes
```

The above log indicates an instance of access where a doctor (DOC12345) is granted access to the records of patient PAT67890. The timestamp provides a non-repudiable proof of access, which can be crucial for audits and compliance checks.

Supplementary to access control, blockchain networks in healthcare can benefit from the integration of other technology solutions like AI (artificial intelligence) for dynamic access control, data analytics, and anomaly detection to further enhance security measures.

Despite the promising aspects of blockchain in enhancing the security and privacy of medical records, several challenges persist, including scalability concerns given the large volume of data generated and stored, and the variable speed of transactions, which can impact the performance of the system. However, as blockchain technology matures and solutions to these challenges are developed, its potential to revolutionize the healthcare data security landscape becomes increasingly feasible.

Thus, the intersection of blockchain with healthcare data management not only provides robust mechanisms to secure data but also fosters a new paradigm in the digital healthcare infrastructure where patient privacy is paramount and data integrity is uncompromised. With the ongoing advancements in blockchain technology and increasing recognition of its benefits in the healthcare sector, a progressive shift toward its broader adoption is anticipated.

9.4 Ensuring Data Interoperability with Blockchain

Data interoperability within the healthcare sector encompasses the ability to share and utilize health-related information across various systems, platforms, and organizations effectively and accurately. Healthcare data comes in diverse formats and structures, encompassing electronic health records (EHRs), diagnostic data, treatment details, and more, originating from disparate sources. The challenge of interoperability in healthcare is not just in linking these different data types, but also in ensuring the aggregated information is secure, consistent, and privacy-preserving. This is where blockchain technology comes into play.

Blockchain offers a decentralized ledger that is immutable and transparent, providing a verifiable and traceable means of recording and sharing data. For interoperability, it can serve as a unified platform that enables secure, real-time data exchange while maintaining compliance with health data regulations including HIPAA in the United States and GDPR in Europe.

- **Standardization of Data**: For blockchain to facilitate interoperability, data must adhere to standardized formats that ensure consistency across different systems. Blockchain networks can enforce these standards by only accepting data that conforms to specific schemas and rules.

- **Patient Identity Verification**: Blockchain can enhance the accuracy of patient identification across different systems. A blockchain-driven universal patient identifier could be created, underpinned by key data elements that authenticate the identity of a patient consistently across all healthcare touchpoints.

- **Data Access and Permissions**: Access control is critical in a healthcare system where multiple entities, such as doctors, laboratories, and insurance companies, need differentiated access to patient data. Smart contracts on blockchain can automatically enforce policies around who can view or modify the data, under what circumstances, and track these interactions.

Implementing blockchain facilitates the creation of a single, immutable history of health data transactions, accessible by authorized entities without the risk of data tampering or inconsistency. To demonstrate how blockchain could be implemented in a real-world healthcare data exchange scenario, consider the following example:

```
# Example: A Blockchain-Based Healthcare Data Exchange System
# This basic example demonstrates how patient data can be added to a blockchain.

class Block:
    def __init__(self, previous_hash, patient_id, data):
        self.previous_hash = previous_hash
        self.patient_id = patient_id
        self.data = data
        self.block_hash = self.hash_block()

    def hash_block(self):
        # Simple hash function for demonstration
        import hashlib
        hash = hashlib.sha256()
        hash.update(str(self.previous_hash).encode('utf-8'))
        hash.update(str(self.patient_id).encode('utf-8'))
        hash.update(str(self.data).encode('utf-8'))
        return hash.hexdigest()

# Creating blocks and adding them to the blockchain
genesis_block = Block("initial", "0001", {"diagnosis": "flu"})
second_block = Block(genesis_block.block_hash, "0002", {"diagnosis": "allergy"})

print("Genesis Block Hash:", genesis_block.block_hash)
print("Second Block Hash:", second_block.block_hash)
```

Genesis Block Hash: c1a5d305449df110e68d301d43f62a9f85b85a21adcc77b8bd300c75547b9555
Second Block Hash: afbe72fcee83f0de30948cf1bb1154c07a2e8cb77c01459437b12df0a2d954f2

In this code snippet, the Block class is used to model blocks in the blockchain. Each block contains a previous hash, a patient identifier, and the patient data in a protected format. The hash of each block is a cryptographic combination of its contents, ensuring data integrity and lineage.

By maintaining each patient's health record as a series of linked blocks, we not only provide a complete audit trail but also secure the data against unauthorized tampering. The hashes serve as proofs of integrity, while blockchain's decentralized nature eliminates single points of failure.

To advance blockchain's role in healthcare data interoperability, further developments are necessary in standardizing data formats and enhancing blockchain protocols to accommodate high transaction volumes and ensure data privacy. Integrating advanced encryption methods for data security, along with consensus mechanisms that comply with healthcare regulatory requirements, will be essential. This integration enables healthcare systems not just to overcome interoperability challenges but also to innovate in patient care and operational efficiencies.

9.5 Blockchain for Drug Traceability in the Pharmaceutical Industry

The pharmaceutical industry faces critical challenges in securing drug supply chains, stemming largely from counterfeiting, theft, tampering, and stringent regulatory compliance. Blockchain technology offers a robust solution by facilitating a transparent, immutable, and auditable record-keeping system that can significantly enhance traceability and security in the drug supply chain.

In understanding the application of blockchain for drug traceability, it's essential to delineate the typical journey of pharmaceuticals from production to consumption. Pharmaceutical products pass through multiple checkpoints—including manufacturers, distributors, retailers, and healthcare providers—before reaching the consumer. Each stage in this supply chain can benefit from the deployment of blockchain technology to secure and streamline processes.

Provenance and Authentication

At the initiation of the supply chain, blockchain provides a mechanism for recording the origin of each drug batch. By storing manufacturing data, including time, location, and raw materials used, on a blockchain, pharmaceutical companies create an indelible record that can be referenced to verify the authenticity of products at any checkpoint throughout the supply chain. This immutable ledger is not only critical for proving provenance but also essential in cases of recall or for identifying the source of counterfeit drugs.

For instance, each package or batch can be assigned a unique digital identifier that is recorded on the blockchain. This identifier can then be scanned and verified against the blockchain data at each point in the supply chain, thereby ensuring that the product reaching the consumer is genuine and unaltered.

Regulatory Compliance and Transparency

Regulatory bodies in the pharmaceutical sector mandate strict regulations to ensure the safety and efficacy of drugs distributed in the market. Blockchain technology facilitates compliance with these regulatory requirements by providing a transparent system where entries cannot be changed once recorded. Regulatory agencies can be granted access to the blockchain, allowing for real-time auditing without the need to be physically present at the manufacturing or distribution sites.

Streamlining Recalls

Drug recalls are complex and typically urgent. Blockchain technology can expedite the recall process by enabling precise tracking of drug batches across the supply chain. In the event of a recall, companies can quickly identify and isolate affected batches, effectively reducing the risk to public health and the associated costs.

Combating Counterfeiting

Counterfeit drugs constitute a significant and dangerous issue within the pharmaceutical industry. The World Health Organization estimates that counterfeit medicine accounts for approximately 10% of the global trade in pharmaceuticals. Blockchain's transparent and immutable record-keeping helps combat this menace by making it nearly impossible for counterfeit drugs to infiltrate the supply chain unnoticed.

To illustrate, suppose a counterfeit batch tries to enter the legitimate supply chain. The absence of a verifiable digital identifier on the blockchain immediately exposes the batch as counterfeit. Thus, blockchain acts as a deterrent to counterfeiting, significantly enhancing the safety and integrity of pharmaceutical products.

Integration with Existing IT Infrastructure

One of the preliminary challenges to blockchain adoption in pharmaceutical traceability is the integration with existing IT systems. Effective implementation requires interfaces that allow seamless communication between the blockchain and the legacy systems used by different stakeholders in the supply chain. Such integration is vital to ensure that the benefits of blockchain can be realized without disrupting existing workflows significantly.

To summarize, the deployment of blockchain technology in the pharmaceutical industry not only enhances drug traceability, risk management, and control but also provides a foundation for building trust with consumers by ensuring the authenticity, safety, and efficacy of pharmaceutical products. Moreover, blockchain empowers regulatory bodies to enforce compliance more robustly and provides the tools necessary to respond swiftly in crisis situations such as drug recalls. The extended visibility and control that blockchain introduces into the pharmaceutical supply chain ultimately lead to a safer public health environment and more efficient regulatory compliance. This transformation, driven by blockchain technology, heralds a new era in the pharmaceutical industry, characterized by increased efficiency, security, and confidence in pharmaceutical products.

9.6 Use of Smart Contracts in Healthcare Services

Smart contracts, self-executing contractual states stored on the blockchain, present numerous possibilities for automating and enhancing various aspects of healthcare services. These contracts are programmed to automatically execute, control, or document legally relevant events and actions according to the terms of a contract or an agreement.

Automating Administrative Processes

One of the significant benefits of using smart contracts in healthcare is the automation of administrative processes. Traditionally, these processes have been plagued by inefficiencies due to manual paperwork, complex approval sequences, and the involvement of multiple stakeholders, leading to delays and increased costs. Smart contracts can streamline these processes by enforcing rules and requirements digitally.

For example, claims processing in health insurance can be automated through smart contracts. Upon the occurrence of a claim event, the smart contract can verify the validity of the claim against the policy rules, automate approvals, and trigger the payment process, all without manual intervention. This not only speeds up the process but also reduces errors and the potential for fraudulent claims.

```
contract HealthInsurance {
    mapping(address => uint) public balances;

    function claimInsurance(address _policyHolder, uint _amount) public {
        require(balances[_policyHolder] >= _amount);
        balances[_policyHolder] -= _amount;
        payable(_policyHolder).transfer(_amount);
    }
}
```

Improving Compliance and Data Integrity

Ensuring compliance with regulatory norms and maintaining data integrity is paramount in the healthcare sector. Smart contracts can be beneficial in this respect by recording and securing data exchanges and processing steps on an immutable ledger.

For instance, the consent management process for sharing patient data across different healthcare providers, a crucial aspect dictated by laws such as the Health Insurance Portability and Accountability Act (HIPAA) in the United States, can be managed via smart contracts. These contracts ensure that patient data is shared only after explicit consent has been recorded on the blockchain, providing a tamper-proof audit trail.

```
contract PatientConsent {
    struct Consent {
        bool approved;
        uint timestamp;
    }
```

```
7     mapping(address => mapping(address => Consent)) public consents; // patient to
          provider mapping
8
9     function giveConsent(address _provider) public {
10        consents[msg.sender][_provider] = Consent(true, block.timestamp);
11    }
12
13    function checkConsent(address _patient, address _provider) public view returns
          (bool) {
14        return consents[_patient][_provider].approved;
15    }
16 }
```

Enhanced Patient Management

Smart contracts facilitate better coordination and management of patient pathways, especially for chronic diseases requiring regular monitoring and complex treatment regimens. They can automate the scheduling of treatments, drugs dispense, and even follow-ups based on predefined criteria.

For example, a smart contract could be programmed to release medication doses from a smart dispenser only when certain conditions are met, such as adherence to a treatment plan confirmed through a patient's check-ins or sensor data indicating the need for medication.

```
1  contract MedicationManagement {
2     function dispenseMedication(address _patient, string memory _medication, uint
          _dose) public {
3         // Logic to validate patient adherence and condition
4         emit MedicationDispensed(_patient, _medication, _dose);
5     }
6  }
```

The use of smart contracts also extends to remote patient monitoring, enhancing the capacity for healthcare systems to provide continuous care without necessitating physical presence. This is particularly relevant in rural or underserved regions where access to healthcare providers is limited. Through data collected from wearable or implantable devices, smart contracts can automatically process and respond to patient data, facilitating timely medical interventions if abnormalities are detected.

```
Event Response:
    PatientID: 12345
    Alert Type: Heart Rate Elevation
    Timestamp: 2023-09-15T12:07:22Z
    Recommended Action: Immediate clinical review
```

The integration of smart contracts in healthcare services undeniably enhances not only the efficiency and transparency of administrative processes but also significantly elevates the level of patient care. Moreover, the inherent characteristics of blockchain technology, such as decentralization, immutability, and security, align well with the stringent requirements of health data management, making smart contracts an invaluable tool in the modernization of healthcare systems.

9.7 Blockchain for Clinical Trials and Research Data

Blockchain technology offers unprecedented opportunities to enhance the reliability, transparency, and traceability of clinical trials and research data in healthcare. The decentralized nature of blockchain allows for the immutable recording of clinical trial protocols, ensuring that any changes to the methodology are transparently recorded and timestamped. This is crucial in maintaining data integrity and proving adherence to original study designs, which regulatory bodies rigorously scrutinize.

Immutable Data Recording

The use of blockchain in clinical trials begins with the creation of a predefined protocol, which is stored on the blockchain. Each subsequent step of the trial — from patient enrollment through to the final analysis — is also recorded on the blockchain, creating an indelible audit trail. This process inherently guards against data tampering and ensures a high level of data fidelity.

```
// Example: Smart contract code to register new clinical trial
contract ClinicalTrialRegistry {
    struct Trial {
        string trialID;
        string protocolSummary;
        uint startDate;
        address registrant;
    }

    mapping(string => Trial) public trials;

    function registerTrial(string memory _trialID, string memory _protocolSummary) public {
        trials[_trialID] = Trial(_trialID, _protocolSummary, block.timestamp, msg.sender);
    }
}
```

As depicted above, a smart contract can effectively function to register each clinical trial protocol. The registerTrial function records key details about each trial, including an identifier, summary of the protocol, the registration timestamp, and the registrant's address.

Enhanced Patient Confidentiality and Consent Management

Blockchain also significantly enhances patient confidentiality and consent management, critical aspects of modern clinical trials. By employing cryptographic techniques such as hashing and private keys, patient identities can be anonymized while allowing selective permissions to access detailed data as required.

For instance, a blockchain-based system can be designed to require patient consent recorded directly on the blockchain before their data is used or shared. This consent can be managed and updated by the patient, providing a dynamic and patient-centered approach to consent that traditional systems struggle to offer.

```
Transaction Record:
    Patient ID: HASHED_VALUE
    Consent Status: True
    Timestamp: 1678905600
```

The above output example represents how patient consent can be recorded. By using a hashed value for the patient ID, personal identifying information remains confidential, and the consent status clearly reflects the patient's current permission state.

Data Interoperability and Integration

Integrating blockchain into clinical trials facilitates greater data interoperability between disparate systems and stakeholders. Since the blockchain ledger provides a single source of truth, all parties — regulatory bodies, research organizations, healthcare providers, and even patients — can access the same consistent information, which enhances collaboration and accelerates the pace of research.

```
// Example: Querying blockchain for trial data
function getTrialData(string memory _trialID) public view returns (string memory
    protocolSummary, uint startDate, address registrant) {
    Trial memory trial = trials[_trialID];
    return (trial.protocolSummary, trial.startDate, trial.registrant);
}
```

By implementing functions like `getTrialData`, stakeholders can easily access trial data. This function facilitates the recovery of comprehensive trial information by providing the trial identifier, crucial for ensuring transparency and verifiability in clinical research.

Challenges to Overcome

While blockchain proposes substantial improvements for clinical trials, several challenges need addressing. The key issues include the scalability of blockchain solutions, which must handle large volumes of data generated in trials, and the integration of this technology with existing clinical data management systems, which are often outdated and not designed for blockchain compatibility.

Furthermore, regulatory acceptance of blockchain-enabled methodologies is still in the early stages. As such, continuous collaboration with regulatory authorities is essential to ensure that blockchain solutions comply with the stringent standards of clinical research and patient safety.

As blockchain technology advances and its application in clinical trials becomes more refined, its full potential to revolutionize this aspect of healthcare will be realized, paving the way for more efficient, transparent, and secure clinical research.

9.8 Improving Health Insurance Claims Processing through Blockchain

Health insurance claims processing is a critical component of the healthcare industry, often characterized by complexities involving claim creation, processing, adjustments, and payments. Blockchain technology offers a robust solution to streamline these processes by providing decentralized, transparent, and immutable record-keeping.

A primary way blockchain improves claims processing is through the enhancement of data integrity and fraud prevention. Each transaction on the blockchain is time-stamped and added to the ledger after consensus among participants, thereby reducing the risk of duplicate claims or false information. A practical implementation involves each claim being recorded as a block. The structure of these blocks includes essential attributes such as claimant information, treatment details, billing

9.8. IMPROVING HEALTH INSURANCE CLAIMS PROCESSING THROUGH BLOCKCHAIN

amount, and timestamps.

```
class HealthInsuranceClaim{
   private String claimantID;
   private String treatmentDetails;
   private double billingAmount;
   private long timestamp;

   // Constructor and access methods
}
```

Another key aspect is the use of smart contracts in blockchain. Smart contracts are self-executing contracts where the terms between buyer and seller are directly written into lines of code. These can be used to automate claim adjudications based on predefined criteria, reducing the need for manual intervention and thereby accelerating processing times. For instance, a smart contract could automatically verify claim legitimacy and release payments if the claim satisfies certain contractual conditions.

```
contract HealthInsurance{
   function processClaim(uint claimID) public {
      HealthInsuranceClaim claim = claims[claimID];
      if(verifyClaim(claim)){
         settlePayment(claim);
      }
   }
   // Additional methods for verification and payment
}
```

Furthermore, blockchain technology fosters transparency and accessibility, allowing all relevant parties to access claim data through a permissioned blockchain framework. This not only includes the insurers and healthcare providers but also the patients, who gain visibility into the claim's status and can ensure their claim is handled fairly. Implementation of permissioned blockchain ensures that each participant has the necessary rights to access only the data they are privy to, therefore maintaining confidentiality and compliance with regulatory requirements such as the Health Insurance Portability and Accountability Act (HIPAA).

The operational efficiency brought by blockchain to health insurance claims processing also significantly reduces transaction costs. Traditional processes involve numerous intermediaries, each adding layers of communication and complicating fee structures. Blockchain's peer-to-peer nature eliminates many of these intermediaries, simplifying the process and cutting costs.

```
{
    "ClaimID": "12345",
    "Status": "Payment Settled",
    "Timestamp": "1609459200"
}
```

Despite these advancements, the integration of blockchain technology in health insurance claims must address specific challenges such as scalability and transaction speed, particularly when handling a vast number of claims. The architecture must support a high throughput of transactions to be viable on a large scale.

Implementing blockchain in health insurance claims processing requires thoughtful consideration of the existing infrastructure and the potential need for significant alterations. Nevertheless, the benefits of improved efficiency, reduced fraud, and enhanced user satisfaction present a compelling case for its adoption. As the industry continues to evaluate and pilot blockchain solutions, we may see a broad transformation in how health insurance claims are processed, potentially setting a new standard in the industry.

9.9 Regulatory and Compliance Concerns in Healthcare Blockchain

The integration of blockchain technology within healthcare settings implicates various regulatory and compliance issues that must be carefully navigated. As a decentralized and immutable ledger, blockchain offers significant benefits in terms of record-keeping and data integrity. However, these features also introduce complexities in compliance with established healthcare regulations, such as the Health Insurance Portability and Accountability Act (HIPAA) in the United States, the General Data Protection Regulation (GDPR) in the European Union, and other national and international frameworks.

HIPAA Compliance and Blockchain: HIPAA, a critical regulatory framework in the U.S., mandates the protection and confidential handling of protected health information (PHI). Key to HIPAA compliance is ensuring that PHI access is restricted to authorized individuals and that the integrity and confidentiality of patient data are maintained. Blockchain's features, such as decentralization, immutability, and encryption, can enhance data security. However, the immutable nature of blockchain can conflict with HIPAA's requirements for amendable and forgettable PHI, wherein patients can request changes or deletions to their health records.

- **Use of Permissioned Blockchains:** To address such issues, healthcare applications on the blockchain might consider using permissioned ledgers, where access controls are strictly enforced, and participants are pre-selected and vetted, thus upholding HIPAA's access control requirements.

- **Encryption and Pseudonymization Techniques:** Techniques such as advanced encryption and pseudonymization can be employed to protect data while ensuring that it remains amendable and forgettable, thus aiding in HIPAA compliance.

Adhering to GDPR Regulations: The GDPR imposes stringent regulations on data privacy and users' rights over their personal data, emphasizing consent, right to access, and the right to be forgotten. The transparent and immutable nature of blockchain can be at odds with such requirements, particularly the right to erasure.

- **Implementation of Off-Chain Solutions:** One way of reconciling blockchain with GDPR is to store personal data off-chain while using the blockchain for logging consent and anonymized data transactions.

Intersecting Blockchain with Other Regulatory Standards: Beyond HIPAA and GDPR, healthcare applications using blockchain technology must also consider other pertinent legal frameworks, such as the Federal Drug Administration (FDA) regulations for drug traceability, electronic health record standards, and international norms like the Data Protection Directive in other jurisdictions.

Blockchain's ability to maintain a cryptographically secure, tamper-proof ledger is appealing for compliance with these regulations as long as the implementation is carefully designed to accommodate legal requirements. For instance, incorporating mechanisms to enable selective transparency and data modification could help meet complex regulatory landscapes.

Legal and Regulatory Challenges Ahead: Healthcare organizations adopting blockchain must also prepare to address legal ambiguities and the pace of regulatory changes. Blockchain is a rapidly evolving technology, and regulations concerning its use are still in development. This dynamic creates a challenging environment for healthcare providers, technology developers, and regulators, all of whom need to maintain ongoing dialogue to ensure that advancements in blockchain technology align with legal and regulatory requirements.

Healthcare organizations using blockchain must ensure they have robust legal counsel equipped to navigate these challenges. They need to engage in continuous education about changing regulations and actively participate in shaping these laws, ensuring practical and compliant applications of blockchain technology in healthcare contexts. This proactive approach not only minimizes the risk of non-compliance but also leverages blockchain technology to enhance the trust and efficiency of healthcare services.

9.10 Case Studies: Blockchain Impact on Healthcare Organizations

In this section, we examine several case studies where blockchain technology has been applied in healthcare organizations to address specific challenges, demonstrating practical applications and tangible benefits. These real-world examples underscore the diverse capabilities of blockchain in enhancing data security, ensuring privacy, improving operational efficiencies, and maintaining compliance in complex regulatory landscapes.

Case Study 1: Patient Data Management in Estonia

Estonia integrated blockchain technology into e-Health Record (EHR) systems to secure patient data and control access. The healthcare system in Estonia utilizes KSI Blockchain to provide integrity for healthcare data and logs all access to the system. This integration supports transparency and auditability, essential aspects in a healthcare environment where data sensitivity is paramount.

- **Implementation Process**: Integration involved setting up a blockchain layer on top of existing EHR systems to ensure that each entry is time-stamped and linked to previous records. This addition prevents unauthorized alteration of the records – an example of effective data immutability implementation.

- **Outcome**: The blockchain system improved security and restored patient trust in the digital handling of medical records. It also streamlined compliance with the European Union's General Data Protection Regulation (GDPR).

Case Study 2: Improving Supply Chain Integrity in the Pharmaceutical Industry

A notable application of blockchain technology is seen in improving the pharmaceutical supply chain. A consortium led by major pharmaceutical companies deployed a blockchain-based system to track and verify the legitimacy of drugs, from manufacture to final delivery.

```
Blockchain Ledger Entry:
{
    "drug_id": "XKL23",
    "timestamp": "2022-03-15T03:24:00Z",
    "status": "shipped",
    "origin": "Manufacturing Site A",
    "destination": "Pharmacy B"
}
```

- **Implementation Process**: The process involved stakeholders from different stages of the supply chain joining the blockchain network. Each stakeholder acts as a node, and they validate transactions based on consensus, ensuring authenticity and transparency throughout the supply chain.

- **Outcome**: Reduction in counterfeit drugs entering the supply chain, enhanced ability to recall defective batches swiftly, and an overall increase in consumer trust and safety.

Case Study 3: Facilitating Clinical Trials and Research

A multi-institutional research initiative targeted at enhancing the management and verification of data in clinical trials adopted blockchain technology. The collaborative nature of clinical research, coupled with the need for tamperproof data, made blockchain an appropriate solution.

```
Blockchain Data Verification Log:
[2023-01-30 09:00:10] Data entry verified.
[2023-01-30 09:01:15] Data entry verified.
[2023-01-30 09:20:25] Data modification attempted, rejected.
```

- **Implementation Process**: The blockchain integration involved creating a decentralized ledger that could record data entries from diverse sources, each timestamped and verified independently.

- **Outcome**: This deployment resulted in an immutable record of trial data, facilitating data monitoring for integrity, reducing the time needed for data verification, and supporting swift compilation and reporting.

Each of these case studies highlights how blockchain technology can be adapted to various aspects of healthcare, benefiting from improved security, operational efficiency, and compliance with regulatory requirements. The diversity in the applications—from securing patient data, ensuring drug traceability, to facilitating reliable clinical research—reflects the versatility and robustness of blockchain in tackling healthcare's complex challenges. These examples provide a valuable framework for organizations considering blockchain implementation in similar arenas.

9.11 Future Directions for Blockchain in the Healthcare Industry

The transformative influence of blockchain technology on the healthcare sector is an ongoing process, with many emerging trends likely shaping the future landscape. As we have seen significant advancements in areas such as patient data management and drug traceability, further exploration and probable innovation paths can be identified. These future directions not only highlight the potential growth of blockchain applications but also ensure more robust and patient-centric healthcare systems.

Given recent advancements, one essential future direction is the expansion of blockchain into genomic data management. With human genomics rapidly becoming a tool for precision medicine, the security and privacy of such data become paramount. The application of blockchain can create a decentralized and tamper-proof repository for genomic data, mitigating risks related to unauthorized access and tampering. Here is a pseudocode example demonstrating the potential blockchain-based integrity verification process for genomic data.

9.11. FUTURE DIRECTIONS FOR BLOCKCHAIN IN THE HEALTHCARE INDUSTRY

Algorithm 12: Pseudocode for Blockchain-based Genomic Data Management

Data: New genomic data entry
Result: Validation and addition of genomic data to blockchain

1 **begin**
2   Initialize blockchain
3   Calculate hash of new genomic data
4   **if** *hash matches existing blocks* **then**
5   Reject data entry as duplicate
6   **else**
7   Create new block
8   Link new block with hash of the latest block
9   Append to blockchain
10   Broadcast new block addition to network

Another promising area is leveraging blockchain for more extensive and real-time bio-surveillance systems. Particularly in the context of global health emergencies like pandemics, blockchain can facilitate the fast, transparent, and secure sharing of data across borders. This enables health organizations to track disease outbreaks more efficiently and formulate swift responses based on real-time data. This application not only reduces the spread but also aids in the prompt distribution of necessary medical supplies and vaccines.

Blockchain also bodes well for enhancing patient empowerment and involvement in their own health care processes. Through decentralized health records, patients can access and control their data, decide whom to share it with, and even potentially monetize their data by providing consent to pharmaceutical research. Integration with emerging technologies such as AI and the Internet of Things (IoT) could further enhance personalized healthcare. Below is an illustrative example showing how a patient might interact with their blockchain-based health records.

```
// Example of a patient accessing health records
function accessRecords(patientID) {
   var records = blockchain.getRecords(patientID);
   return records;
}
```

From the regulatory perspective, progressing into the future will require development of new frameworks that address blockchain-specific issues in healthcare. These include ensuring compliance with global data protection regulations, like GDPR in Europe or HIPAA in the United States, and adapting to the decentralized nature of blockchain.

- Compliance adaptation to decentralized architectures
- Increased scrutiny to ensure data immutability does not conflict with the right to be forgotten
- Guidelines for interoperability between different blockchain healthcare applications

As the technology matures and more use cases become viable, blockchain stands poised to offer substantially more to the healthcare industry. Together with complementary technologies and regulatory evolution, blockchain can aid in realizing a healthcare ecosystem that is not only inter-linked and efficient but also more centric to the needs and privacy of patients.

Chapter 10

Integrating Blockchain with Existing IT Infrastructure

This chapter addresses the practical considerations and methodologies for integrating blockchain technology with existing IT infrastructure. It explores strategic planning, compatibility issues, and the necessary technical adjustments required for blockchain implementation. The discussion includes an analysis of the potential benefits such as increased data integrity and efficiency, alongside the challenges like scalability and maintenance. The chapter aims to provide a roadmap for organizations to successfully adopt blockchain, enhancing their existing systems while minimizing disruption.

10.1 Assessing Current IT Infrastructure for Blockchain Integration

The initial step towards integrating blockchain technology into an existing IT infrastructure is a comprehensive assessment of the current systems. This assessment focuses on understanding the capability of the existing infrastructure to support blockchain functionalities and identifying potential upgrades or modifications that might be necessary.

Infrastructure Analysis

To begin with, the IT infrastructure must be reviewed to determine its current state and readiness for blockchain implementation. This includes an evaluation of hardware capabilities, software environments, network architecture, and data storage solutions. Each component plays a crucial role in ensuring the successful adoption and operation of blockchain technology.

Hardware Capabilities

The assessment should start with the hardware capabilities, as blockchain applications often require robust processing power for tasks such as transaction validation and block creation. The current hardware should be evaluated for its CPU throughput, memory capacity, and storage speed. Should the existing hardware be insufficient, it may necessitate an upgrade to more powerful servers or distributed systems that can handle the increased workload associated with blockchain operations.

Software Environment

On the software side, the operating systems and the middleware used across the enterprise need to be compatible with blockchain technologies. This includes ensuring that the necessary cryptographic libraries are supported and up-to-date. Additionally, any existing applications should be reviewed to ascertain if their current programming languages and environments are adaptable for blockchain integration, or if they will require complete redevelopment.

Network Architecture

Network architecture is critical as blockchain relies heavily on network efficiency to transmit data across nodes efficiently. An analysis must be conducted on the current state of the network infrastructure to ensure that it can manage the high bandwidth usage and maintain low latency communication which is pivotal in blockchain operations.

Data Storage Solutions

Evaluating data storage solutions involves checking the scalability and security of the current database systems. Blockchain databases, being decentralized, demand data storage solutions that can support redundancy, immutability, and extensive data replication. This evaluation will help determine whether new distributed database systems are required or if the existing databases can be adapted.

Capability Maturity Model

Further, the integration process should adopt a well-defined capability maturity model to stage the assessment and integration process methodically. This model helps in identifying the maturity level of the IT infrastructure in handling blockchain technology—from initial understanding and exploration (Level 1) to optimized processes that fully integrate blockchain into the business operations (Level 5).

- **Level 1: Initial** - Basic awareness of blockchain technology and its potential impact on the current IT structure.

- **Level 2: Managed** - Planning phase with pilot testing, recognizing the gaps in the current infrastructure that hinder blockchain integration.

- **Level 3: Defined** - Design and development of blockchain solutions are started, focusing on addressing the identified infrastructure gaps.

- **Level 4: Quantitatively Managed** - Controlled implementation and performance monitoring of blockchain solutions, with ongoing adjustments for optimal performance.

- **Level 5: Optimizing** - Full-scale integration, with refinements and enhancements being continuously implemented based on feedback and evolving needs.

The thorough understanding gained from this initial assessment provides a foundation for detailing the specific technical requirements and strategic planning needed for blockchain integration. This initial phase is critical as it sets the parameters for subsequent steps in the blockchain adoption process, essentially providing a blueprint that aligns the technology with enterprise-specific needs. The outcome of this assessment will serve as a guideline for detailed planning and execution phases covered in the subsequent sections of this chapter.

10.2 Key Considerations Before Integrating Blockchain

Before embarking on the integration of blockchain technology into an existing IT infrastructure, several pivotal considerations must be assessed to ensure a successful deployment. These include understanding the alignment of blockchain technology with the business objectives, determining the scalability requirements, evaluating security implications, considering the legal and regulatory environment, and anticipating the impact on system performance.

Alignment with Business Objectives

One of the primary considerations is the alignment of blockchain technology with overarching business objectives. Organizations must define clear goals that the introduction of blockchain aims to achieve. These objectives often encompass enhancing transparency, improving the efficiency of transactions, reducing costs, or increasing security. For instance, if an organization aims to enhance supply chain transparency, blockchain can be implemented to create a more resilient and transparent supply chain network.

```
Example Business Objectives for Blockchain Integration:
- Reduce transaction costs by 30% within the first year
- Increase data transparency across international borders
- Enhance customer trust through improved data integrity
```

Scalability Requirements

Scalability is a critical factor for organizations to consider before integrating blockchain. The chosen blockchain solution must be capable of handling increasing workloads and transaction volumes that correspond with business growth without compromising performance. There are two dimensions of scalability to be considered: vertical scaling, which involves adding more resources to the existing network nodes, and horizontal scaling, which involves adding more nodes to the network.

10.2. KEY CONSIDERATIONS BEFORE INTEGRATING BLOCKCHAIN

```
1  // Example of a scalability requirement specification
2  function adjustNodeResources(uint additionalMemory, uint additionalCPUs) {
3      currentMemory += additionalMemory;
4      currentCPUs += additionalCPUs;
5  }
```

Security Implications

Security is paramount in any IT deployment, more so with blockchain technology due to its distributed nature. The decentralized aspect of blockchain can both improve security, by removing single points of failure, and introduce unique security challenges such as the risk of 51% attacks or smart contract vulnerabilities. Organizations must ensure that the blockchain implementation is fortified with robust security measures tailored to the specific architecture chosen.

```
Potential Blockchain Security Measures:
- Regular smart contract audits
- Implementation of robust encryption practices
- Continuous network monitoring for unusual activity
```

Legal and Regulatory Environment

Legal and regulatory considerations are also crucial when integrating blockchain technology. Depending on the jurisdiction and industry, there may be specific laws and regulations regarding data privacy, transaction transparency, or technology deployment that must be adhered to. It is imperative for organizations to conduct thorough legal assessments to ensure compliance with relevant regulatory requirements.

- Data storage and transfer regulations
- Financial and transactional legislation
- Technology-specific guidelines and standards

Impact on System Performance

Lastly, organizations must consider the impact of blockchain on the existing IT system's performance. Blockchain networks, especially those that use consensus mechanisms like Proof of Work, can consume substantial computational and power resources, potentially impacting the performance of other critical systems. Careful planning and resource allocation are necessary to mitigate any adverse effects on system performance.

```
1  // Example of checking system resource utilize before blockchain integration
2  if (blockchainNode.canAllocateResources(requiredMemory, requiredCPU)) {
3      blockchainNode.initiate();
4  } else {
5      throw new ResourceAllocationException("Insufficient resources for blockchain
           integration.");
6  }
```

These considerations form the foundation for decision-making regarding blockchain integration. A thorough understanding and evaluation of these factors will guide organizations in tailoring a blockchain solution that meets their specific needs while enhancing their current IT operations. This approach not only ensures a smoother integration process but also helps in maximizing the benefits of blockchain technology in enhancing organizational efficiency and integrity.

10.3 Blockchain Integration Strategies

Integrating blockchain technology into existing IT infrastructure requires a well-considered strategy that accounts for technological compatibility, business processes, and organizational goals. This section delves into the core strategies that organizations can employ to ensure seamless and effective integration of blockchain solutions with existing systems.

Selecting the Appropriate Blockchain Type: Organizations must first decide between a public, private, or consortium blockchain. Each type has distinct characteristics and implications for integration:

- Public blockchain systems like Bitcoin and Ethereum offer high levels of transparency and security but may present challenges in terms of scalability and data privacy.

- Private blockchain systems provide more control over participants and transactions, which can be advantageous for enterprise use cases requiring privacy and permissioned access.

- Consortium blockchains are partially decentralized and ideal for businesses that operate in groups where trust must be distributed among distinct entities.

10.3. BLOCKCHAIN INTEGRATION STRATEGIES

Integration through APIs: Application Programming Interfaces (APIs) are crucial for integrating blockchain with existing applications. They serve as a bridge, facilitating communication between the blockchain network and enterprise systems without extensive modifications to existing software.

```
// Example of a simple blockchain API call
GET /api/v1/blockchain/transactions?id=12345
```

This example illustrates how APIs allow for retrieving data from a blockchain, enabling applications to interact with blockchain data effectively. Organizations should develop or utilize existing robust APIs that support a wide range of functionalities such as transaction writing, identity verification, and data querying.

Middleware Solutions: Middleware acts as a connecting layer between blockchain platforms and enterprise applications. It handles the complexity of blockchain protocols by providing a set of tools and services that abstract the underlying blockchain infrastructure from business applications. Middleware can manage smart contracts, support event handling, and synchronize data across distributed ledgers and existing databases.

Developing a Phased Implementation Plan: Implementing blockchain should be a phased process:

1. **Pilot Project:** Start with a pilot project that addresses a specific business process where blockchain could add value. Monitor performance and gather insights.

2. **Scaling:** Based on pilot results, gradually scale the solution to other parts of the business.

3. **Full Integration:** Once the blockchain solution is proven at scale, it can be fully integrated into the IT infrastructure with greater confidence.

Ensuring Scalability and Interoperability: Scalability and interoperability are fundamental to the success of blockchain integration. Techniques such as sharding (dividing a blockchain into smaller manageable parts) or using off-chain solutions can address scalability. For interoperability, employing protocols like the Interledger Protocol (ILP) allows different blockchain systems to communicate.

Smart Contract Deployment: Smart contracts automate transaction processes. When integrating a blockchain:

```
1  // Example of a smart contract function
2  function transferOwnership(address newOwner) public {
3     require(msg.sender == owner);
4     owner = newOwner;
5  }
```

In this code snippet, ownership of a digital asset or property is transferred only if executed by the current owner, showcasing how smart contracts enforce business rules.

Organizations must thoroughly test smart contracts to prevent breaches or unintended actions. Regular audits by internal and external security experts are advisable to maintain the integrity and security of smart contracts.

Training and Change Management: It is essential to conduct proper training and change management activities to help staff adapt to new technological frameworks. Comprehensive training on the blockchain platform's operation, security practices, and on how to interact with new interfaces ensures smooth integration and operations.

By carefully selecting the blockchain type, leveraging APIs, employing middleware, and developing a phase-based implementation strategy, you can integrate blockchain into the existing systems effectively. The role of smart contracts and the importance of training and change management are also crucial to enhance the integration process. Through meticulous planning and execution, blockchain can be woven into the fabric of existing IT architectures in a manner that augments the capabilities of the systems while fostering innovation and efficiency.

10.4 Technical Requirements for Blockchain Deployment

Embedding blockchain technology within an existing IT infrastructure mandates a comprehensive assessment of the technical prerequisites. This section delves deeply into the core technical requirements necessary for successful blockchain deployment, including hardware specifications, software requirements, network configurations, and security protocols.

Hardware Specifications

The hardware requirements for blockchain systems can vary significantly depending on the specific blockchain architecture (e.g., permissioned versus permissionless) and the scale of the operation. Below are the key hardware considerations:

- **Processor Power (CPU):** Blockchain operations, especially those involving consensus mechanisms such as Proof of Work (PoW), are computationally intensive. High-performance CPUs are thus essential for efficiently processing transactions and maintaining ledger synchronicity.

- **Memory (RAM):** Adequate RAM is critical for the fast retrieval and handling of transactions during the consensus process. Insufficient memory can lead to bottlenecks, slowing down the transaction processing rate and overall system performance.

- **Storage Capacity:** The choice of storage depends on the blockchain's nature. Permissionless blockchains typically require more storage space due to the ever-growing size of the ledger. Solid State Drives (SSDs) are preferred for their speed over Hard Disk Drives (HDDs).

- **Network Bandwidth:** Sufficient bandwidth is crucial to handle potentially high volumes of transaction data and peer-to-peer communication across the blockchain network. The required bandwidth varies with the transaction payload size and the rate of transactions.

Software Requirements

Blockchain deployment necessitates specific software tools and platforms, which may include:

- **Blockchain Platform:** Depending on the enterprise needs, selecting an appropriate blockchain platform is critical. Options include Ethereum, Hyperledger Fabric, R3 Corda, and others, each supporting different features such as smart contracts, privacy options, and consensus mechanisms.

- **Cryptographic Libraries:** Security in blockchain is pivotal and relies heavily on cryptographic standards. Libraries such as

OpenSSL provide tools necessary for encryption and decryption, which are crucial for creating and verifying digital signatures.

- **Development Tools:** Tools and Integrated Development Environments (IDEs) like Truffle for Ethereum, or the Hyperledger Composer, are indispensable for application development and testing on blockchain networks.

Network Configuration

- **Node Configuration:** The blockchain network consists of nodes, each of which needs to be properly configured to comply with the network's requirements. This includes setting up full nodes, which hold a complete copy of transaction history, or lightweight nodes, which hold only essential information needed to validate transactions.

- **Consensus Protocol Configuration:** Each blockchain has a consensus mechanism, whether it be PoW, Proof of Stake (PoS), or another protocol. Effective deployment requires careful configuration of these protocols to ensure network reliability and security.

- **Network Security:** Ensuring secure communication between nodes involves configuring firewalls, intrusion detection systems (IDS), and proper authentication methods to prevent unauthorized access and safeguard data integrity on the network.

Security Protocols

Security remains a paramount concern in blockchain deployments. Essential security measures include:

- **Data Encryption:** Implementing data encryption at rest and in transit to protect sensitive data. Advanced Encryption Standard (AES) and Secure Sockets Layer (SSL)/Transport Layer Security (TLS) are commonly used encryption standards.

- **Regular Audits:** Conducting regular security audits and penetration testing to identify and mitigate vulnerabilities.

- **Access Controls:** Setting up strict access controls to ensure that only authorized entities have the ability to modify the blockchain or access sensitive information.

By rigorously addressing these technical requirements, enterprises can establish a robust foundation for blockchain deployment, paving the way for enhanced data integrity and operational efficiencies. The successful implementation of these specifications not only integrates blockchain seamlessly with existing IT infrastructure but also leverages its potential to the fullest, ensuring a strategic advantage in the technological landscape.

10.5 Handling Data Migration and Interoperability Issues

Data migration to a blockchain system encompasses both the transfer of existing data into a new blockchain infrastructure and the ongoing process of ensuring interoperability between the blockchain and conventional IT systems. This section addresses the methodologies, common challenges, and best practices essential for executing a smooth transition and ensuring continuous interaction between disparate systems.

Methodologies for Data Migration to Blockchain

To begin, it's essential to outline a structured approach towards migrating data onto a blockchain. The primary steps include data auditing, mapping, extraction, transformation, and loading.

- **Data Auditing**: This initial step involves reviewing the existing data to ascertain its accuracy, consistency, and completeness. Any discrepancies or quality issues must be resolved before migration to ensure the integrity of data on the blockchain.

- **Data Mapping**: Critical for determining how data from the existing system will fit into the new blockchain system. This includes defining how each piece of data is represented on the blockchain, what data becomes part of the blockchain ledger, and how relational data is handled.

- **Extraction**: Involves pulling data out from the current systems. Special care should be taken to maintain data integrity during this process.

- **Transformation**: Data often needs to be transformed or reformatted to meet the data input requirements of the blockchain. This could include encryption, hashing, or fragmenting data into suitable sizes.

- **Loading**: The final step involves importing the transformed data into the blockchain. This should be done in a secure and controlled manner to avoid creating bottlenecks in the network or compromising the data's integrity.

Interoperability Challenges and Solutions

Interoperability between blockchain systems and existing IT infrastructure is critical for applications that require data to flow seamlessly from traditional databases to blockchain networks and vice versa.

```
Blockchain Technology Layer Exchange Framework (BTLEF)
{
   Initialize communication interfaces for both blockchain and existing IT systems;
   Ensure data format compatibility;
   Implement data transformation protocols;
   Establish continuous synchronization mechanisms;
   Monitor and manage data transmission reliability;
}
```

Factors to consider in interoperability:

- **Data Format Compatibility**: Ensure that data formats are compatible or can be converted through middleware or during the transformation phase of the migration process.

- **Communication Protocols**: Both systems need to employ a common set of communication protocols or be equipped with translation facilities that allow them to send and receive data.

- **Security Protocols**: Adequate security measures must be in place to protect data during transfer between systems. This includes using encryption and secure channels.

- **Performance and Throughput**: The impact on system performance and data throughput must be evaluated and optimized to prevent bottlenecks.

Handling the integration of a blockchain with existing IT infrastructure demands a comprehensive understanding of both technological assets and organizational workflow to mitigate data migration risks. Effective communication, iterative testing during migration, and ensuring interoperability are integral to aligning blockchain technology within existing IT paradigms. It is evident that while the integration presents notable challenges, a systematic, well-planned approach can vastly reduce risk and enhance the operational coherence of the organization's data ecosystem.

10.6 Modifying Existing Applications to Work with Blockchain

The integration of blockchain technology into existing applications necessitates both strategic planning and technical adaptation. Such modifications serve to ensure that legacy systems can effectively interact with new blockchain frameworks, thereby leveraging the aforementioned technology's benefits such as increased security, transparency, and traceability.

Firstly, it is imperative to understand that modification typically involves the application's data handling and storage mechanisms. Legacy applications often use centralized databases, whereas blockchain introduces a decentralized ledger system. To bridge this gap, the application architecture must evolve to support interactions with a blockchain network.

- Assess the data flow within the application and determine critical points where data integrity is paramount.
- Identify processes that will benefit most from decentralization and enhanced security.
- Prepare the application for additional latency that might occur due to the consensus mechanisms inherent in blockchain technologies.

Database Integration

One of the greatest challenges lies in modifying the application's database to work with a blockchain. This usually means enabling the

CHAPTER 10. INTEGRATING BLOCKCHAIN WITH EXISTING IT INFRASTRUCTURE

application to interact with both traditional relational databases and blockchain's distributed ledger.

To integrate a blockchain ledger with an existing application, developers must implement APIs that facilitate data transactions between the legacy database systems and the blockchain network. Here is a simplified example of API implementation in Python that interacts with a blockchain network:

```
1  import requests
2
3  def get_blockchain_data(block_id):
4      response = requests.get(f'http://example_blockchain.com/block/{block_id}')
5      return response.json()
6
7  def post_transaction_to_blockchain(transaction_data):
8      response = requests.post('http://example_blockchain.com/transactions/new', json
           =transaction_data)
9      return response.status_code
```

Updating Business Logic

The business logic of the application, which defines how data is processed and managed, may also require reconfiguration to incorporate blockchain logic. This involves ensuring that business transactions involving the ledger are valid and secured through appropriate cryptographic methods.

Consider the following pseudocode implementing business logic that confirms a transaction's validity before adding it to the blockchain:

Algorithm 13: AddTransactionToBlock

Input: transaction_data
Output: success or failure

1 **begin**
   // Validate transaction
2 is_valid ← validate_transaction(transaction_data)
3 **if** *is_valid* **then**
4 | block.add(transaction_data)
5 | return success
6 **else**
7 | return failure
8 **end**
9 **end**

Security Enhancements

Security is a pivotal aspect of blockchain integration. Legacy applications must enhance their security features to align with the high security standards of blockchain technology. This involves employing advanced authentication mechanisms, improving data encryption, and ensuring that data integrity checks are robust.

One illustrative aspect of security enhancement is the use of cryptographic hashing for data integrity:

```
import hashlib

def hash_data(data):
    return hashlib.sha256(data.encode()).hexdigest()
```

The output after hashing a particular string "Example Data" would be shown as follows:

```
6f24be10e407263b216333a35d7f5a3f208334f45ddf501215b93f7e448e1360
```

Interface Adjustments

Finally, adjustments to the user interface and user experience designs of existing applications are essential to accommodate new functionalities introduced by blockchain integration. These modifications aim to ensure that interactions with the blockchain are seamless and intuitive for end-users.

Adapting existing applications to work with blockchain technologies is not trivial. It requires a well-thought-out strategy that focuses on technical adjustments, reassessments of business logic, security enhancements, and interface redesign. By following these guidelines, organizations can ensure that their applications not only maintain their operational integrity and user base but also gain the full range of benefits that blockchain technology offers.

10.7 Securing the Blockchain within Existing IT Ecosystems

When integrating blockchain technology into an existing IT ecosystem, security is paramount. Blockchain, by its nature, offers enhanced security features due to its decentralized structure and cryptographic processes. However, the interface between existing systems and the new blockchain components necessitates additional security measures to ensure both systems' integrity and security.

First, it is critical to analyze the security protocols currently in place within the IT infrastructure. This involves not only identifying the technologies used, such as firewalls, anti-malware systems, and intrusion detection systems, but also understanding the existing data management and access control policies. The process includes the following necessary actions:

- Review of current network access policies and their compatibility with blockchain's decentralized nature.

- Assessment of the encryption methods in use and their adequacy for securing data transactions on the blockchain.

- Evaluation of existing data integrity checks compared to those applied in blockchain operations.

Following this analysis, specific attention must be directed toward the integration points between the blockchain and existing systems. These points represent potential vulnerabilities as data transfers between different environments. To manage these risks, several security protocols should be implemented:

- Establishing secure APIs (Application Programming Interfaces) which act as the communication bridge between blockchain and the current IT systems. These APIs should be designed to prevent attacks such as SQL injection and to authenticate properly between different environments.

- Using robust encryption protocols to secure data in transit. Implementing SSL/TLS for data transmitted over the network is a critical security measure.

- Designing a comprehensive role-based access control (RBAC) system to manage permissions for who can write or read the blockchain. This helps in maintaining rigid access structures required by business processes.

On the blockchain side, the use of smart contracts provides a programmable approach to enforcing business rules and security policies.

10.7. SECURING THE BLOCKCHAIN WITHIN EXISTING IT ECOSYSTEMS

Smart contracts must be rigorously tested since they operate automatically based on the code's logic, which if flawed, might lead to security breaches. This requires:

```
1  // Example of a simple smart contract in Solidity
2
3  pragma solidity ^0.5.0;
4
5  contract SimpleContract {
6      uint256 public value;
7
8      function setValue(uint256 newValue) public {
9          value = newValue;
10     }
11 }
```

Here, the `setValue` function allows users to modify the `value` variable, which is placed publicly on the blockchain. Ensuring that only authorized parties can call this function is crucial. Techniques such as using cryptographic signatures for transactions or setting modifiers in smart contracts can enforce this.

The next significant concern is the storage and protection of private keys used in blockchain transactions. Deploying secure key management systems and hardware security modules can help in managing cryptographic keys throughout their lifecycle, including creation, storage, use, and destruction.

The physical security of the facilities where blockchain nodes are hosted cannot be overlooked. Secure locations with controlled access prevent unauthorized physical access, thus ensuring the hardware and data are not tampered with.

```
Block height: 556100
Hash: 0000000000000000001308cd5ab00fade276fb23204c6a35c3c9c4abd4b00f
Previous block hash: 0000000000000000002cb969a3892feced6a842e7504143eb1f4f5d4a7174077
Merkle root: 4acd4e01f1475b00ea59a569048b7dde593b4fcb5c90b5df2c866d8fd3098eac
Time: 2021-02-19 10:37 UTC
```

The example above presents a typical output from a blockchain explorer, reflecting a block's critical information. Each block contains transactions securely encrypted and can be verified publicly, maintaining transparency and preventing malicious alterations.

To conclude, securing a blockchain when integrating it into an existing IT ecosystem involves layered security practices focusing on both technological and procedural adaptations. Ensuring the secure exchange of data via APIs, adequately managing access rights, and the secure storage and handling of cryptographic keys are essential steps towards this integration. Each layer of security serves to fortify the system, sustaining the blockchain's inherent strengths while protecting it from new vulnerabilities introduced during integration. This dual approach not only preserves the functionality of the current systems but also leverages the innovative capabilities of blockchain technology.

10.8 Monitoring and Managing Blockchain Operations

Monitoring and managing blockchain operations is paramount for ensuring smooth integration of blockchain technology with existing IT infrastructures. This section delineates strategies for monitoring network activity and managing nodes within the blockchain, ensuring optimal performance and addressing issues as they arise.

Effective monitoring of blockchain operations begins with the establishment of key performance indicators (KPIs) that are aligned with the organization's objectives. It is essential to monitor various aspects such as transaction throughput, block generation time, and network latency. Additionally, monitoring should cover security aspects like node health, consensus process effectiveness, and abnormal transaction patterns that could indicate security threats.

A commonly adopted tool for blockchain monitoring is the use of specialized blockchain explorers. These platforms provide a user-friendly interface to observe live blockchain operations without interacting directly with the blockchain nodes. They display information about blocks, transactions, and wallet balances. For more detailed insights into the performance and health of the blockchain network, organizations can utilize analytics platforms that aggregate data over time to identify trends and anomalies.

```python
# Example of a simple monitoring script in Python
import requests

def check_node_status(node_url):
    try:
        response = requests.get(node_url)
        if response.status_code == 200:
            return "Node is active and reachable"
        else:
            return "Issue with node connectivity"
    except requests.exceptions.RequestException:
        return "Failed to connect to node"

# Example usage
node_status = check_node_status("http://exampleblockchainnode.com/api")
print(node_status)
```

10.8. MONITORING AND MANAGING BLOCKCHAIN OPERATIONS

```
Node is active and reachable
```

For managing the blockchain, it is crucial to establish a robust governance framework. This includes defining roles and permissions for different participants within the network to facilitate effective management and adherence to compliance standards. Blockchain node management tools can provide significant assistance in this regard. These tools help in performing tasks such as adding or removing nodes, updating blockchain software, and managing forks if they occur.

Another critical aspect is the management of smart contracts which are self-executing contracts with the terms of the agreement directly written into code. The lifecycle of a smart contract includes development, testing, deployment, monitoring, and maintenance. It is recommended that smart contracts undergo thorough testing environments before being deployed on the main network. Once deployed, the contracts must be constantly monitored to ensure they execute as intended and do not expose the network to risks.

```
1   # Example smart contract deployment script
2   from web3 import Web3
3
4   w3 = Web3(Web3.HTTPProvider('http://example.ethereum.node'))
5   contract = w3.eth.contract(address='ContractAddress', abi='ContractABI')
6
7   def deploy_contract(transaction):
8       tx_hash = contract.constructor().transact(transaction)
9       tx_receipt = w3.eth.waitForTransactionReceipt(tx_hash)
10      return tx_receipt.contractAddress
11
12  # Transaction information
13  transaction = {
14      'from': 'YourAccountAddress',
15      'gas': 2000000,
16      'gasPrice': '50 gwei',
17      'nonce': w3.eth.getTransactionCount('YourAccountAddress')
18  }
19
20  new_contract_address = deploy_contract(transaction)
21  print(new_contract_address)
```

0xdAc17F958D2ee523a2206206994597C13D831ec7

Utilizing these methods within an IT ecosystem requires the IT team to possess or acquire a specific skill set that includes understanding blockchain technology and smart contract coding and auditing. Workshops and training sessions can be effective in upskilling the existing IT staff to handle these new responsibilities.

Additionally, it is advisable for organizations to employ a dedicated blockchain operations team. This team will focus on the continuous evaluation of blockchain performance metrics compared against the set benchmarks, ensuring that the blockchain integration adds value to the organization's existing IT infrastructure and aligns with its overall business goals. This approach not only mitigates risks but also maximizes the efficacy of the blockchain operations throughout their lifecycle, ensuring they meet the desired objectives and propel the organization towards a more secure and efficient future.

10.9 Training and Support for Blockchain Integration

Training and support form a critical component of the blockchain integration process within existing IT infrastructure. Effective training ensures that staff are well-versed on blockchain functionalities and are capable of leveraging its benefits maximally, while support structures are essential for the ongoing maintenance and troubleshooting of blockchain systems.

Developing a Comprehensive Training Program: The first step toward effective integration is the development of a comprehensive training program that is tailored to the needs of various stakeholders within the organization. This program should cover the following key areas:

- **Blockchain Basics:** Concepts of blockchain technology, such as distributed ledgers, consensus mechanisms, smart contracts, and cryptographic hash functions.

- **Operational Training:** Functional training on how blockchain will influence daily operations and specific role-based training for technical staff on handling blockchain operations.

- **Development Training:** For IT staff and software developers, detailed sessions on the blockchain development environment, APIs, and integration points are crucial.

- **Security Practices:** Training on the security aspects of blockchain, including data security, transaction security, and potential vulnerabilities.

This training should leverage diverse formats, such as workshops, webinars, and e-learning modules, to ensure broad accessibility and comprehension. It is essential to assess knowledge retention and application through regular evaluations and refresher training sessions.

10.9. TRAINING AND SUPPORT FOR BLOCKCHAIN INTEGRATION

Establishing a Support Framework: The establishment of a robust support framework is vital to address the technical challenges that arise post-integration. This framework should consist of:

- **Internal Support Team:** A dedicated team that understands the intricacies of the blockchain environment and can offer first-hand troubleshooting and problem-solving.

- **External Experts:** Partnerships with blockchain experts and consultants who can provide specialized insights and solutions for complex issues.

- **Community Engagement:** Leverage the broader blockchain community, which can offer assistance, plugins, and tools that enhance the operational efficiency.

Documentation plays a pivotal role in both training and support. Detailed records of system configurations, operational procedures, and problem resolution logs are indispensable. These documents should be regularly updated and easily accessible to ensure they can effectively guide and educate staff as well as support personnel in resolving any issues promptly.

Utilizing Feedback Mechanisms: To continuously improve the training and support offered, it is necessary to implement feedback mechanisms. Regular feedback sessions should be conducted to understand the training efficacy and identify the support challenges faced by staff. This feedback should be systematically analyzed and used to make informed adjustments to both the training curriculum and support processes.

Effective training and support not only facilitate a smooth transition during blockchain integration but also empower the organization's workforce to efficiently manage and optimize blockchain solutions. By investing in comprehensive training programs and constructing robust support systems, enterprises can enhance the reliability and effectiveness of their blockchain initiatives, which ultimately contributes to their overall strategic objectives and technological advancement. This approach ensures that the workforce is not merely equipped to use the technology but is also proficient in optimizing its use to drive business growth and innovation.

10.10 Evaluating the Impact of Blockchain on IT Operations

The deployment of blockchain technology within an existing IT infrastructure invariably leads to a variety of significant impacts on IT operations, which necessitate a thorough assessment. This evaluation is fundamental for ensuring the ongoing stability, performance, and adaptability of IT services post-integration. The broad areas influenced include operational reliability, system performance metrics, cost implications, and required personnel skill sets.

Operational Reliability

Integrating blockchain technology often enhances operational reliability due to its inherent design, which promotes data integrity and fault tolerance. To systematically evaluate these enhancements, one should monitor the decrement in system downtime, the frequency of data inconsistencies, and the rate of transaction disputes pre- and post-integration. A notable increase in reliability can be observed through reduced rollback scenarios and correction interventions necessitated by data errors.

System Performance Metrics

Blockchain implementations can have complex effects on performance metrics. The addition of blockchain layers to existing systems potentially introduces latency and may reduce transactional throughput due to the cryptographic operations required. It is critical to measure the impact of these factors through metrics such as transaction processing speed, system response time, and network latency.

Graphical representations created using the `TikZ` package can vividly illustrate these changes:

10.10. EVALUATING THE IMPACT OF BLOCKCHAIN ON IT OPERATIONS

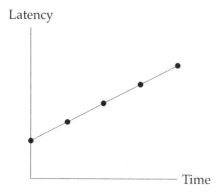

Cost Implications

The cost impact of blockchain implementation encompasses both initial and operational costs. These include but are not limited to hardware upgrades, software licensing, and increased energy consumption in maintaining node operations across the network. To effectively manage costs, IT managers need to perform a detailed cost-benefit analysis taking into account the total cost of ownership (TCO) and the anticipated return on investment (ROI) concerning enhanced security, improved trust, and efficiency gains.

Requirement of Personnel Skill Sets

The introduction of blockchain necessitates the acquisition of specific technical skills within the IT team, especially pertaining to blockchain technology fundamentals, smart contract development, and system integration techniques. IT operations teams need to undergo substantial training and, in some cases, bolstering through new hires with relevant expertise.

A structured training program could be outlined as follows:

- Introduction to Blockchain Fundamentals
- Advanced Training on Smart Contracts and Consensus Algorithms
- Hands-on Integration Techniques
- Ongoing Support and Troubleshooting

Every aspect aforementioned requires precise tracking and evaluation protocols to ensure that all adjustments to the IT systems align with organizational objectives and are sustainable in the long term. Moreover, these evaluations assist in creating a feedback loop that informs continuous improvement cycles, potentially refining blockchain integration strategies over time to better serve the demands of organizational IT operations.

10.11 Case Studies: Successful Integrations of Blockchain in Existing IT Infrastructures

This section presents several case studies that exemplify successful integration of blockchain technology into existing IT infrastructures across different industries. Each case study provides insights into the strategic planning, implementation processes, and the outcomes of blockchain adoption.

Banking Sector: Improved Transaction Processing and Security

A prominent multinational bank undertook a blockchain integration to enhance the security and efficiency of its transaction processing system. The bank implemented a private blockchain, leveraging smart contracts to automate transactions and reduce reliance on intermediaries.

- **Challenges**: The main challenges included ensuring compatibility with legacy banking systems and meeting stringent regulatory requirements for financial transactions.

- **Implementation Strategy**: The strategy involved developing a custom blockchain solution that interfaces seamlessly with existing transaction processing systems. A phased rollout was adopted to minimize disruption to ongoing operations.

- **Results**: The integration resulted in a 30% reduction in transaction processing times and a significant decrease in fraud incidents. The blockchain system provided a more transparent and secure framework for handling transactions, which also aided in regulatory reporting and compliance.

```
contract TransactionProcessor {
    function processTransaction(uint amount, string sender, string receiver) public
    {
        // Transaction processing logic
    }
}
```

Healthcare Sector: Enhancing Patient Data Management

A healthcare provider implemented blockchain to improve the management and security of its patient records. The goal was to create a decentralized and tamper-proof repository of patient information that could be accessed securely by authorized personnel.

- **Challenges**: Integration with existing electronic health record (EHR) systems and ensuring patient data privacy were major challenges.

- **Implementation Strategy**: The solution involved creating a permissioned blockchain network that links various stakeholders such as hospitals, clinics, and insurance companies.

- **Results**: The blockchain network enabled seamless and secure sharing of patient data across different service providers, reducing duplicate tests and errors in patient care. Additionally, it enhanced compliance with health data protection regulations.

```
contract PatientRecord {
    function addRecord(string patientId, string recordDetails) public {
        // Add patient record
    }
}
```

Supply Chain Management: Increasing Transparency and Efficiency

A global retail company adopted blockchain to manage its complex supply chain that spanned multiple countries and involved numerous vendors and distributors. The objective was to increase transparency and efficiency in the supply chain by tracking goods from production to delivery.

- **Challenges**: Ensuring all parties in the supply chain adopted the technology and managed the increased data load were significant challenges.

- **Implementation Strategy**: A blockchain-based tracking system was developed to record each step in the supply chain. All parties involved were given access to the blockchain, which allowed for real-time tracking and verification of goods.

- **Results**: The integration led to improved inventory management, reduced losses from counterfeit goods, and better compliance with safety regulations. The real-time data available on the blockchain also enabled quicker decision-making processes.

```
1  contract SupplyChainTracker {
2      function updateItemStatus(string itemId, string status) public {
3          // Update item status in the supply chain
4      }
5  }
```

The case studies underscore the versatility and benefits of integrating blockchain technology with existing IT infrastructures. The success across different sectors demonstrates blockchain's potential to address specific operational challenges and enhance overall efficiency and security. Through strategic planning and careful implementation, these organizations have set a precedent for others considering blockchain technology to modernize their operations.

Chapter 11

Legal and Regulatory Considerations of Blockchain

This chapter delves into the essential legal and regulatory frameworks that shape the adoption and operation of blockchain technology. It examines the evolving landscape of blockchain-related legislation, highlighting compliance issues, intellectual property rights, and the implications of decentralized models for traditional legal systems. The discussion emphasizes the necessity for enterprises to stay informed about jurisdictional variances and regulatory updates to navigate the complex legal dimensions of blockchain technology effectively.

11.1 Understanding the Legal Framework Surrounding Blockchain

The legal framework surrounding blockchain is a composite structure of various legal principles, regulatory measures, and jurisdictional statutes that together define the operational, contractual, and compliance obligations of entities utilizing this technology.

The initial aspect that needs attention is the classification and definition of blockchain and its components in legal terms. Despite its technological nuances, blockchain functions as a ledger technology that can be integrated into different sectors and thus, the legal definition might vary. For example, in some jurisdictions, digital assets such as cryptocurrencies are classified under commodity trading, while others might recognize them under securities or as a digital currency.

Further exploration is required on the legislative actions aimed at blockchain technology. Many governments globally have begun instituting frameworks that explicitly mention blockchain technology. For example, the state of Wyoming in the United States has passed several legislations tailored to create a conducive environment for blockchain technology and digital assets. These laws address digital asset custody through banks and clarity on the legal status of digital assets as personal property.

Moreover, understanding the legal intricacies involves recognizing the crucial role of smart contracts on blockchain platforms. Smart contracts are self-executing contracts wherein the terms between buyer and seller are directly written into code. The legal recognition of smart contracts is not ubiquitous and varies significantly across different jurisdictions. Challenges persist in fitting smart contracts within traditional contract law frameworks, particularly around the issues of contract formation, execution, and enforceability. An understanding of the Electronic Signatures in Global and National Commerce Act (ESIGN) in the United States and the Electronic Commerce Directive in the EU can provide significant insights into how electronic agreements are recognized and enforced.

Legal interpretations and case law also play crucial roles in shaping blockchain's legal framework. Courts in various jurisdictions have tackled cases involving blockchain and cryptocurrency, setting precedents that may influence future legal considerations. For instance, case law surrounding the application of blockchain-based evidence in legal proceedings and the enforcement of blockchain-based arbitration decisions is beginning to form.

The question of jurisdiction and the transnational nature of blockchain transactions bring forward complex legal challenges. Blockchain can operate across borders without the need for intermediary oversight, which creates a tension between the technology and traditional legal systems which are typically confined to specific geographic and jurisdictional boundaries. Determining the appropriate jurisdiction in disputes involving blockchain technology requires an understanding of the domicile of the parties involved, the location of the server nodes, among other factors.

Finally, international cooperation and harmonization of legal standards are essential given the global operation of blockchain. Current efforts such as the European Blockchain Partnership, which aims to establish a European Blockchain Services Infrastructure, showcase initiatives at regional levels. However, broader international frameworks and guidelines, akin to those established by the Financial Action Task Force (FATF) on cryptocurrencies, are still evolving.

This section reveals that the legal framework surrounding blockchain is multi-faceted and still under development. Enterprises looking to adopt blockchain technology should actively engage with ongoing legal dialogues, adapt to the rapid regulatory changes, and seek legal expertise to navigate this complex landscape effectively.

11.2 Global Regulatory Landscape for Blockchain Technology

The regulatory landscape for blockchain technology is as diverse and complex as the technology itself. Across different jurisdictions, regulatory approaches to blockchain and cryptocurrencies vary significantly, influenced by local economic policies, prevailing legal systems, and cultural attitudes towards technology and finance.

In the United States, the Securities and Exchange Commission (SEC) and the Commodity Futures Trading Commission (CFTC) have taken prominent roles in defining the regulatory environment for blockchain-based derivatives, tokens, and cryptocurrencies. For instance, the SEC has issued guidance indicating that certain tokens may be considered securities and thus fall under securities laws. This determination depends on the specifics of how the tokens are issued and the expectations set about their utility and return on investment.

- The SEC's "Framework for 'Investment Contract' Analysis of Digital Assets" is a critical document that provides insight into how they evaluate cryptocurrencies under the traditional tests used by U.S. courts (most notably, the Howey Test).

- The CFTC regards cryptocurrencies as commodities and therefore asserts its jurisdiction to regulate derivatives based on them,

CHAPTER 11. LEGAL AND REGULATORY CONSIDERATIONS OF BLOCKCHAIN

such as futures and swaps.

In Europe, the regulatory environment is somewhat unified under the European Union, which has been proactive through its regulatory body, the European Securities and Markets Authority (ESMA). ESMA has focused on the risks associated with cryptocurrency investments, emphasizing the importance of clear disclosures to consumers. Further, the Fifth Anti-Money Laundering Directive (5AMLD) in the EU has extended AML regulations to cover crypto exchanges and wallet providers, requiring these services to perform customer due diligence and submit suspicious activity reports.

Asia presents a mixed picture, with countries like Japan and South Korea having well-defined regulatory frameworks that encourage innovation while ensuring investor protection. Japan, for instance, officially recognizes cryptocurrencies and regulates them under the Payment Services Act, which requires all cryptocurrency exchanges to be registered and maintain rigorous security standards.

- Japan's Financial Services Agency (FSA) has issued licenses to multiple cryptocurrency exchanges, promoting a secure and regulated environment for cryptocurrency transactions.

Conversely, China has taken a more restrictive stance. The People's Bank of China (PBOC) has banned initial coin offerings (ICOs) and shut down local cryptocurrency exchanges, reflecting the government's concern over financial risks and capital outflows associated with cryptocurrencies.

```
# Example of how regulatory decisions can impact blockchain markets
def regulatory_impact_example(country):
    if country == 'China':
        return "Significant market drop due to ICO ban and closure of exchanges"
    elif country == 'Japan':
        return "Market growth supported by regulatory acceptance and innovation"
```

Each of these approaches reflects a different balance in regulatory priorities, from consumer protection and financial stability to fostering innovation and competitiveness in the global technology marketplace. Enterprises operating within or across these jurisdictions must navigate a complex array of regulatory expectations, ensuring compliance while seizing operational and strategic opportunities offered by blockchain technologies.

11.3 Contract Law and Smart Contracts: Legal Recognition

The legal landscape governing smart contracts is evolving, driven by the broader adoption of blockchain technology in various sectors. Smart contracts are self-executing contracts with the terms of the agreement directly written into lines of code. The code and the agreements contained therein exist across a distributed, decentralized blockchain network.

In examining the legal recognition of smart contracts, it is essential to differentiate between the concepts of traditional contracts and smart contracts. Traditional contracts are agreements that create legal obligations which are enforceable by law. They typically involve offer, acceptance, and consideration between two or more parties. Smart contracts, by contrast, automate the execution of these agreements and ensure compliance through blockchain technology. They are designed to automatically execute, control, or document legally relevant events and actions according to the terms of a contract or an agreement.

Enforceability of Smart Contracts: Critically, for any contract to be enforceable, it must meet the criteria of being a valid legal agreement. This includes intention to create legal relations, offer and acceptance, consideration, capacity of parties, and legality of purpose. Smart contracts facilitate these elements in varied ways:

- Intention to Create Legal Relations: In smart contracts, this is typically indicated by the deployment of the contract on the blockchain, where it is visible and accessible by relevant parties.

- Offer and Acceptance: These are coded into the contract, with terms being accepted once a party initiates the transaction that triggers the contract.

- Consideration: Digitally represented assets or access rights can serve as consideration, transferred automatically upon fulfilling the contract terms.

- Capacity of Parties: As with traditional contracts, parties need to have the legal capacity to enter agreements. Smart contracts do not inherently validate this but rely on the parties to ensure compliance.

- Legality of Purpose: Smart contracts must be designed to execute legal purposes and not engage in or facilitate illegal activities.

Legal jurisdictions are increasingly recognizing these elements in the context of blockchain and smart contracts. However, variations exist across different legal systems regarding the extent to which these automated contracts are regarded as legally binding.

Legislation and Smart Contracts: Some jurisdictions have begun amending their laws or introducing new regulations to accommodate the unique aspects of smart contracts. For instance, the state of Arizona, USA, passed a law in 2017 that recognizes smart contracts and blockchain signatures as legally valid and enforceable. Similarly, the European Union's General Data Protection Regulation (GDPR) has implications for smart contracts, particularly concerning the storage and processing of personal data.

Challenges in Legal Recognition: Despite the advancements, several challenges impede the full legal recognition and adoption of smart contracts:

- Ambiguity in Code: Legal disputes might arise from ambiguities in code interpretation, where the execution of smart contracts might not reflect parties' true intent.
- Modification and Termination: Traditional contracts allow modifications and termination under mutual agreement or specific conditions, which are rigid and challenging to implement in smart contracts without predefined mechanisms.
- Jurisdictional Issues: Since blockchain operates on a global scale without adhering to specific geographic boundaries, determining the applicable jurisdiction and law for disputes can be complex.

Efforts to integrate legal frameworks with technological innovations in smart contracts must address these challenges. Education and collaboration between legal professionals and technologists are crucial to developing smart contracts that not only ensure compliance and enforceability but also maintain the flexibility and efficiency that blockchain technology offers. As the legal environment adapts to these digital contracts, regulatory clarity will likely increase, leading to broader acceptance and implementation in various contractual scenarios.

11.4 Privacy Laws and Data Protection in Blockchain Systems

The intersection of blockchain technology with privacy laws and data protection regulations presents a complex landscape that enterprises must navigate carefully. First, it is imperative to understand that the very architecture of blockchain—that is, its reliance on a decentralized, immutable ledger—poses unique challenges for compliance with privacy regulations such as the General Data Protection Regulation (GDPR) in the European Union, the California Consumer Privacy Act (CCPA) in the United States, and other similar legislation globally.

One of the core principles underpinning privacy regulations is the right of individuals to control their personal data, including the rights to access, correct, and erase their data. However, the immutable nature of blockchain contradicts the concept of data erasure (or the right to be forgotten) as once information is added to the blockchain, it cannot be altered or deleted.

- Enterprises must consider designs that allow compliance without compromising the blockchain's inherent traits. A common approach involves storing personal data off-chain while maintaining references (hashes of data) on-chain. This method leverages blockchain for integrity verification without exposing the actual data.

- Another crucial aspect is the anonymization of data before it is ever written to the blockchain, ensuring that the data cannot be traced back to an individual. This can help mitigate privacy concerns but must be handled with care to ensure true anonymization.

Additional complications arise from the decentralized nature of many blockchain implementations. Here, data is not stored in a single location but is distributed across numerous nodes, which may span multiple jurisdictions with differing privacy laws.

- Enterprises must navigate these jurisdictional variances carefully, often implementing data governance frameworks that are dynamic and responsive to changes in law across these locations.

- Ensuring all nodes comply with the strictest privacy standards can offer a practical solution, albeit one that may limit the flexibility or efficiency of the blockchain system.

From a technical perspective, blockchain developers can employ various methods to enhance privacy and compliance:

- Techniques such as zero-knowledge proofs allow transaction validation without revealing any underlying data.

- Segregation of duties can be architected into the blockchain, where different nodes undertake distinct roles, potentially making it easier to manage data according to privacy requirements.

```
Example of Privacy-Preserving Transaction Verification:
Transaction is validated.
No personal data is revealed.
Only a confirmation of the transaction's validity is recorded on the blockchain.
```

Legal professionals and blockchain developers must work together closely to ensure that technology solutions align with legal requirements. This interdisciplinary approach not only aids in compliance but also drives innovations in how blockchain can be utilized in a privacy-friendly manner.

Furthermore, the ongoing evolution of privacy laws must be meticulously monitored. Future legislative changes could introduce new compliance requirements, but they may also provide opportunities for enhancing the blockchain's functionality within the legal frameworks. The proactive involvement in standards development and blockchain regulation is recommended for enterprises aiming to influence policy-making processes that affect this technology sector.

Thus, adherence to privacy laws in blockchain systems is not only about compliance but about understanding the balance between technological features and regulatory requirements. Enterprises, equipped with advanced solutions and a thorough understanding of both domains, can leverage blockchain's benefits while respecting individual privacy rights and obligations under law.

11.5 Regulatory Compliance in Financial Blockchain Applications

Financial blockchain applications are subject to a complex matrix of regulatory requirements, which vary significantly across different jurisdictions. Understanding and adhering to these regulations is crucial for enterprises to operate legally and reap the benefits of blockchain technology in the financial sector.

In the United States, the Securities and Exchange Commission (SEC) and the Commodity Futures Trading Commission (CFTC) are two key regulatory bodies that impact blockchain applications relating to securities and commodities trading respectively. The SEC has emphasized that if a blockchain token qualifies as a security, it must comply with federal securities laws. The criteria put forth in the Howey Test (used to determine what constitutes an investment contract and thus a security) are central to this determination process.

```
// Example of a Howey Test application to a blockchain token
if (isAnInvestment && expectationOfProfits && derivesFromTheEffortsOfOthers) {
  complyWithSecuritiesRegulations();
}
```

Output:
Ensure compliance with SEC regulations

In Europe, the General Data Protection Regulation (GDPR) poses challenges for blockchain implementations, particularly with the immutable and decentralized nature of blockchain which might contravene certain requirements of data rights like the right to be forgotten. Enterprises must devise strategies to reconcile the conflict between GDPR's requirements and blockchain features.

- Assess whether blockchain data can be considered personal data under GDPR.
- Implement measures to anonymize data to ensure GDPR compliance.
- Address data storage and transfer mechanisms given the transborder nature of blockchain.

Furthermore, Anti-Money Laundering (AML) laws and the necessity for Know Your Customer (KYC) procedures are pivotal in financial blockchain applications. Various jurisdictions have extended AML and

KYC frameworks to include transactions involving cryptocurrencies and other blockchain-based assets. This regulatory measure aims to mitigate potential misuse of the technologies for illegal activities, thus enhancing the integrity of financial transactions conducted through blockchain.

```
// Code snippet for integrating AML and KYC procedures in a blockchain application
function verifyTransaction(sender, receiver, amount) {
    if (kycCompliance(sender) && kycCompliance(receiver) && !
        isSuspiciousTransaction(amount)) {
        processTransaction(sender, receiver, amount);
    } else {
        flagTransaction(sender, receiver, amount);
    }
}
```

Output:
Transaction flagged for further verification

Jurisdictional discrepancies stand out as a particular complication. The decentralized plane of blockchain allows for cross-border operations, inevitably causing overlapping and potentially conflicting regulations. Enterprises must engage with legal experts to navigate these complexities, ensuring compliance not only at a local or national level but also in consideration of international laws where applicable.

Regarding the future outlook, as blockchain technology continues to evolve, regulatory frameworks are also expected to adapt. Financial regulators worldwide are increasingly recognizing the need for updated and more comprehensive rules that address the specific challenges and opportunities presented by blockchain technologies.

This dynamic and fast-evolving regulatory landscape necessitates continued vigilance and adaptability on the part of enterprises using blockchain to power their financial applications. Staying informed and proactive in regulatory compliance is not merely about legal necessity but is fundamental to gaining and maintaining trust in blockchain applications as viable and sustainable financial solutions.

11.6 Intellectual Property Issues in Blockchain Development

Intellectual Property (IP) issues present unique challenges and opportunities within the realm of blockchain technology. The decentralized and often open-source nature of blockchain platforms can conflict with traditional IP regimes, which are designed to protect individual creativity and innovation.

Identification of IP Assets in Blockchain

The definition and identification of IP assets in blockchain development are not straightforward. Typically, IP assets in blockchain include, but are not limited to:

- Software code and architecture underlying the blockchain;
- Individual smart contracts and their code;
- Documentation and graphical user interfaces;
- Cryptographic methods and algorithms;
- Distributed applications (dApps) built on top of platforms like Ethereum.

The decentralized creation and maintenance of these assets with contributions from various stakeholders complicate the application of classic IP protection mechanisms like copyrights, patents, and trademarks.

Copyright Challenges in Blockchain

Blockchains inherently involve the creation of software. This software, whether it constitutes the core protocol, smart contracts, or dApps, generally qualifies for copyright protection. The technical specifics, however, present complications. Given the open-source nature of much blockchain software, developers often release their code under permissive licenses that allow for free use, modification, and distribution.

Here is an example of copyright-related pseudo code for a basic smart contract written in Solidity:

```
pragma solidity ^0.5.0;

contract SampleContract {
    string public constant COPYRIGHT_NOTICE = "Copyright (c) 2023, Sample Author";

    function transferOwnership(address newOwner) public returns (bool success) {
        // Ownership transfer code
        return true;
    }
}
```

The `COPYRIGHT_NOTICE` in this contract is an assertion of copyright within the code. However, the enforcement of this copyright in decentralized and distributed environments can be problematic.

Patenting Blockchain Innovations

Patents protect new inventions and are a key area of concern in blockchain development. Blockchain-based patents have surged as firms attempt to capitalize on the commercial applications of blockchain technology. The patentability criteria—novelty, non-obviousness, and utility—must be met, and the specific implementation of the blockchain technology must be detailed clearly in the patent application.

For example, a method for enhancing blockchain scalability may be patented, provided it offers a novel solution not obvious to someone skilled in the art. The application must describe the invention sufficiently enough that another developer could reproduce the method.

Below is a simplified pseudocode for a patentable blockchain scalability method:

Algorithm 14: Example of a blockchain scalability enhancement method

Result: Reduced transaction processing time
1. initialization;
2. **while** *Transaction received* **do**
3. | identify block;
4. | apply sharding mechanism;
5. | distribute transaction across nodes;
6. | validate transaction concurrently;
7. **end**

Trademark Issues in Blockchain

Trademarks protect brand names, logos, and other identifiers from being used in ways that can confuse consumers. In blockchain, trademarks might apply to platform names, cryptocurrency names, or other service marks. The decentralized aspect of blockchain raises significant challenges for trademark enforcement. For instance, if a decentralized autonomous organization (DAO) that is not a legal entity uses a trademark, determining the responsible party for any infringement becomes complex.

Trade Secrets and Blockchain

Maintaining the confidentiality of trade secrets, such as proprietary algorithms or business processes implemented on a blockchain, is inherently difficult in a technology designed for transparency. Utilizing permissioned blockchains can mitigate this issue, as they restrict access to the data and operations within the network.

Collaborative Creation and IP Ownership

The collaborative and often anonymous contributions to blockchain projects pose substantial challenges for assigning and enforcing IP ownership. In many blockchain projects, the lack of clear agreements about IP ownership and rights to modify or redistribute the code can lead to disputes. Establishing clear contracts and governance frameworks at the outset of the project is vital for preventing such issues.

This section analyzed the pressing IP concerns in blockchain development, highlighting the complex interplay between innovation in blockchain technology and existing IP laws. The adaptability of IP laws to encompass new technologies like blockchain will be crucial as enterprises continue to explore and expand these innovations. Moving forward, legal professionals and blockchain developers will need to craft nuanced IP strategies that address these unique challenges.

11.7 Cross-border Transactions and Jurisdictional Challenges

The advent of blockchain technology has revolutionized the way transactions are conducted across borders, offering advantages such as reduced transaction times and costs, enhanced security, and increased transparency. However, these benefits are accompanied by significant legal challenges, particularly in the realm of jurisdictional conflicts and the enforcement of laws across different countries.

One primary challenge in dealing with cross-border blockchain transactions is the determination of applicable law. Traditional legal systems are territorially bound, but blockchain operates on a global scale, without regard to national borders. This makes it difficult to ascertain which jurisdiction's laws apply to a particular transaction, contract, or activity conducted via blockchain.

For instance, consider a scenario where a blockchain transaction involves parties located in Country A and Country B, and the distributed ledger is maintained by nodes located in multiple countries. The complexity arises when a legal issue requires adjudication. Questions about which country's courts have the authority to hear the case, which laws are applicable, and how judgments can be enforced across jurisdictions become significantly complex.

- Determination of the responsible jurisdiction for regulatory purposes
- Enforcement of legal judgments across different jurisdictions
- Recognition and enforcement of rights and obligations that arise from blockchain transactions

Legal scholars and practitioners have suggested several approaches to address these challenges. One approach is the use of "choice of law" clauses in smart contracts, which explicitly state the governing law and jurisdiction. However, the enforceability of such clauses across all involved jurisdictions remains a subject of debate.

```
// Example of a choice of law clause embedded in a smart contract
pragma solidity ^0.5.1;
contract CrossBorderContract {
    // Governing law and jurisdiction clause
    string public constant governingLaw = "Laws of Country A";
    string public constant jurisdiction = "Court of District 9 in Country A";

    // Contract details
    function transactionDetails() public pure returns (string memory) {
        return "This contract is governed by the laws of Country A and any disputes
            will be resolved in the Court of District 9 in Country A.";
    }
}
```

Furthermore, blockchain technology's inherent characteristic of decentralization poses additional challenges for legal enforcement. The absence of a central authority in decentralized blockchains means there is no central point of compliance or control. This decentralization complicates the ability of any single country to enforce its laws or regulations unilaterally.

A possible solution to some of these jurisdictional challenges could be the development of international treaties or agreements specifically designed for blockchain-enabled transactions. These treaties could provide harmonized legal standards and cooperative enforcement mechanisms. However, the creation and implementation of such treaties would require extensive international collaboration and a deep understanding of blockchain technology and its implications for traditional legal concepts such as sovereignty and jurisdiction.

As the blockchain ecosystem continues to evolve, so too must the legal frameworks that govern it. The legal community, regulators, and blockchain developers must engage in continued dialogue and cooperation to address the challenges posed by cross-border blockchain transactions. Only through collaborative efforts can the full potential of blockchain technology be realized, while simultaneously respecting the legal rights and protections necessary in a globally connected world.

11.8 Legal Concerns with Decentralization and Anonymity

Decentralization and anonymity are foundational attributes of many blockchain systems. These features, while providing significant benefits in terms of security and user privacy, also pose substantial legal challenges. The central issue stems from the difficulty in attributing actions or transactions to specific individuals, a scenario that complicates legal accountability and compliance.

One of the primary legal challenges introduced by decentralization is the absence of a central governing body. Traditional systems, whether financial, organizational, or governmental, typically operate under clear regulatory and supervisory frameworks. In a decentralized blockchain, however, there is no central authority to oversee operations or ensure compliance with local and international laws. This situation raises questions concerning the enforcement of legal agreements and the ability to pursue recourse against wrongful actions.

For instance, in case of fraudulent transactions on a decentralized blockchain, attributing the actions to an individual or entity can be exceedingly challenging. The pseudonymous nature of blockchain complicates the tracking of individuals involved in illegal activities, such as money laundering or financing of terrorism. Here is an example of a blockchain transaction:

```
Transaction ID: 7a7b1593
From: 1A8zP1EPicaTq9A8MrmCFXsrZWqPxZ1j1B
To: 3J98t1WpEZ73CNmQviecrnyiWrnqRhWNLy
Amount: 2.5 BTC
```

Given the above transaction, identifying the actual individuals behind the addresses without additional data from outside the blockchain can prove impossible. This anonymity not only enables privacy but also opens avenues for escaping legal accountability.

Furthermore, the global nature of blockchain platforms introduces complexities concerning jurisdiction. Which country's laws apply to a transaction or contract executed via a decentralized system that spans multiple countries? The typical answer depends on the jurisdictions involved in the transaction, but this is complicated when the identities of the parties are shielded or unknown.

The lack of clarity around jurisdiction can also impede the application of tax laws. For instance, if an individual gains a significant profit from cryptocurrency transactions on a decentralized exchange, determining the taxable entity and appropriate jurisdiction for tax purposes poses substantial challenges without clear guidelines or cooperation across nations.

To approach these issues, some countries have started to implement specific legal frameworks to better define the legal status of blockchain transactions. For example, modifications to anti-money laundering (AML) laws include mandates requiring cryptocurrency exchanges to perform customer due diligence, akin to traditional financial institutions. However, these regulations vary significantly between jurisdictions, creating a patchwork of compliance requirements.

Legal scholars and practitioners have proposed the development of decentralized legal frameworks, adjusted to the operational methodologies of blockchain systems. These proposals suggest a form of legal evolution to accommodate decentralized structures without stymying innovation:

- Introduction of universal standards for identity verification on blockchain networks.
- Enhanced cooperation between international law enforcement agencies for blockchain monitoring.
- Developing smart contracts that include enforceable legal terms by default.

Such steps, while theoretically sound, must be implemented strategically to address both the decentralized nature of the technology and the privacy concerns of its users. The delicate balance between effective legal regulation and the preservation of the benefits of decentralization and anonymity remain a pivotal point in ongoing legal debates surrounding blockchain technology. The eventual solutions will likely be a combination of technological, legislative, and international cooperation, tailoring the laws to adapt without relinquishing the core advantages of blockchain technology.

11.9 Blockchain and Anti-Money Laundering (AML) Regulations

The integration of blockchain technology into financial systems has brought about a paradigm shift in how financial transactions are conducted and regulated globally. One of the significant areas affected by this integration is the enforcement of Anti-Money Laundering (AML) regulations. Blockchain's inherent characteristics such as decentralization, transparency, and immutability place it at the nexus of AML regulatory frameworks.

For blockchain operators and financial institutions leveraging this technology, there is a compelling need to understand how AML rules apply to blockchain transactions and the strategies for compliance. AML regulations are designed to prevent the laundering of illegally obtained money through financial systems. Given blockchain's ability to facilitate fast and cross-border transactions, it poses unique AML risks that need to be vigilantly managed.

The Role of Anonymity and Pseudonymity: On blockchain networks, transactions often occur either anonymously or under pseudonyms through the use of public addresses. This feature can impede the traceability of funds, thereby attracting financial activities linked to money laundering. Regulatory bodies have started to address this issue by enforcing "Know Your Customer" (KYC) procedures on blockchain-operated businesses. These entities are required to verify the identity of their customers before enabling transactions which helps align the operations with standard AML requirements.

Regulatory Developments across Jurisdictions: Different countries have adopted varying approaches to blockchain and AML regulations. For instance, the Financial Action Task Force (FATF), an intergovernmental organization, has issued guidelines recommending that virtual asset service providers (VASPs), including blockchain companies, be subjected to AML regulations akin to traditional financial institutions. These guidelines suggest measures such as monitoring and reporting suspicious transactions, which is instrumental in curtailing the potential misuse of cryptocurrencies.

Technology-Enabled AML Solutions: The unique attributes of blockchain also offer potential AML solutions. The transparency of the blockchain ledger permits the tracing of transaction histories unequivocally. This capability can be utilized to develop and implement advanced monitoring systems for suspicious activities. Moreover, blockchain can support the creation of shared databases among regulated entities, facilitating more effective cross-referencing of data, which could enhance the detection of financial crimes across platforms and borders.

```
// Example of a smart contract function for monitoring transactions
function monitorTransactions(address user) public returns (bool) {
    uint256 transactionVolume = getTransactionVolume(user);
    if(transactionVolume > threshold) {
        reportToRegulator(user);
        return true;
    }
    return false;
}
```

The code sample illustrates a possible blockchain application where transactions of a particular volume are flagged and information is automatically sent to regulators. This function forms part of a decentralized application (DApp) that could assist VASPs in complying with AML regulations.

Challenges in Implementing AML Regulations on Blockchain: Despite the benefits, there are several challenges in the effective implementation of AML regulations in blockchain environments. The decentralized nature of blockchain can complicate the enforcement of jurisdiction-based regulations, as the technology does not inherently respect geopolitical boundaries. Additionally, the variation in regulatory landscapes across different regions can lead to inconsistencies in AML enforcement and compliance.

Effective AML practices in the context of blockchain require a balanced approach that respects the principles of innovation and privacy while upholding essential regulatory standards. In moving forward, it is crucial for regulatory authorities and blockchain enterprises to engage in continuous dialogue, adapt to technological advancements, and collaboratively develop frameworks that mitigate money laundering risks without stifling the growth and beneficial applications of blockchain technology.

11.10 Consumer Protection and Dispute Resolution Mechanisms

Consumer protection in the context of blockchain technology involves a set of legal challenges and opportunities that stem from the technology's inherent characteristics including decentralization, transparency, and immutability. These features, while beneficial in many aspects, can also pose significant obstacles in the implementation of traditional consumer protection norms.

The primary concern in blockchain-powered applications centers on the clarity and enforceability of terms and conditions. Since smart contracts automate the execution of agreements and operate independently of any single party's control, consumers may find themselves bound by terms that they neither fully understand nor have the practical ability to negotiate. This raises questions about the fairness and equity of such contracts under existing consumer protection laws, which are designed to ensure transparency, fair treatment, and the right to redress.

Effective dispute resolution mechanisms are critical in this environment. Traditional legal processes may not always adapt well or extend effortlessly to decentralized systems. For instance, the identification of a liable party in a blockchain network can be complex due to the dispersed nature of decision-making. Therefore, adapting dispute resolution mechanisms to the blockchain context involves considerations of both jurisdiction and applicable law, which are often uncertain in decentralized systems.

One innovative approach to addressing these challenges is through decentralized autonomous organizations (DAOs) that incorporate governance and dispute resolution directly into the blockchain. Here, the community of users can vote on issues including changes to the code or terms, potentially offering a form of redress that aligns better with the decentralized ethos of blockchain.

In addition to DAOs, several entities have begun to explore the use of blockchain-based arbitration and mediation services. These platforms use smart contracts to enforce arbitration agreements and decisions. The enforcement process is automated, reducing the need for judicial intervention and hopefully, increasing the efficiency and reducing the costs of dispute resolution.

Consider, for instance, the following pseudocode representing a simplified process for blockchain-based arbitration:

Algorithm 15: Simplified Blockchain-based Arbitration Process

Data: DisputeDetails, ArbitratorAddresses, AgreementContract
Result: Resolution

1. initialization
2. **while** *not at end of DisputeDetails* **do**
3.   read current dispute details
4.   agree on an Arbitrator from ArbitratorAddresses
5.   Arbitrator reviews the AgreementContract
6.   decision = makeDecision(DisputeDetails, AgreementContract)
7.   executeDecision(decision)
8.   **if** *party disagrees* **then**
9.   appealDecision()
10.   go to Arbitrator selection

Indeed, blockchain's capacity for immutability could be advantageous in ensuring that arbitration decisions, once made, are not unduly altered. However, the transparency and finality of blockchain also mean that once a dispute is resolved, the outcome is visible and irreversible, potentially impacting the willingness of parties to engage in arbitration.

To foster broader adoption, it is paramount that these mechanisms are communicated clearly to consumers, ensuring they understand both the risks and the remedies available. Educating consumers on how blockchain works and how disputes are resolved can mitigate the risk of dissatisfaction and non-compliance with outcomes.

The integration of consumer protection and dispute resolution mechanisms within blockchain platforms not only enhances trust but also ensures that the technology remains a viable tool for enterprise applications. As blockchain continues to evolve, legal professionals and technologists must collaborate to refine these processes, ensuring they deliver fair outcomes and uphold the principles of consumer protection.

11.11 Future Legal Trends and Potential Regulations for Blockchain

The rapid evolution of blockchain technology necessitates an adaptive legal framework that can address its unique challenges and opportunities. As we move into the future, several key trends in the regulation of blockchain can be anticipated, potentially shaping the way enterprises and governments interact with this technology.

Increased Harmonization of Blockchain Regulations

As blockchain technology does not adhere to traditional geographic boundaries, there is a growing need for harmonization of regulations across jurisdictions. This harmonization can facilitate smoother operations of global blockchain applications such as cross-border payments, international trade, and decentralized markets.

Attempts at creating common standards and frameworks can be seen in the formation of international blockchain consortia that involve regulators, enterprises, and tech communities. These groups are instrumental in forging common understandings and in setting up interoperable frameworks that adhere to regulatory expectations while fostering innovation.

Regulation of Decentralized Autonomous Organizations (DAOs)

Decentralized Autonomous Organizations (DAOs) represent a significant shift in the way organizations can be structured and operated. They run on smart contracts on a blockchain and are absent of centralized leadership. The legal status of DAOs remains a grey area in many jurisdictions.

Future regulations could provide clearer guidelines on the formation, operation, and dissolution of DAOs, potentially recognizing them as legal entities with rights and responsibilities akin to traditional corporations. This would necessitate adjustments in corporate governance laws and may introduce new types of legal responsibilities and audit requirements.

Digital Identity and Blockchain

The use of blockchain for managing digital identities is an emerging area that could see significant legal developments. Blockchain can provide a secure and immutable system for storing personal data for identification purposes. However, this raises concerns regarding privacy, data protection, and the potential misuse of personal data.

Legal frameworks could evolve to specifically regulate how blockchain is used for digital identity management. This could include stipulations on data retrieval processes, the right to be forgotten, and data portability, ensuring adherence to global data protection regulations like the General Data Protection Regulation (GDPR) in the European Union.

Smart Contracts Regulation

Smart contracts are self-executing contracts with the terms of the agreement between buyer and seller being directly written into lines of code. The legal recognition of smart contracts as legitimate and binding agreements is an area likely to see expansive growth in regulatory frameworks.

Regulatory bodies could develop standards and frameworks that define the circumstances under which a smart contract is legally binding. There could also be developments in specifying the legal liabilities in cases of smart contract failures, fraud, or exploitation due to bugs or coding errors.

Tokenization and Securities Law

Tokenization — the process of converting rights to an asset into a digital token on a blockchain — intersects significantly with existing securities laws. As tokens can represent assets like real estate, stocks, or commodities, they may fall under existing regulatory frameworks governing securities.

Expect regulatory trends to increasingly clarify which types of tokens are considered securities, the legal responsibilities of token issuers, and the rights of token holders. This aligns with the broader objective of protecting investors and maintaining transparent and fair markets.

Future legal trends in the blockchain space will likely emphasize regulatory clarity, adaptability to new business models, and the protection of user rights and data. These trends underscore the need for ongoing dialogue between technologists, legal experts, and regulators to ensure that the governance of blockchain technology promotes both innovation and legal certainty. This dialogue is crucial as blockchain continues to challenge traditional legal paradigms and offer new avenues for growth and development.

Made in United States
North Haven, CT
21 April 2025